B R I T A I N I N O L D P H O T O G R A P H S

PENN & TYLERS GREEN

PENN & CHEPPING WYCOMBE PARISH COUNCILS

Compiled By

MILES GREEN, BARBARA HUNT & LIZ TEBBUTT

Written By

MILES GREEN

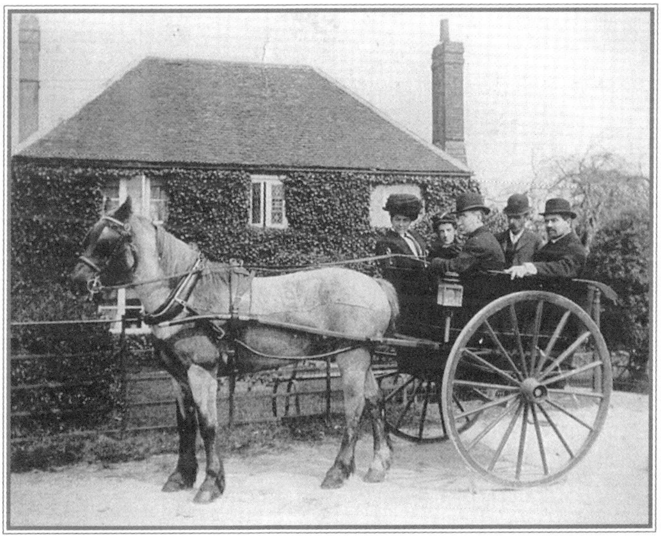

SUTTON PUBLISHING LIMITED

Sutton Publishing Limited
Phoenix Mill · Thrupp · Stroud
Gloucestershire · GL5 2BU

First published 2000

British Library Cataloguing in Publication Data
A catalogue record for this book is available from the British Library.

ISBN 0-7509-1895-0

Typeset in 10.5/13.5 Photina.
Typesetting and origination by
Sutton Publishing Limited.
Printed and bound in England by
J.H. Haynes & Co. Ltd, Sparkford.

Title page photograph: The Wooster family and friends outside Penbury Farmhouse, 1910. The house was built in about 1790. Penbury means the fortified place of Penn and was the manor house of the de la Penne family, overlooking Church Knowl, until the thirteenth century. The farm belonged to the Penn Estate and George Wooster was tenant farmer from 1889 to 1938. A future American President, Herbert Hoover, stayed there in about 1914. There were extensive barns which burnt down in the 1940s or 1950s. (*David Wooster*)

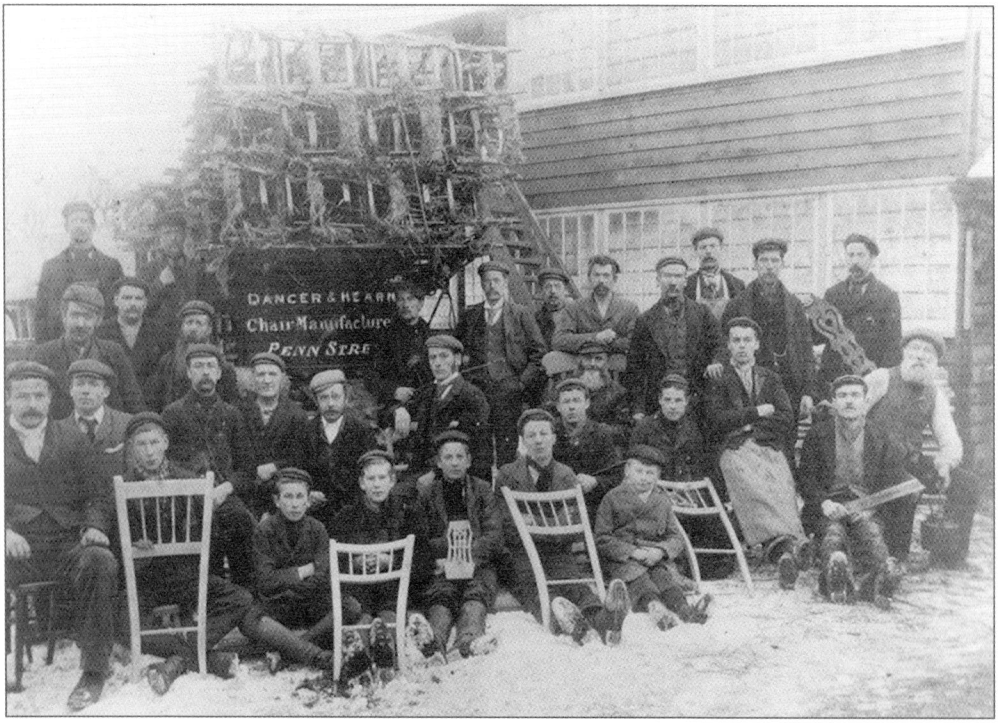

The workforce of Dancer & Hearne, Penn Street, 1895. Alfred Hearne (seated centre) and Albert Hearne behind him (hands in pockets) were the sons of William Hearne, who married the daughter of the landlord of the Hit or Miss and started the firm, in 1840, in a small wooden shed attached to the pub. By 1938 it claimed to be the largest chair factory in Europe, producing 450,000 chairs p.a. with over 300 employees. During the Second World War the factory made wings and tails for de Havilland Mosquitoes, parts of the barges used on D-Day, rifle butts, tent pegs and pick-axe handles.

CONTENTS

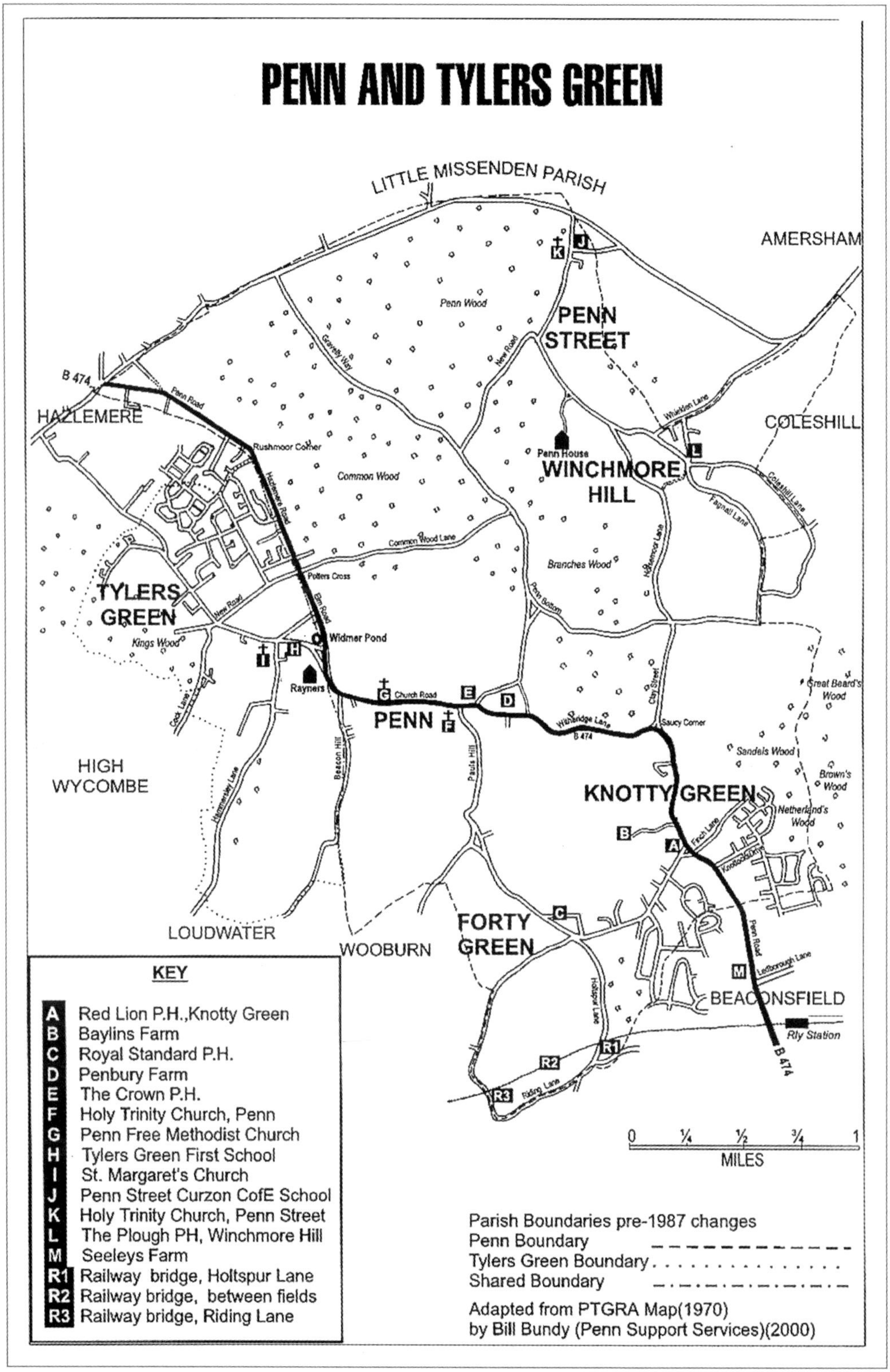
PENN AND TYLERS GREEN
LITTLE MISSENDEN PARISH
AMERSHAM
PENN STREET
Penn Wood
Gravelly Way
New Road
B 474
Penn Road
HAZLEMERE
Rushmoor Corner
Hazlemere Road
Common Wood
Common Wood Lane
Penn House
WINCHMORE HILL
Whielden Lane
COLESHILL
Coleshill Lane
Fagnall Lane
Branches Wood
Potters Cross
TYLERS GREEN
New Road
Elm Road
Kings Wood
Widmer Pond
Rayners
Church Road
PENN
Penn Bottom
Witheridge Lane
Saucy Corner
Great Beard's Wood
Sandels Wood
Brown's Wood
HIGH WYCOMBE
Beacon Hill
Pauls Hill
KNOTTY GREEN
Finch Lane
Netherland's Wood
LOUDWATER
WOOBURN
FORTY GREEN
Penn Road
Ledborough Lane
BEACONSFIELD
Rly Station
Holtspur Lane
Riding Lane
KEY
A Red Lion P.H., Knotty Green
B Baylins Farm
C Royal Standard P.H.
D Penbury Farm
E The Crown P.H.
F Holy Trinity Church, Penn
G Penn Free Methodist Church
H Tylers Green First School
I St. Margaret's Church
J Penn Street Curzon CofE School
K Holy Trinity Church, Penn Street
L The Plough PH, Winchmore Hill
M Seeleys Farm
R1 Railway bridge, Holtspur Lane
R2 Railway bridge, between fields
R3 Railway bridge, Riding Lane
0 ¼ ½ ¾ 1
MILES
Parish Boundaries pre-1987 changes
Penn Boundary
Tylers Green Boundary
Shared Boundary
Adapted from PTGRA Map(1970)
by Bill Bundy (Penn Support Services)(2000)

INTRODUCTION

This book, covering the two parishes of Penn and Tylers Green, was conceived as a celebration of the Millennium. Penn Village and Tylers Green share most of their organisations and facilities and are, in most respects, one community. Knotty Green, Forty Green, Penn Street and Winchmore Hill are all separate hamlets of the civil parish of Penn.

The twentieth century saw two world wars and far-reaching and rapid change of a kind never experienced before. The advent of the Marylebone railway, the car and the bus, together with the sale of all the Rayners and St John's Estates and over half of the Penn Estate, combined to encourage a four- or five-fold increase in population. Two quiet, self-contained, country parishes have had to adapt to very different people and circumstances.

Over the same period, domestic life has been revolutionised by the arrival of mains water, gas, electricity and sewers and by the disappearance of most of the small shops which served even the humblest community. The photographs illustrate all these themes very effectively, and the introduction to each chapter aims to give the reader a sense of where we have come from, for better or for worse.

Penn and Tylers Green have always had more than their fair share of important visitors and residents. Edmund Burke's French school attracted prime ministers, cabinet ministers and the French royal family. The Howe connection has brought a succession of royal visitors from William IV and Queen Adelaide to George V and Queen Mary. Queen Elizabeth the Queen Mother visited the WI in 1940. Disraeli was a regular visitor to Rayners, Herbert Hoover, future President of the USA, stayed at Penbury Farm. Sir Arthur Whitten Brown, first to fly the Atlantic in 1919, is buried in St Margaret's. Lord Dawson of Penn, Alison Uttley, Rupert Davies, Stanley Holloway, Alvar Liddell, David Niven and Terry Pratchett are all closely connected with the two parishes.

Elizabethan and Stuart Londoners used to send their 'nurse children' to Penn to escape the regular epidemics and this idea of 'healthy high lying ground in this most healthy part of the Chilterns' recurs regularly through the centuries. In 1911 the Vicar of Penn wrote: 'As a health resort, Penn is now famous, the death rate being almost the lowest in the kingdom.' Evidence for this assumption included the remarkable longevity of inhabitants such as Mrs Rebecca Clarke, born the year before Trafalgar. She had her first car ride at the age of 106 and was photographed working in a hay field the same day. She died in 1912, aged 108.

ACKNOWLEDGEMENTS

The name of the owner of each photograph is to be found in brackets after the caption. We are most grateful to them, and apologise if we have made any errors in attribution because some pictures have been in the archives for many years. A special mention must also be made of those who have contributed significantly to the sum of local knowledge recorded in the captions and introductions to each chapter:

The Penn Estate – Lady Charlotte Dinan, Earl Howe.

In Penn Village and Tylers Green – Mr and Mrs Peter Barnes, Mr Arthur Brown, Mrs Evelyn Clark, Mrs Barbara Culverhouse, Dr Robin Horn, Mrs Betty Milner, Mr Geoffrey Perfect, Mr and Mrs Harold Wheeler. Together with those now deceased: Mrs Violet Becher, Mrs Lilian Clarke, Miss Pat Cuthbert, Mrs Betty Jollye, Miss Rosamund Mathews, Lady Rose (wife of the 3rd Sir Philip), Mr Ken Stevens, Mrs Edith White.

In Winchmore Hill – Mrs Maureen Seymour and the late Mr Fred Payne.

In Penn Street – Mr Ron Miles, the Revd Nigel Stowe, Mrs Alice Timms.

In Knotty Green and Forty Green – Mr Derek Brydon, Mrs Pat Colley, Mr and Mrs Geoffrey Feast, Mr and Mrs Geoffrey Green, Mr Oliver Heal, Mrs Kay Mellor, Mr and Mrs John Walker, Mr David Wooster.

A bare mention of this kind does not begin to do justice to their generous cooperation, often over many years, or to the value of their first-hand accounts stretching back over the century – in the case of Mrs Edith White, to the Relief of Mafeking, in 1901, when she remembers the men sitting around Widmer Pond singing 'Goodbye Dolly I must leave you'.

The Chepping Wycombe Parish Council (CWPC) photographic archive was started twenty-five years ago by the late Mr Ken Stevens and has been painstakingly administered over the last fifteen years by Mrs Liz Tebbutt. The Penn Parish Council (PPC) archive is comparatively new but growing rapidly. Mr Barry Wright contributed many of the early photographs. Mr Brian Cullip and Mr Eddie Morton have photographed copies of many of the originals for the archives. Mr Bill Bundy has prepared the map on p. 4. Mrs Marrilyn Green has patiently typed up successive drafts which Mr Bill Bundy has transferred to disk for publication. Mrs Jean Rollason has found a good few errors and infelicities missed by the authors

The publishers asked for the text to be as full as possible and the book has turned out to be much more of a pictorial history than was initially envisaged. Factual mistakes will have been made, despite every effort to avoid them, and any corrections, information or new photographs will be gratefully received.

CHAPTER ONE

FROM BEACONSFIELD STATION TO HAZLEMERE

Two elderly ladies, interviewed fifteen years ago, remembered walking from Penn Church to Old Beaconsfield before the arrival of the railway in 1906 which created New Beaconsfield. They passed only the few farms and handful of cottages that can be seen on the 1800 map (p. 48).

The Parliamentary Bill sanctioning the new railway, with a station at Beaconsfield, was passed in 1897. Shortly afterwards Penn Parish Council wrote to the railway company warmly supporting the proposed site for the station and predicting, in all innocence, that 'The Hamlet of Penn including Tylers Green has about 1,500 inhabitants and there are several gentlemen having residences in London who would doubtless use the Beaconsfield Station in their journey to and from London'.

Within a few months of the opening of Beaconsfield station the Parish Council saw the need to widen Witherage Lane at various points, and Earl Howe agreed to give the land and set back his fences. A public meeting approved, and the Parish Council was asked to contribute £125 (approximately £10–20,000 today).

Responsibility for the repair of the roads had been taken over from the Parish Council, only a few years before, by the Highways Surveyor of the new Amersham Rural District Council. There were regular complaints about the abominable state of the road and its antiquated method of repair, with stones gathered from the fields by women 'with hands as hard as iron' and children. They were paid 8*d* a load measured by a cord 3 yards long 'up and over', and the stones were then broken up with hammers and steam-rollered in.

Drainage was poor, with water flowing across the road at various places, including flooding from Penn churchyard down Crown Lane. In 1906 there was anger at the state of the road after the water mains had been put in at Knotty Green, the first time it had been disturbed in this way.

By 1903 there was a motor car at Rayners in Tylers Green (p. 83), and only six months after the railway had opened the 'Motor Garage' at Beaconsfield applied for permission, which was refused, to advertise on the Recreation Ground at Knotty Green. The first motor bus service was started by the Penn Bus Company in 1920. The road was gradually tarmacked during the late 1920s.

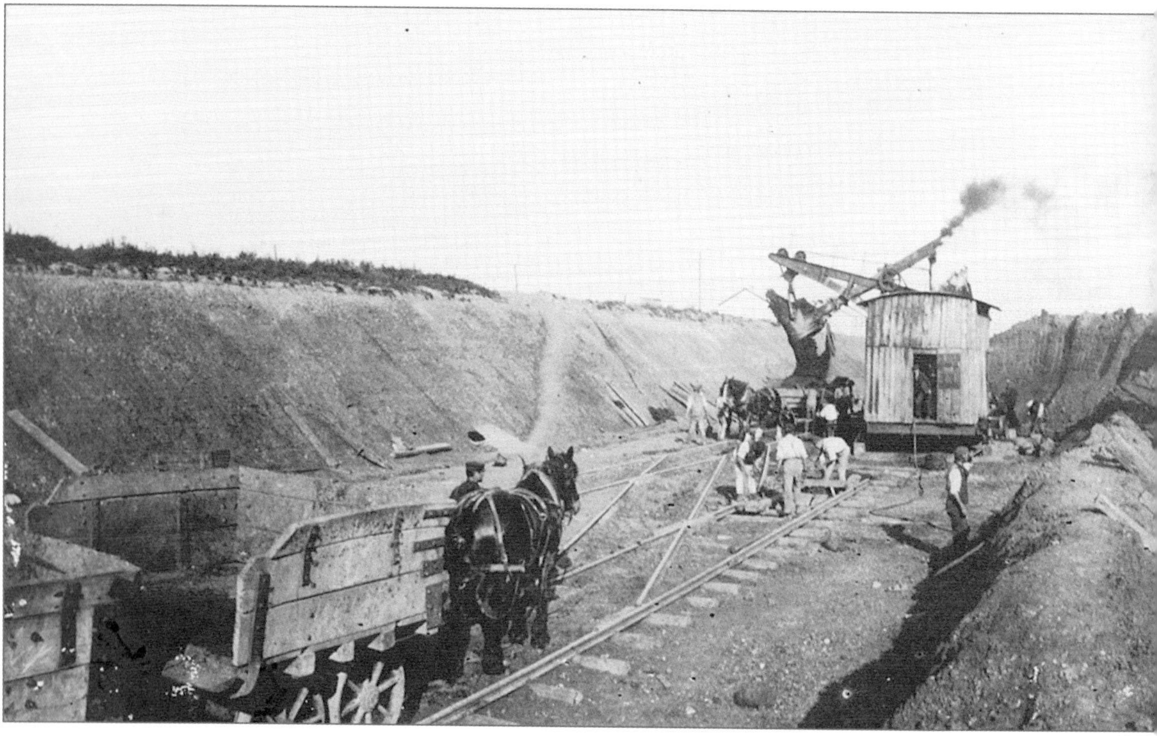

Above: Digging out Beaconsfield station using a combination of horse power and steam shovels, 1905. The photographer is looking towards London. Today's car park was originally a goods yard. A stationmaster's house was built where Boots the chemist now stands. (*David Wooster*)

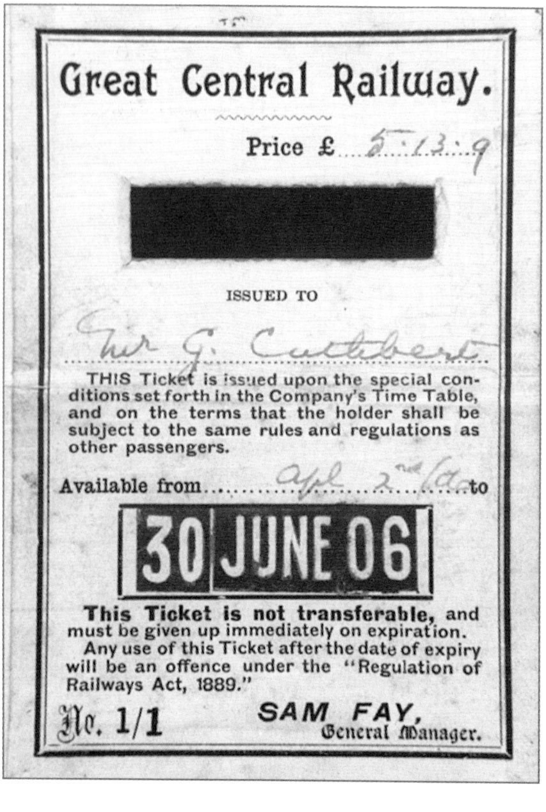

Great Central Railway.

Price £ 5 : 13 : 9

ISSUED TO

Mr G. Cuthbert

THIS Ticket is issued upon the special conditions set forth in the Company's Time Table, and on the terms that the holder shall be subject to the same rules and regulations as other passengers.

Available from Apl 2nd /06 to

30 JUNE 06

This Ticket is not transferable, and must be given up immediately on expiration.
Any use of this Ticket after the date of expiry will be an offence under the "Regulation of Railways Act, 1889."

No. 1/1 SAM FAY, General Manager.

The first quarterly season ticket (first class) between Beaconsfield and Marylebone, issued to Mr G. Cuthbert, on 2 April 1906, cost £5 13*s* 9*d*. Today it costs £847, 149 times more. (*Pat Cuthbert*)

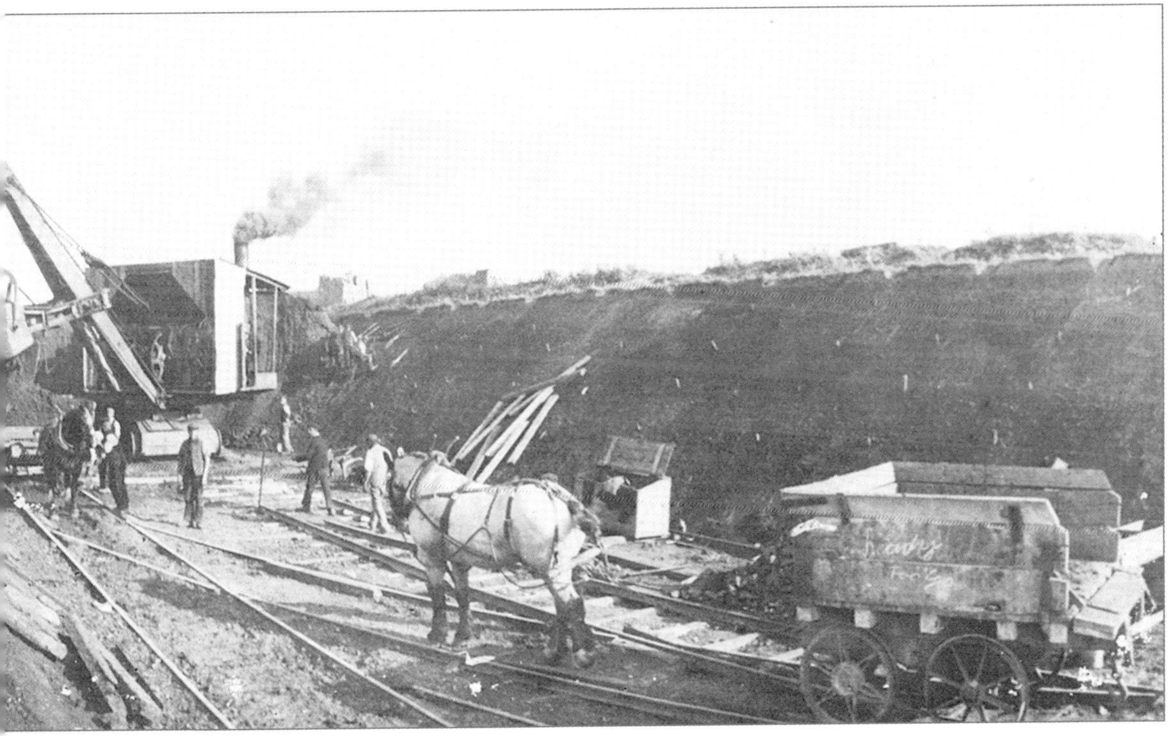

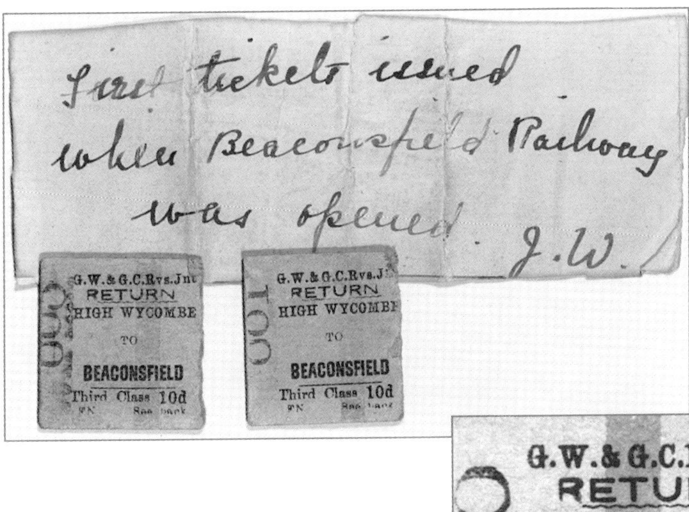

The first two return tickets, Beaconsfield to High Wycombe, on 2 April 1906, cost 10*d*. The handwritten note with the tickets is from Job Wooster of Seeley's Farm (p. 58). (*Beaconsfield and District Historical Society*)

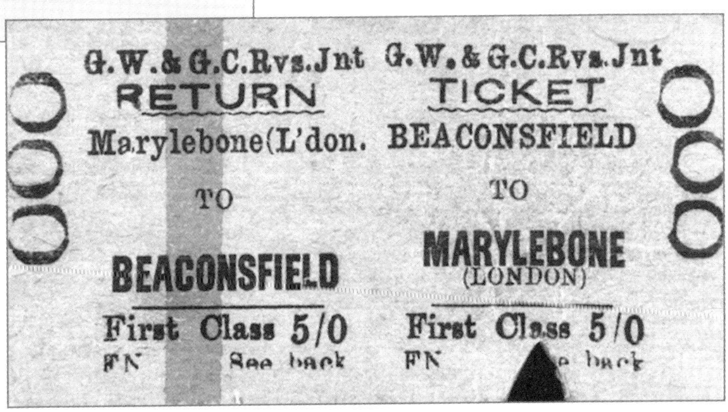

Right: The first return ticket (first class) to Marylebone cost 5*s* in April 1906. Today it costs £18, a 72-fold increase. It was a half-hour service to Marylebone. (*Beaconsfield and District Historical Society*)

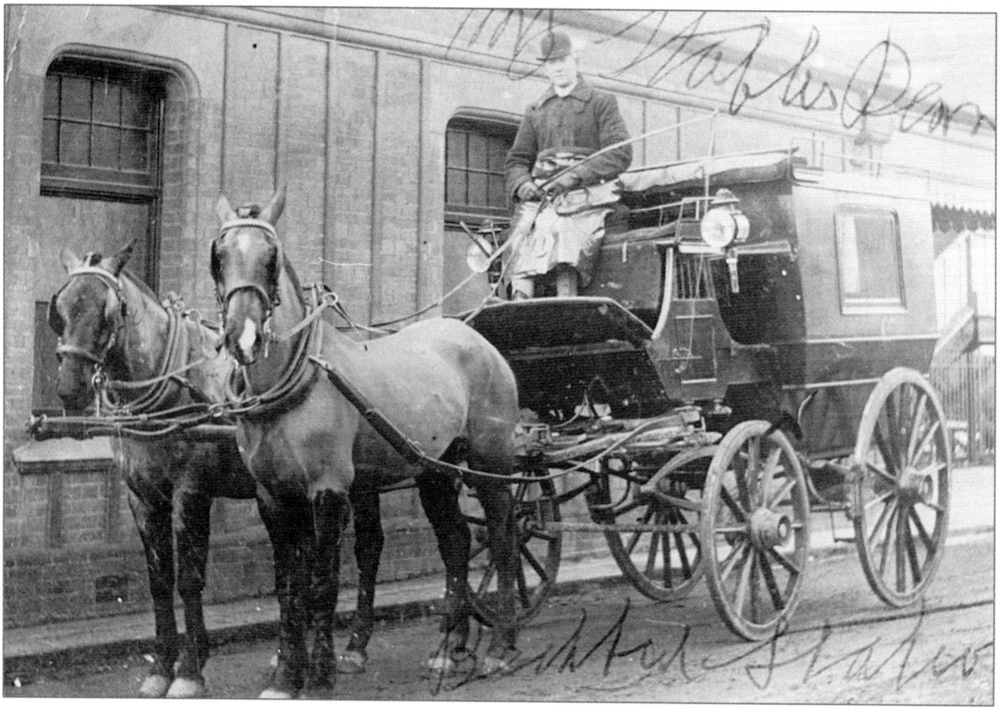

A cab driven by Mr Stickley awaiting passengers for Penn outside the newly built station at Beaconsfield, *c.* 1906. Later a horse bus ran from Mr Reid's stables near the Red Lion, Penn, but only if there were passengers and if the weather was not too bad. It made only two journeys daily, to catch the early morning train and then back in the evening. The first motor bus, of the Penn Bus Company, ran in 1920. (*CWPC*)

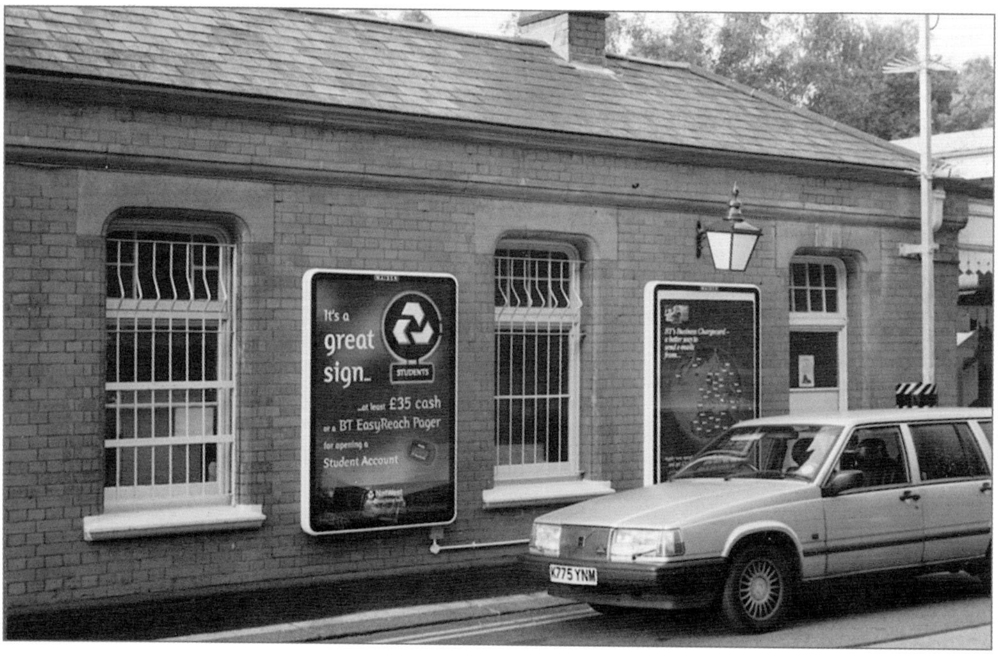

A modern view. (*Eddie Morton*)

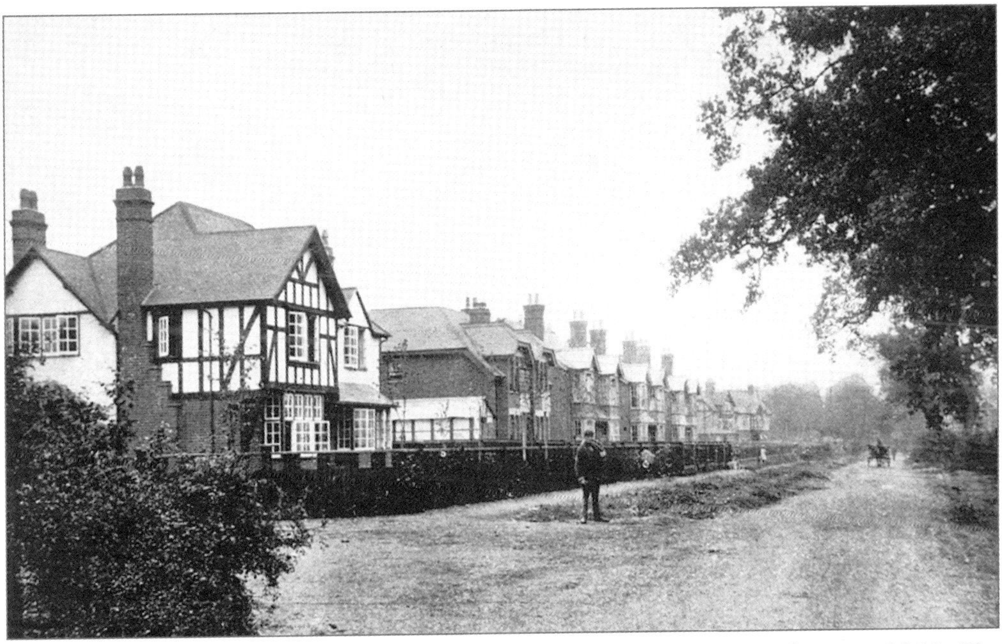

Looking back along the Penn Road from the junction with Ledborough Lane, 1911. The photograph, by Arthur A. White, appeared in an official guide book to Beaconsfield which has an introduction by G.K. Chesterton. The railway hotel can be seen at the end of the row, replaced by Waitrose in about 1980. Today's shops seem to have been built as houses. Enid Blyton lived at Green Hedges, 100 yards along the road towards Penn, from 1938 to 1968, and most of her 'Noddy', 'Famous Five' and 'Secret Seven' books were written there. (*David Wooster*)

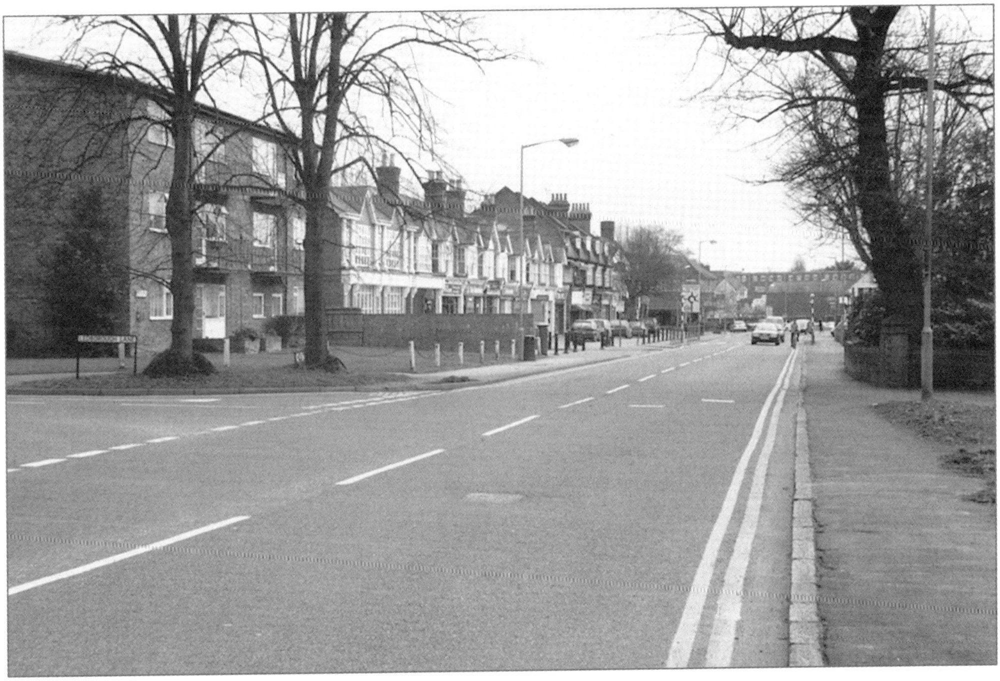

A modern view. (*Eddie Morton*)

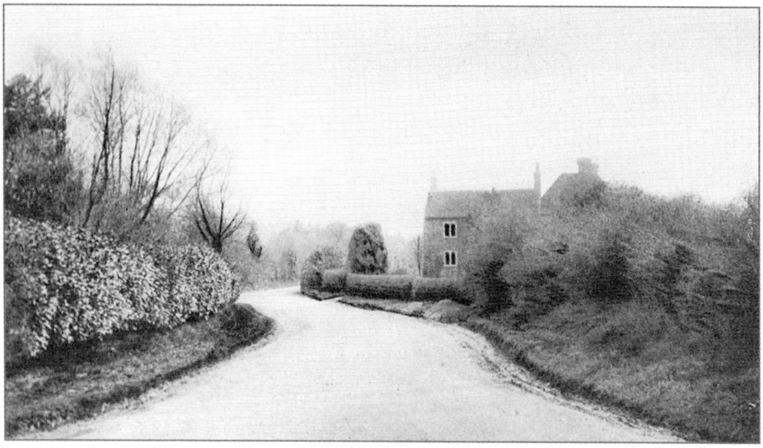

Penn Road, looking towards Beaconsfield from in front of the Red Lion, Knotty Green, *c.* 1920. Orchard House, to the right, burned down in about 1990 and has been replaced by Churchill Close. In 1909 there were complaints about the height of the hedge at Orchard (late Norfolk) House which made the bend in the road dangerous. There was a house on the same site in about 1750. (*Colin Seabright*)

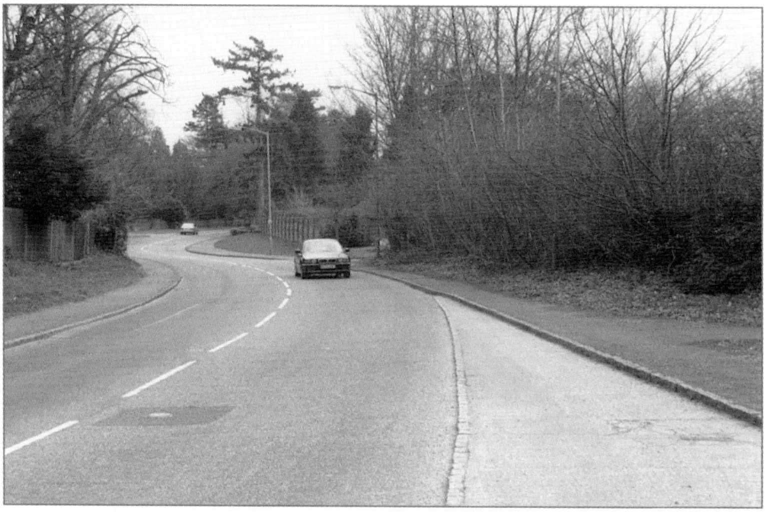

Modern view. (*Eddie Morton*)

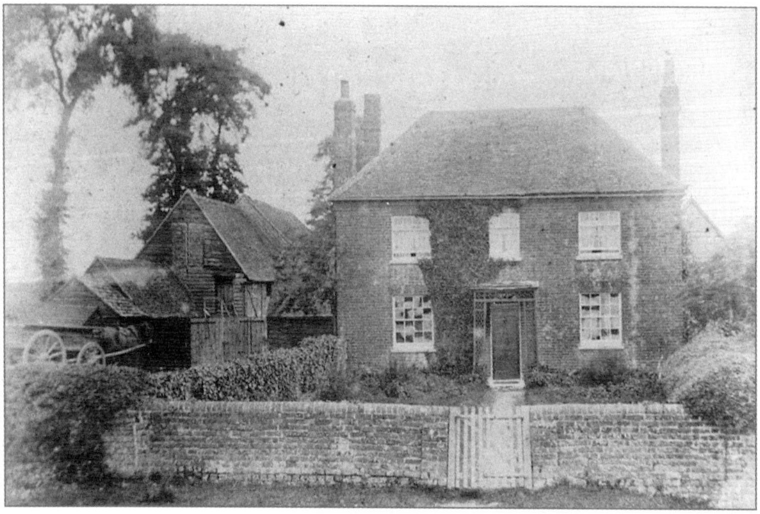

Knotty Green Farm, *c.* 1900. This old farmhouse, built in about 1790, used to stand on the corner of Finch Lane and Penn Road. It ceased to be a farm after much of its land was sold off in 1906 and was purchased by Mr J. Baily Gibson, to whom the Parish Council protested when he decided to fill up the farm pond in 1909. It was greatly extended to become part of a much larger house, all of which was demolished in about 1960. The photograph was provided by David Wooster whose great grandfather, George Wooster, held the farm as the tenant of the Penn Estate. The houses of Farm Grove and Old Farm Close now occupy the site. (*David Wooster*)

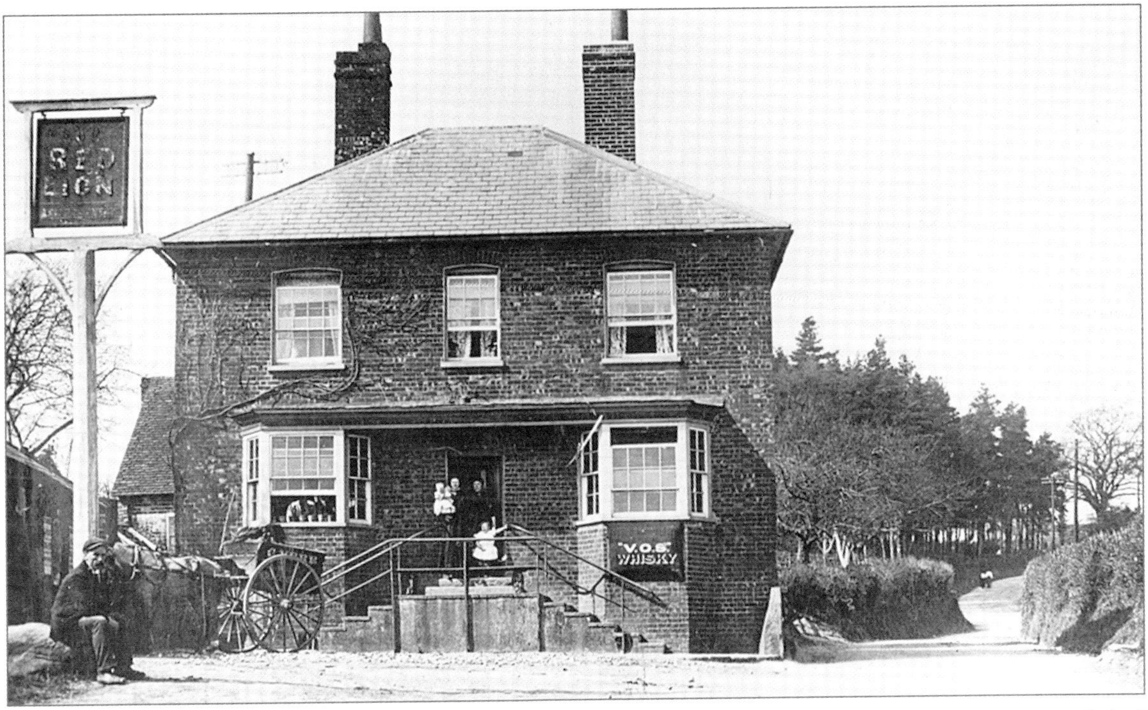

The Red Lion and Penn Road, before 1907. The photograph shows Knotty Green Hill, which was a good deal steeper before the gradient was reduced by taking off the top. There was a stone water trough and a public notice board at the top of the hill, just before the turning to West Witheridge. The road was widened after the arrival of the railway. The Red Lion was included in the county register of alehouse keepers in 1753. (*CWPC*)

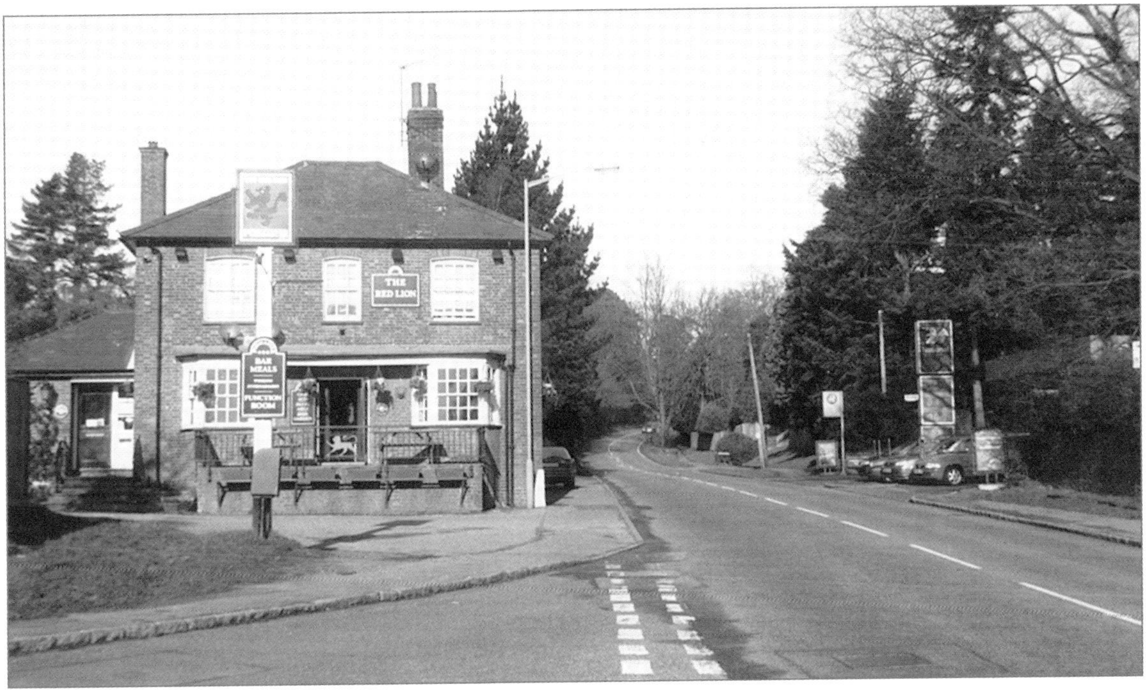

Modern view. (*Eddie Morton*)

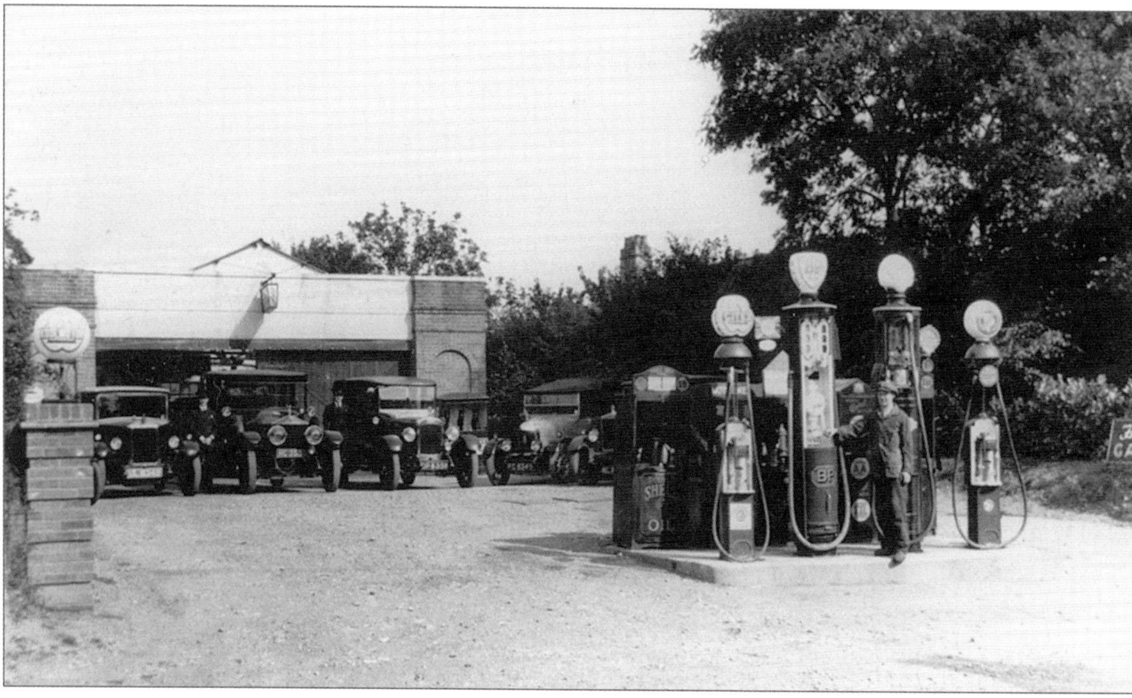

Hallett's Garage (now Knotty Green Garage) in 1931, not long after it was established. Teddy Iles is standing by the petrol pumps, chauffeur Harry Beardsall by the Rolls-Royce and Doug Griffiths by the Austin. (*Knotty Green Garage*)

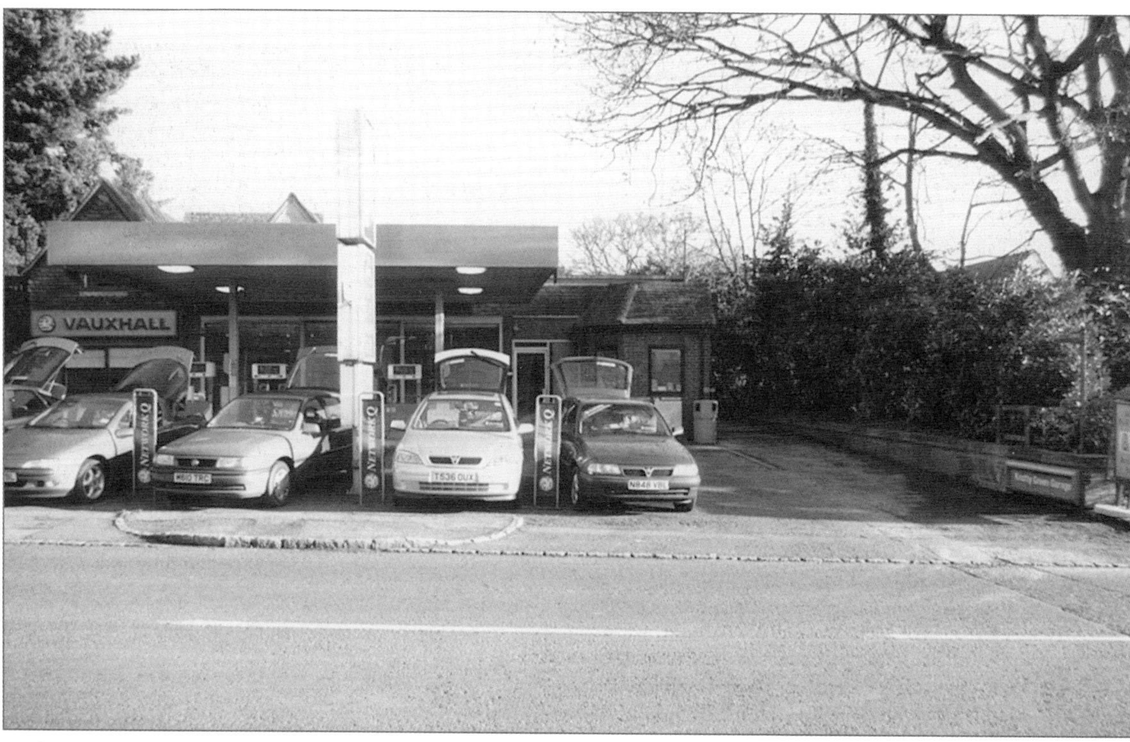

Modern view. (*Eddie Morton*)

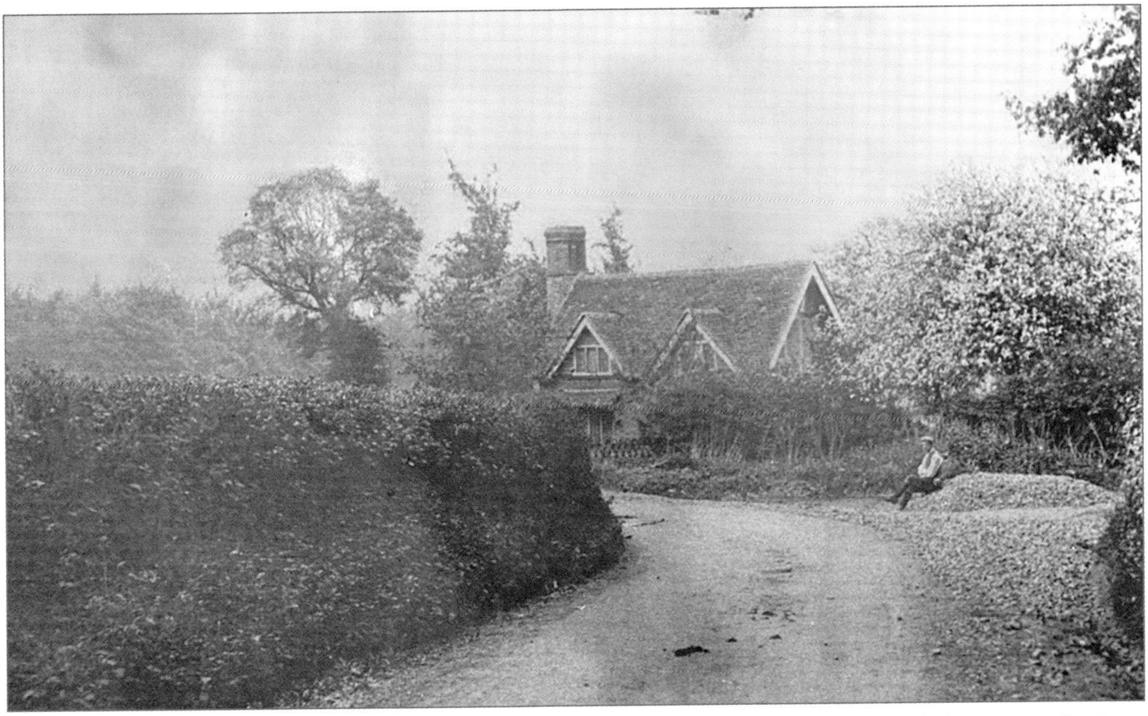

The sharp bend by the Old Cottage (formerly Harley's Cottage), which was a tied cottage belonging to the Penn Estate, early 1900s. Rupert Davies of Maigret TV fame lived in Shearings behind the Old Cottage. Note the stones used for road repair. (*CWPC*)

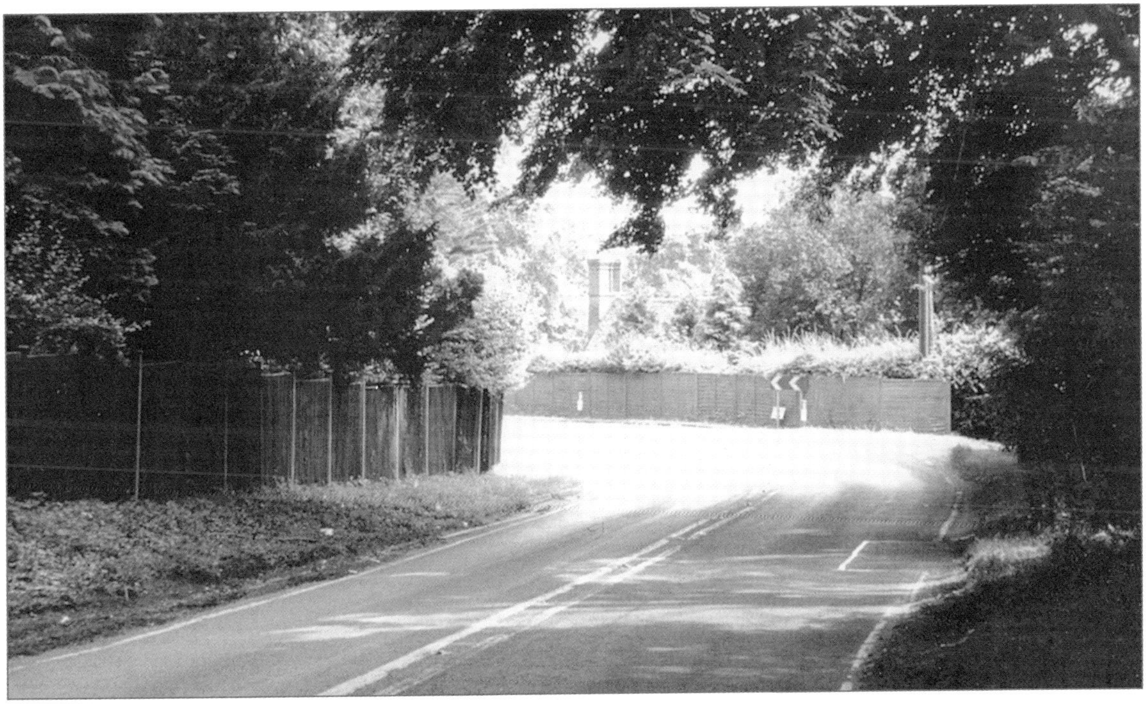

Modern view. (*Eddie Morton*)

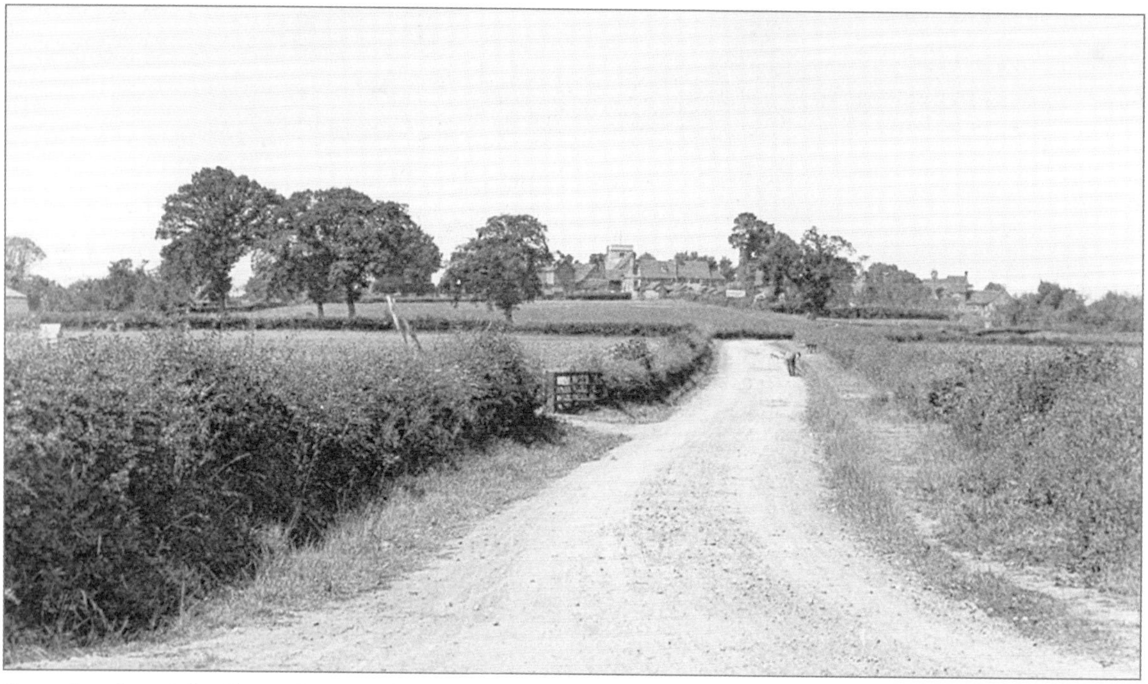

Penn church and the Crown from just beyond Penbury Farm, early 1900s. This stretch of road did not exist until about 150 years ago. Today's road crosses the former farmyard of Penbury Farm, which had a large pond. Witherage Lane (the spelling seems to have changed to 'Witheridge' in the 1920s) ran from Saucy Corner to Penbury, then turned down to Church Knowl and up to an important property known, in 1199, as Withiheg and now known as Puttenham Place. Crown Lane was the way up to Penn Church. (*CWPC*)

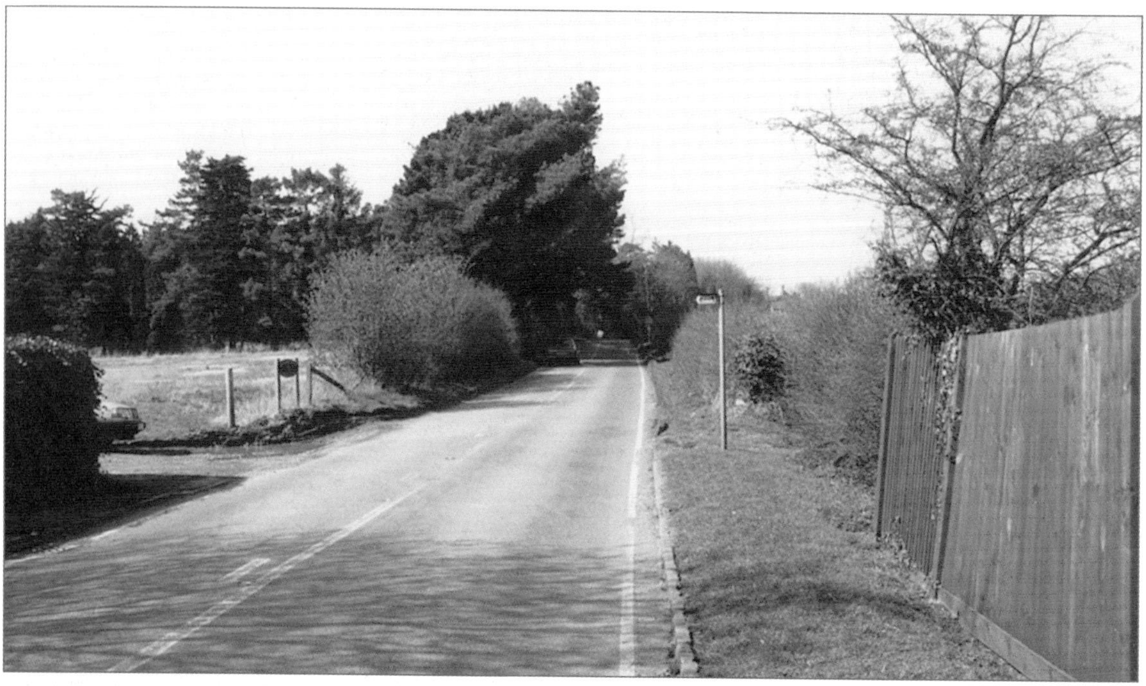

Modern view. (*Eddie Morton*)

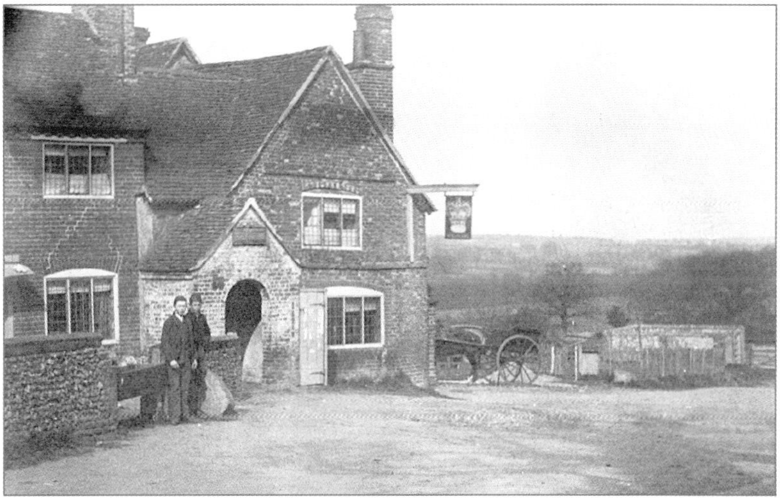

The Crown, before 1907.
A listed building and probably the longest established public house in the parish, the Crown was one of only two alehouses in Penn recorded in a return of 1577. The oldest part of the building is of about that date. The brick and flint pound for stray animals was built in 1870 and removed in 1907. Its predecessor was a wooden structure fixed to the churchyard wall. The Parish Council still get a rent from the present owners of the Crown, for the use of the former pound as a car park. (*CWPC*)

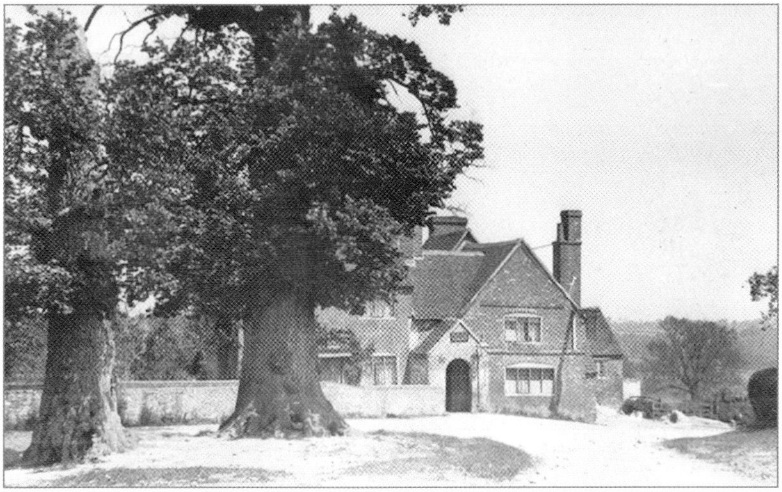

The Crown, showing two 'stock' elms of which only one stump remains, early 1900s. The stocks used to be about where the war memorial stands (erected in 1921) and Owen Fryer, born in 1858 in the Corner Cottage, Pauls Hill (now Stone Cottage), thought he remembered seeing a man in them. At that time there was still a non-uniformed village constable who dealt with minor offences. (*Enid Evered*)

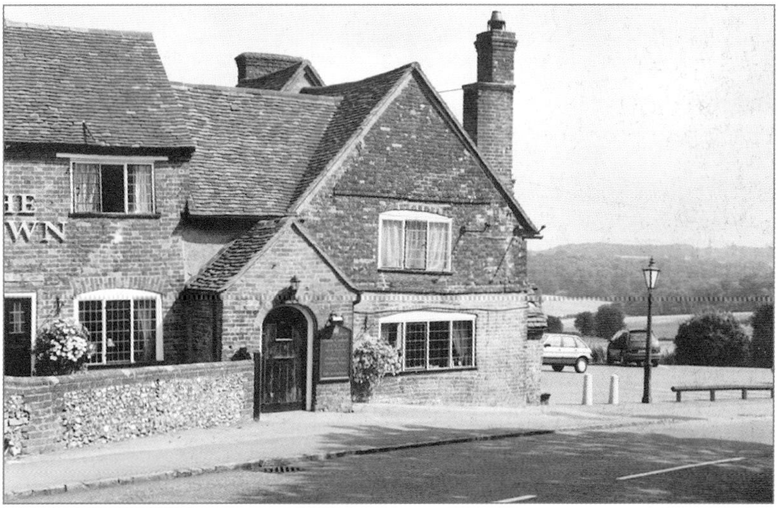

Modern view. (*Eddie Morton*)

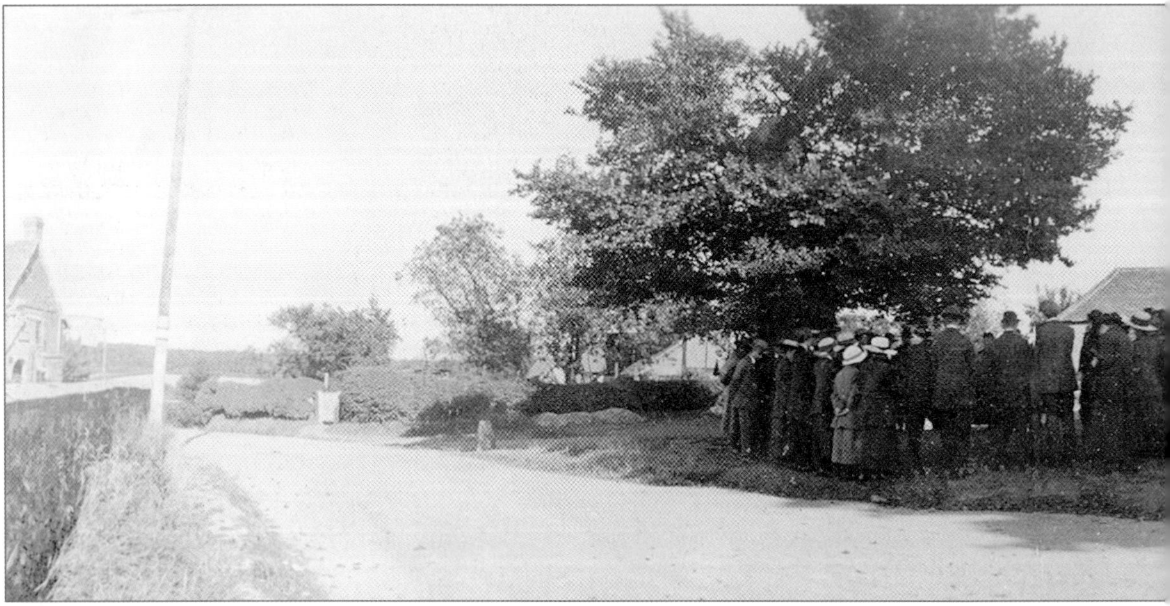

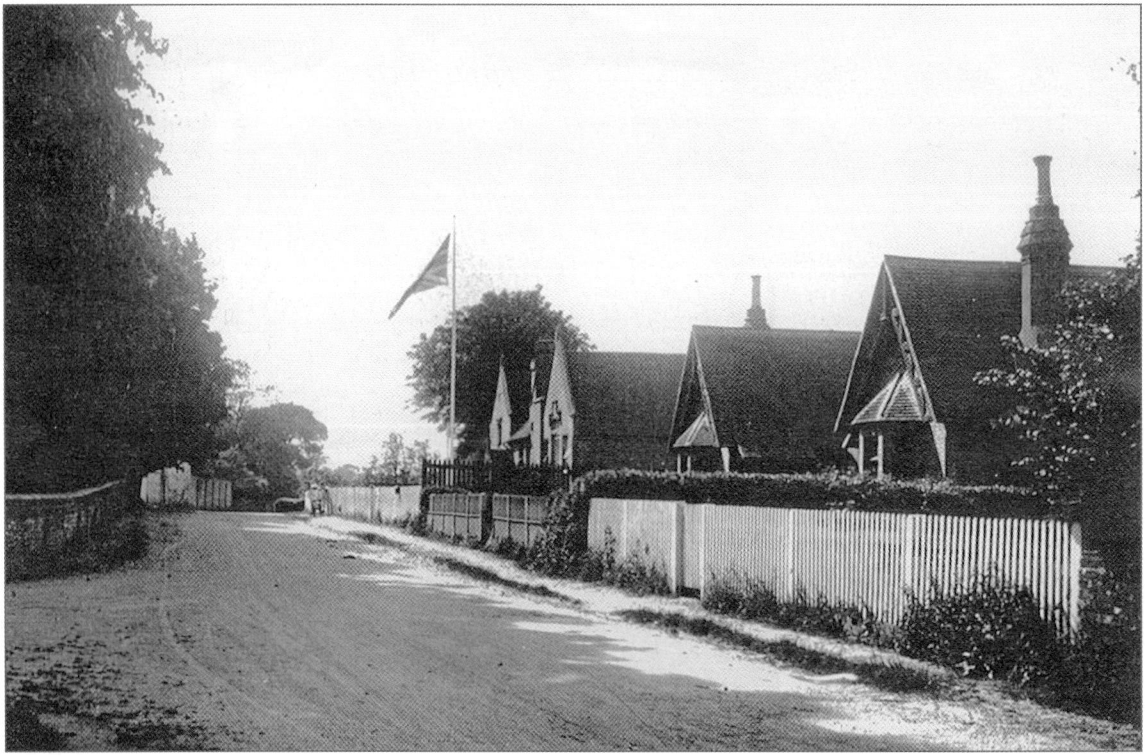

Almshouses and Penn schools, after 1910. The large extension added to the school in 1910, at a cost of £1,250 and paid for by public subscription, can be seen in this photograph. Pupil numbers were increasing sharply as the new railway encouraged house building. The almshouses were built in 1831, paid for by Earl Howe and Thomas Grove immediately after a labourers' revolt and severe rioting in Wycombe Marsh and Loudwater. The almshouses were pulled down in 1969, after much dispute, to make way for the modern flats of Penn Mead. (*Wycombe Museum*)

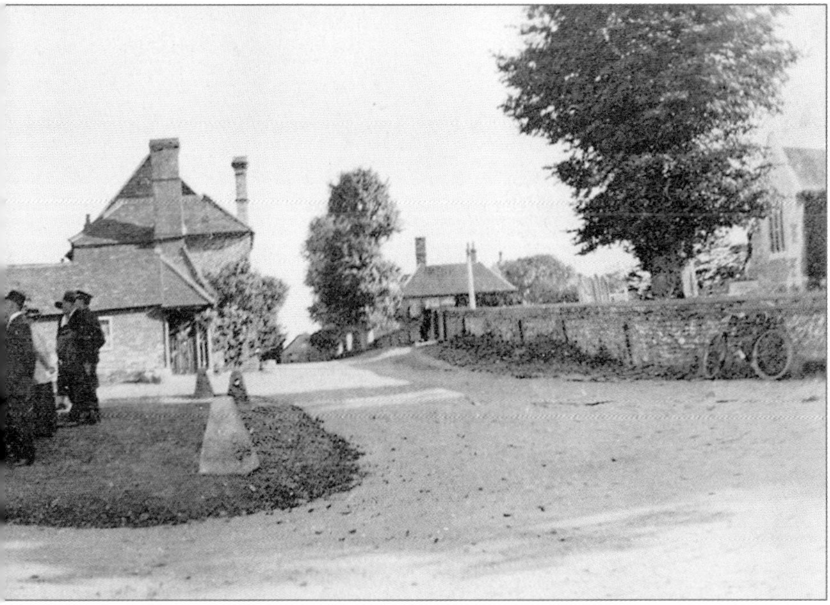

Open Air Holiness Meeting, *c.* 1920. This was a strongly evangelical group run by George Wooster, the tenant of Penbury and four other farms of the Penn Estate. Herbert Hoover, a future President of the United States, shared similar views and stayed at Penbury Farm for a day or two in about 1914. Religious exhortations were placed on Mr Wooster's properties along the road: 'Prepare to meet thy God' appropriately by the steep bend below the farm; 'The Lord will deliver'; 'God Saves' and so on. (*David Wooster*)

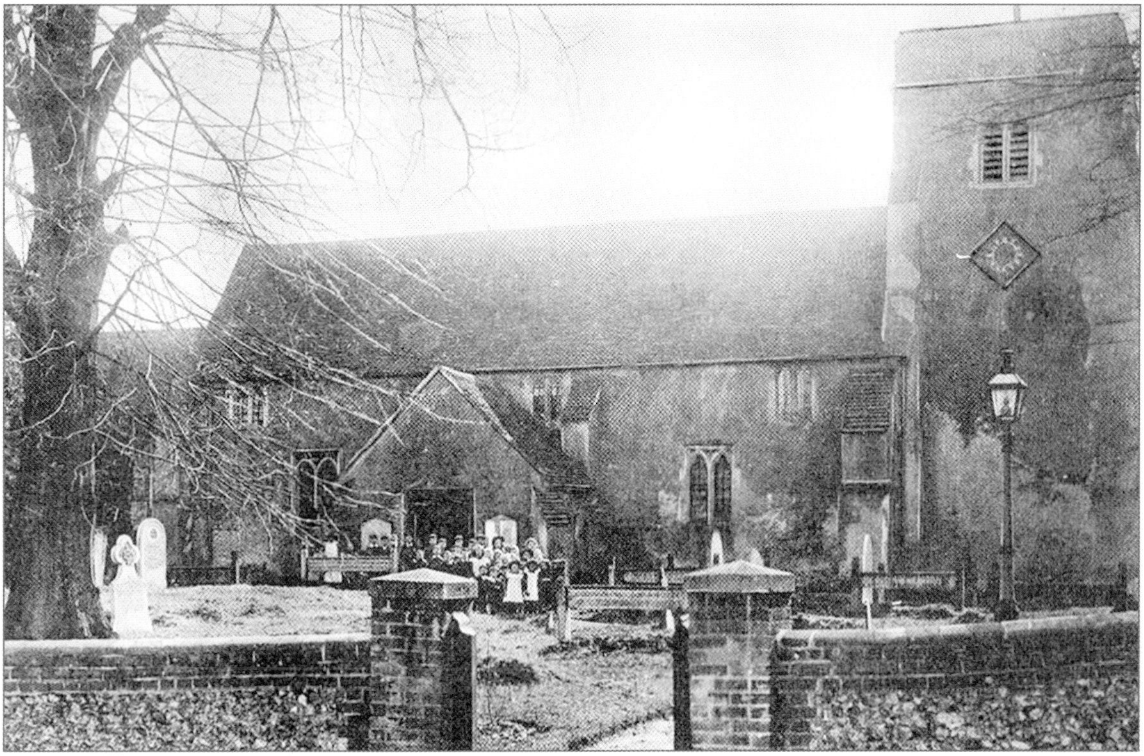

Penn Church, before 1913. This photograph was taken before the lych gate was added in 1913, under the erroneous impression that it was the 700th anniversary of the church. It is probably a little older: the date 1177 was seen on a foundation stone under the chancel by the Revd John Middleton, who was vicar from 1787 to 1808. Earl Howe has inherited the patronage of the church from his Penne forbears who were granted it by Henry VIII, in 1541, as one of many royal rewards for Sybil Penne's role as a nurse and foster mother to the sickly Prince Edward. (*CWPC*)

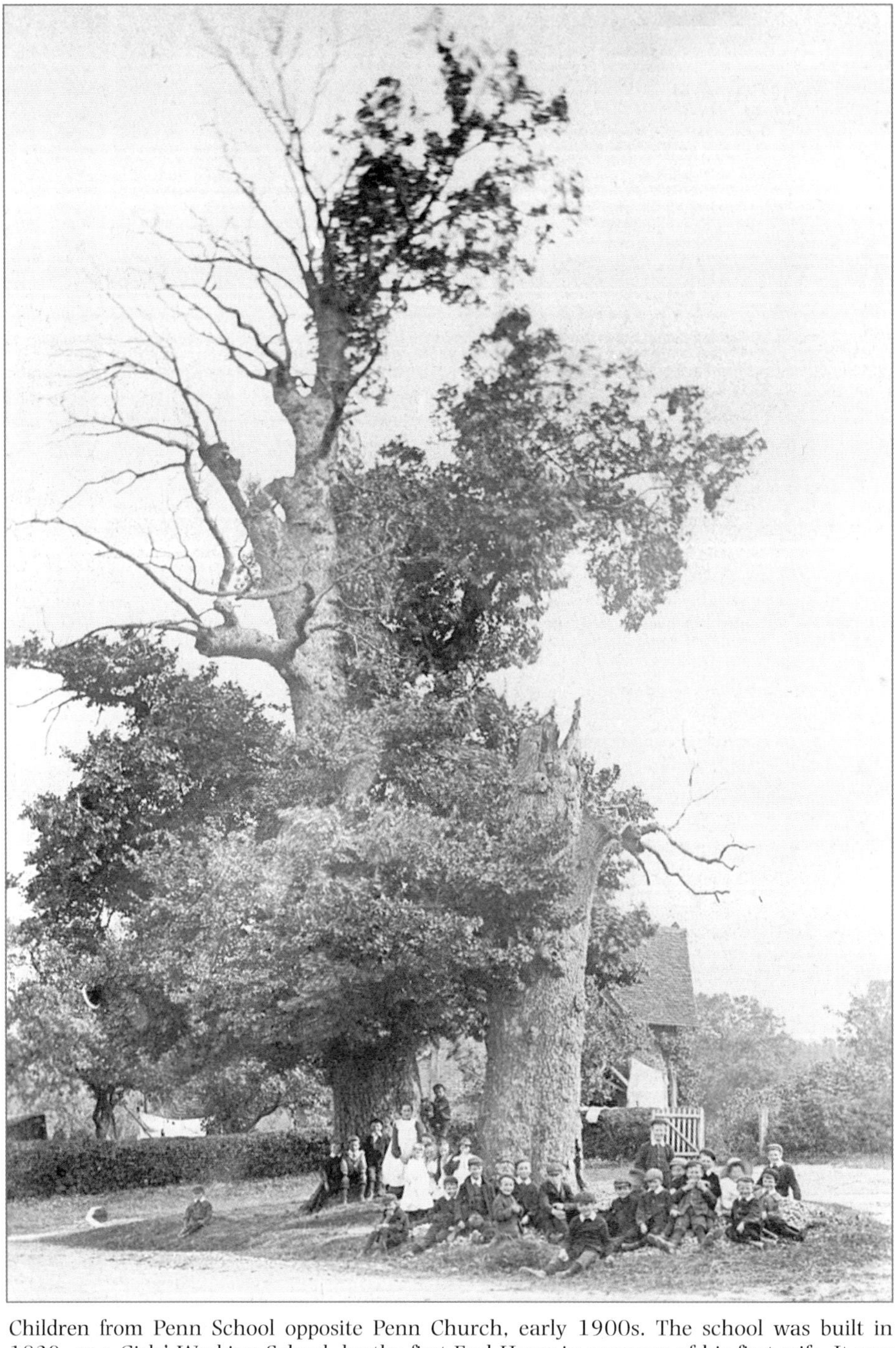

Children from Penn School opposite Penn Church, early 1900s. The school was built in 1839, as a Girls' Working School, by the first Earl Howe in memory of his first wife. It was a Church of England school supported by annual subscription from Earl Howe, other leading parishioners and Queen Adelaide, the wife of William IV. Boys joined the girls after 1875 when their school at Church Knowl was closed, and infants were added when their school at Tylers Green was closed in 1910. Penn School was closed in 1952 because of a shortage of pupils. (*Colin Seabright*)

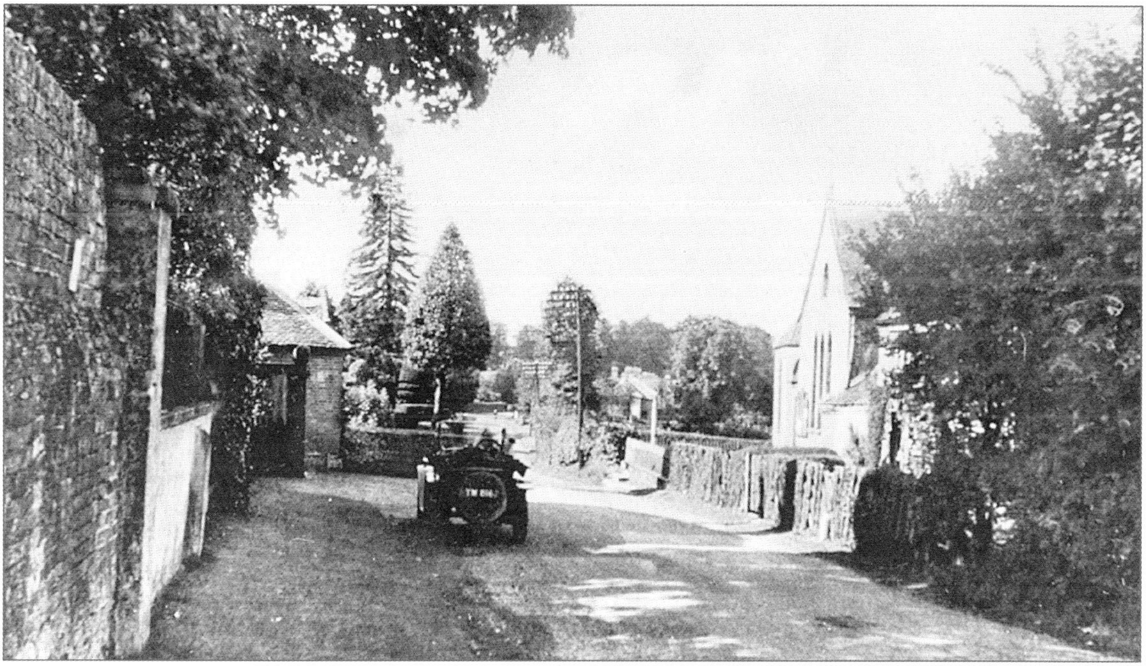

Outside Watercroft, looking towards Tylers Green, 1920s. The road is not yet tarmacked. The Free Methodist church to the right was built in 1808, the first in the Wycombe area. Watercroft, on the left, was built in about 1825. (*CWPC*)

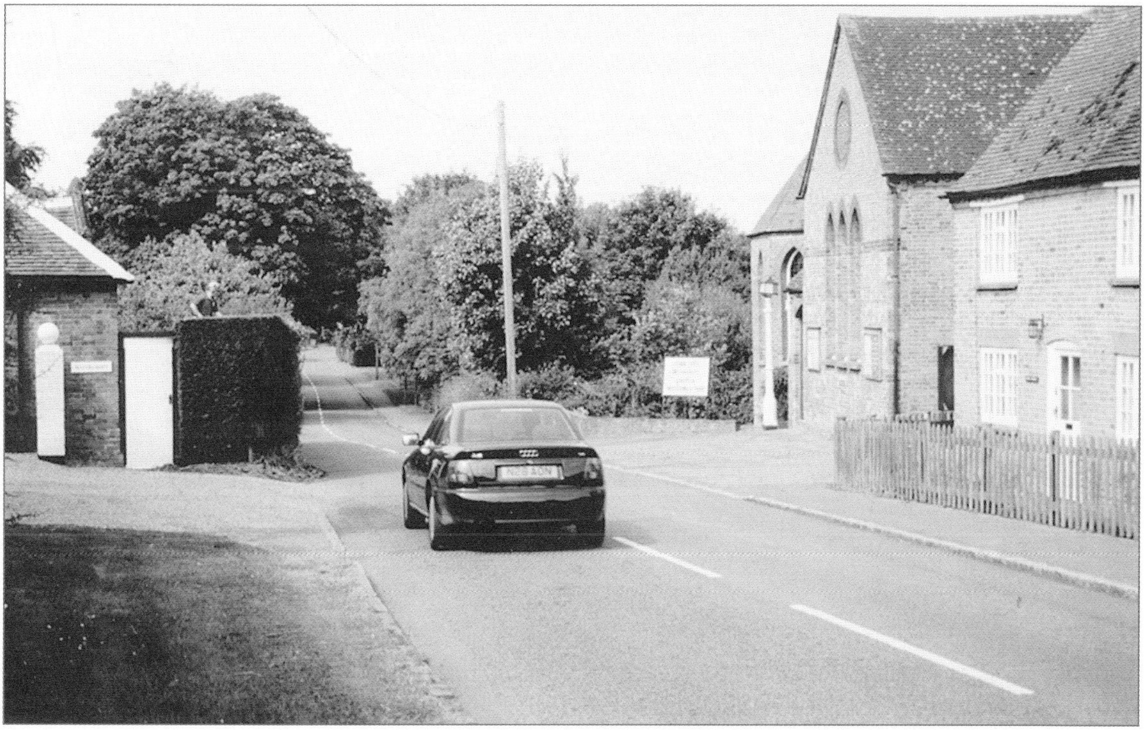

Modern view. (*Eddie Morton*)

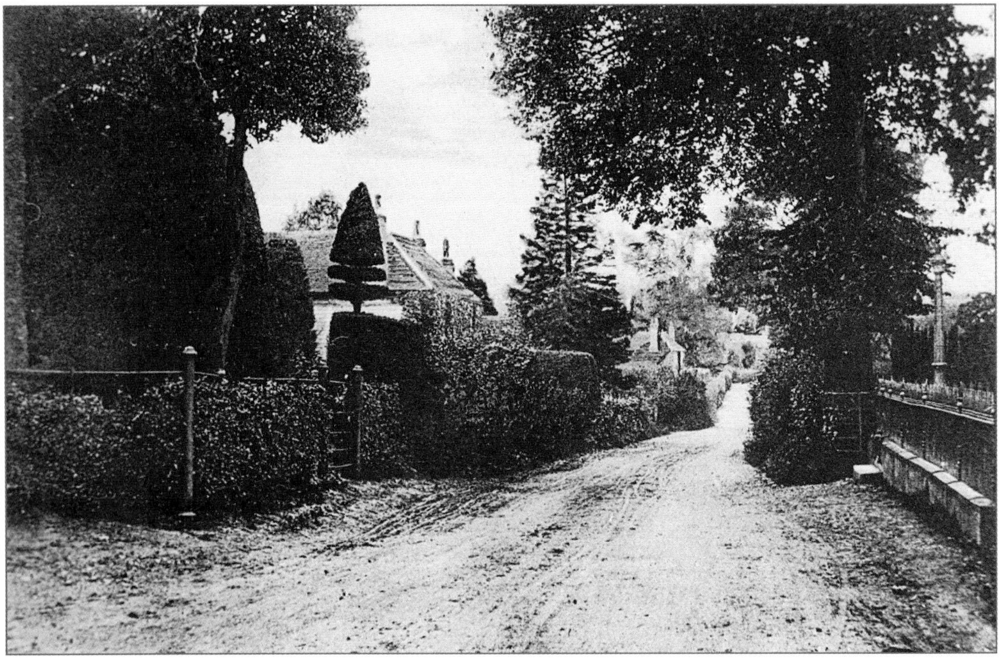

A postcard view from outside the Methodist chapel towards Tylers Green, with Dell Cottage on the left and Stumpwell Cottage further down, 1905. Dell Cottage was owned by Lord Dawson of Penn from before the First World War to 1938. He was George V's physician and issued the famous bulletin in 1935, 'The King's life is moving peacefully towards its close'. He added a large library to the original two small cottages. His family called the house 'library with cottage attached'. The first transatlantic telephone call was made, from Pennsylvania, to Lord Dawson, along a cable run out from Penn post office, on 7 January 1927. (*Mr and Mrs Harold Wheeler*)

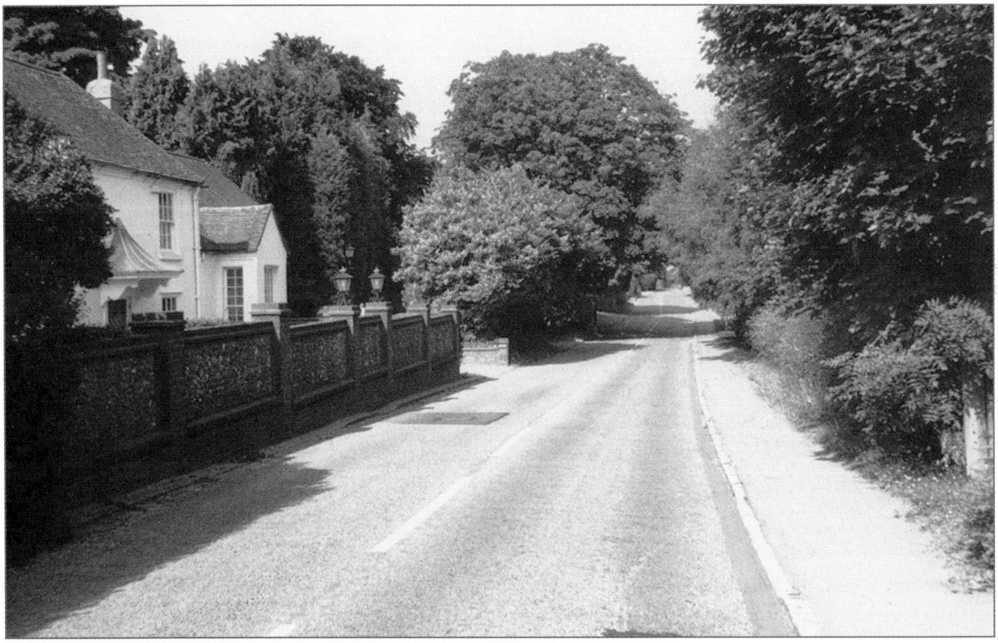

A modern view. (*Eddie Morton*)

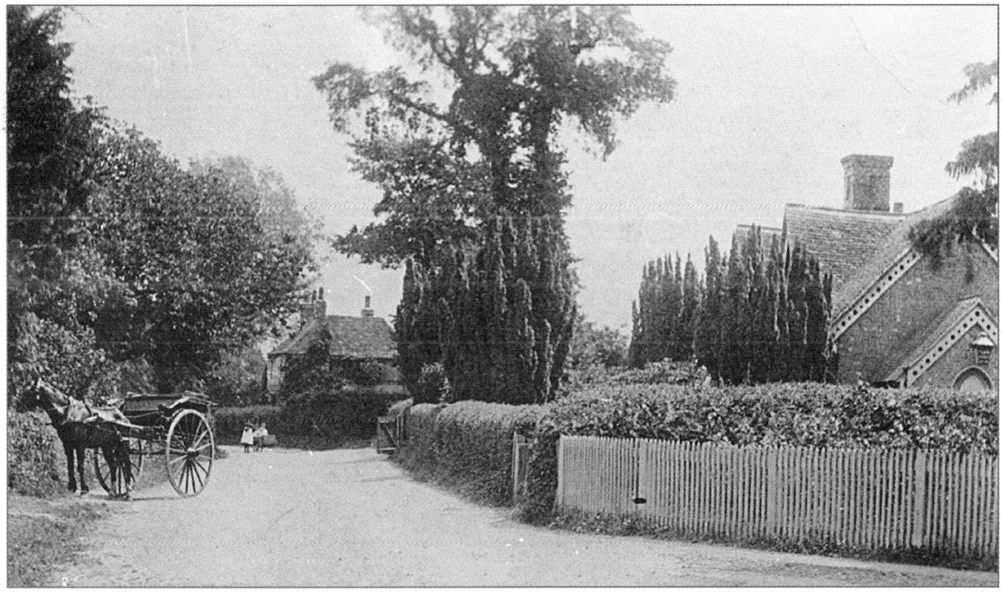

Looking back towards Penn Church from Beacon Hill, early 1900s. The Old Reading Room on the right was built from the bricks of the boys' school at Church Knowl when it was dismantled in 1875. The house was built by Earl Howe as the Penn Institute, a working men's club where the gentry left their periodicals and newspapers and where tea and coffee were available. The aim was to improve the common man and wean him away from the many public houses. It remained open from 1875 until 1960, with only two housekeepers in eighty-five years. The WI used to meet there. The 5th Earl's third wife lived in Stumpwell Cottage, seen at the end of the lane, in the 1960s. (*CWPC*)

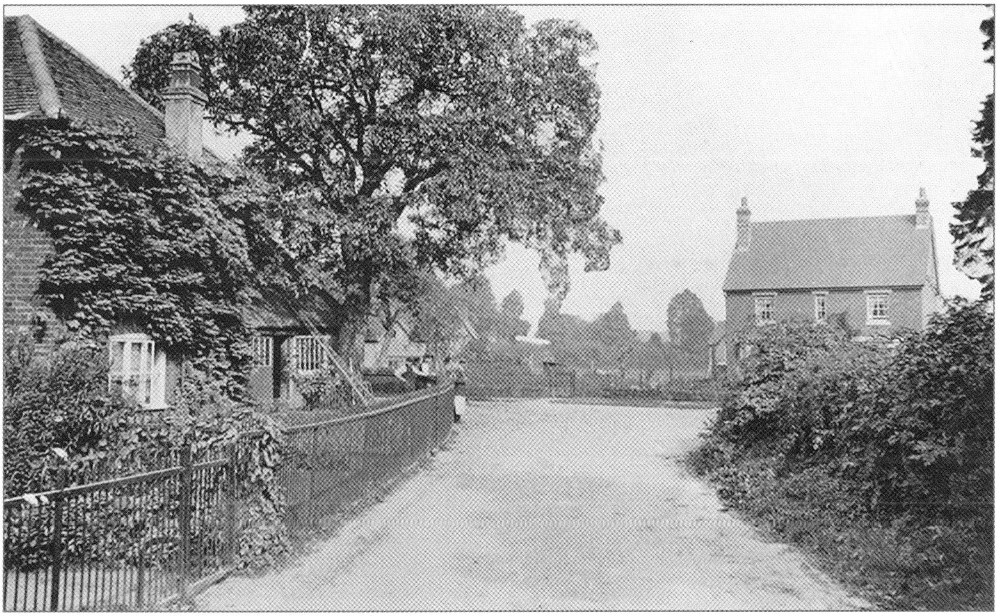

A view from Beacon Hill with the smithy on the left, *c.* 1915. What is now Winter's Garage was still part of the garden of Allendale (now Hampdens), the house to the right which was built in 1906 for Walter Evans, the owner of the smithy. He is shown as telephone no. 6 in the directory for Penn in 1915. (*Colin Seabright*)

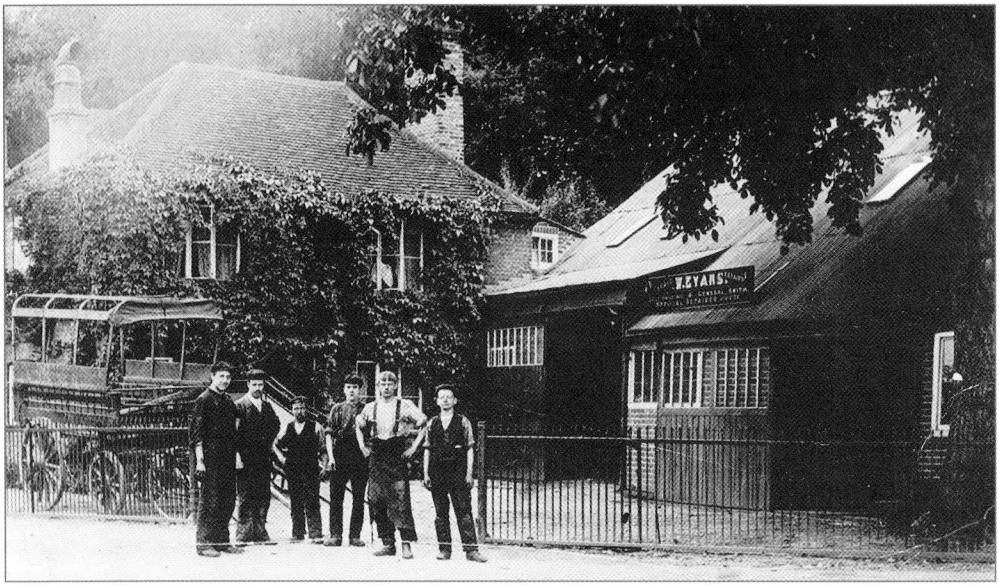

The smithy run by Walter Evans at the corner of Beacon Hill, early 1900s. Wingroves were the blacksmiths here for the century before Walter Evans took over in the 1880s. He also advertised 'private electric light installation' provided by paraffin generators and accumulators before the mains supply arrived. Billy Simmonds is the small man in the centre. George Slade worked for Evans and had taken over by 1920, described as 'motor and agricultural engineer and smith'. He was exempted from military service in 1914 because he was the only blacksmith and was still shoeing farm horses in the 1920s and 1930s. The cottage seems to be late eighteenth century with additions at the front from 1840 and 1860. (*Harold Wheeler*)

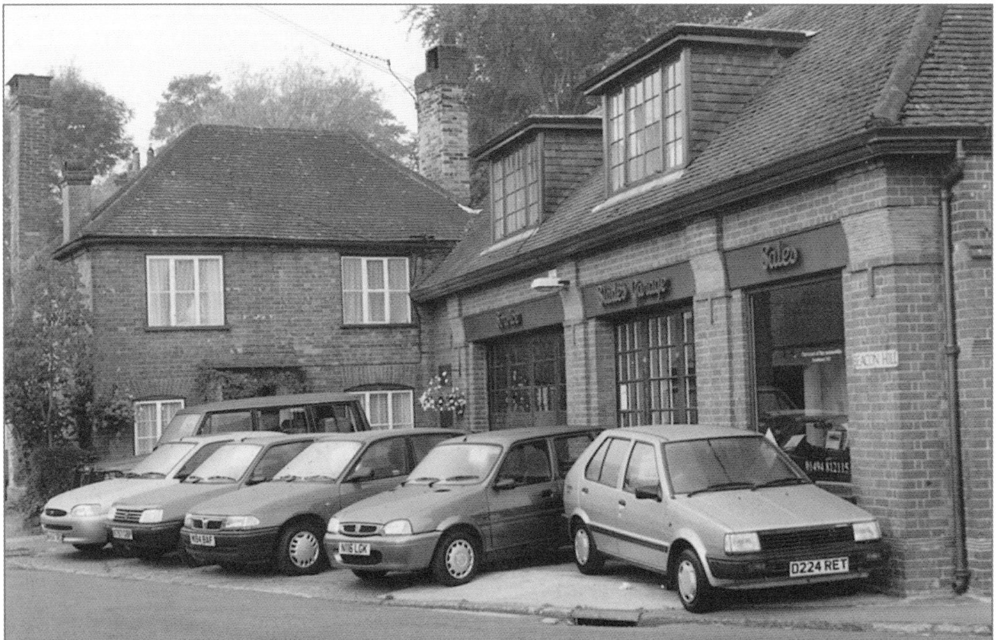

A modern view of Slade's Garage. By the late 1930s the garage was dealing only with cars. (*Eddie Morton*)

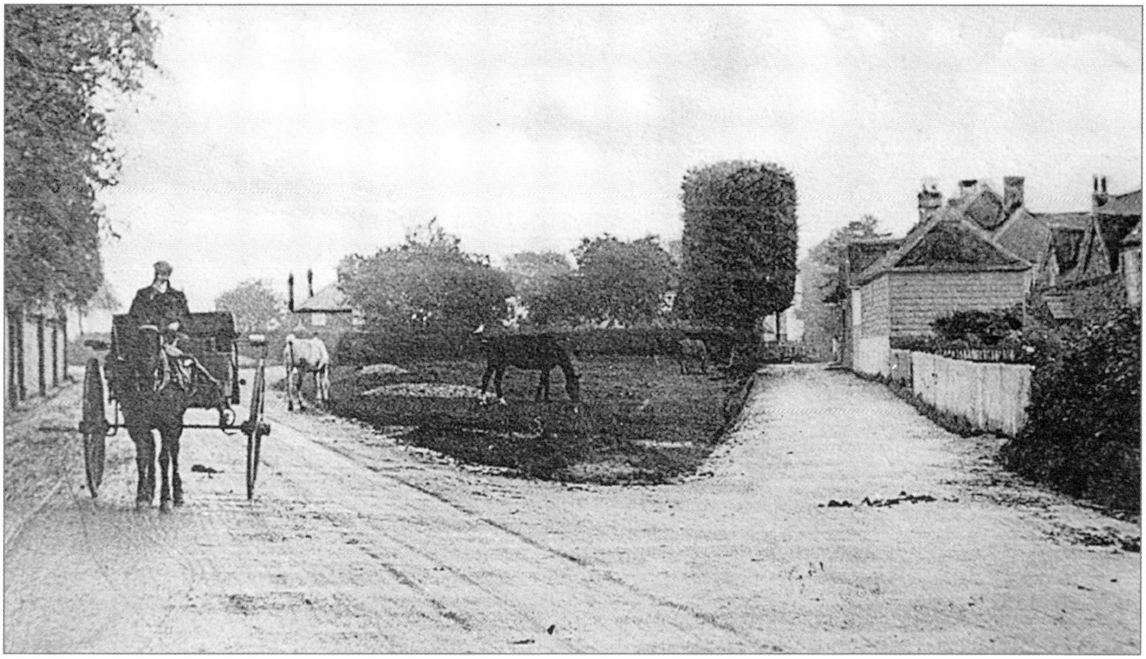

View from the main gates of Rayners, *c.* 1910. Mr Gurney is on his way to his farm at Seer Green. Note that horses were still allowed to graze on the Common and there used to be a gate across the road near the entrance to Rayners to prevent strays. The original road went through the shopping area, the present main road being the 'horse road' which detoured around it. The yew hedge in front of King's the butcher was (erroneously) said to 'part the village'. In fact the parish boundary runs along the line of the horse road. (*CWPC*)

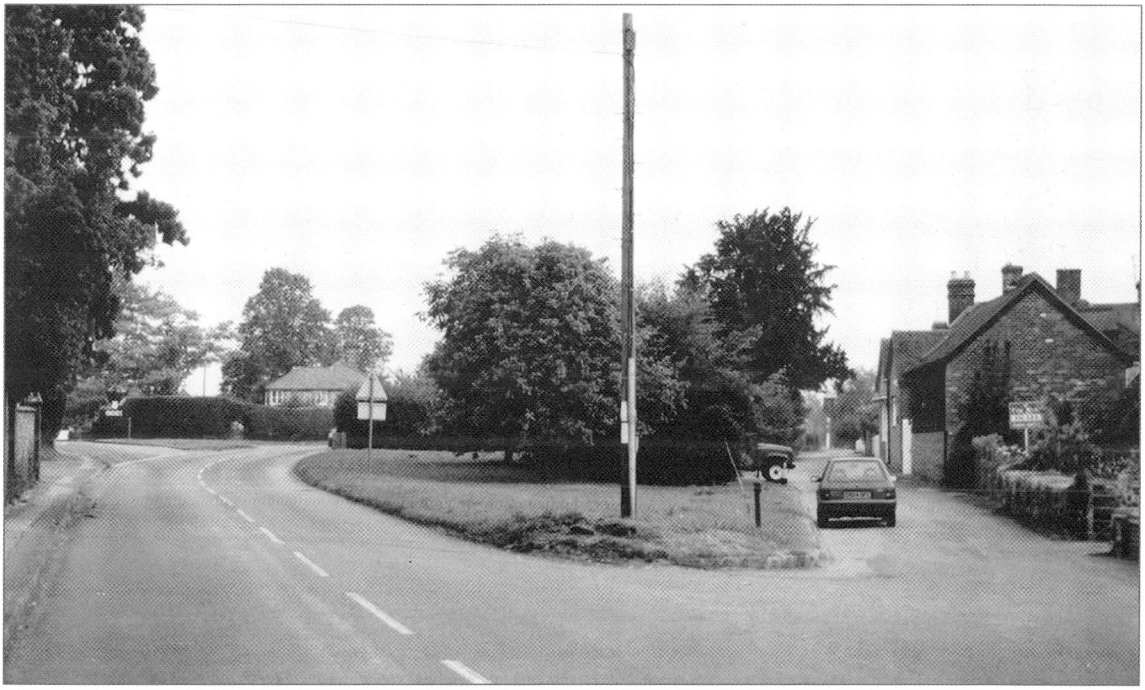

Modern view. (*Eddie Morton*)

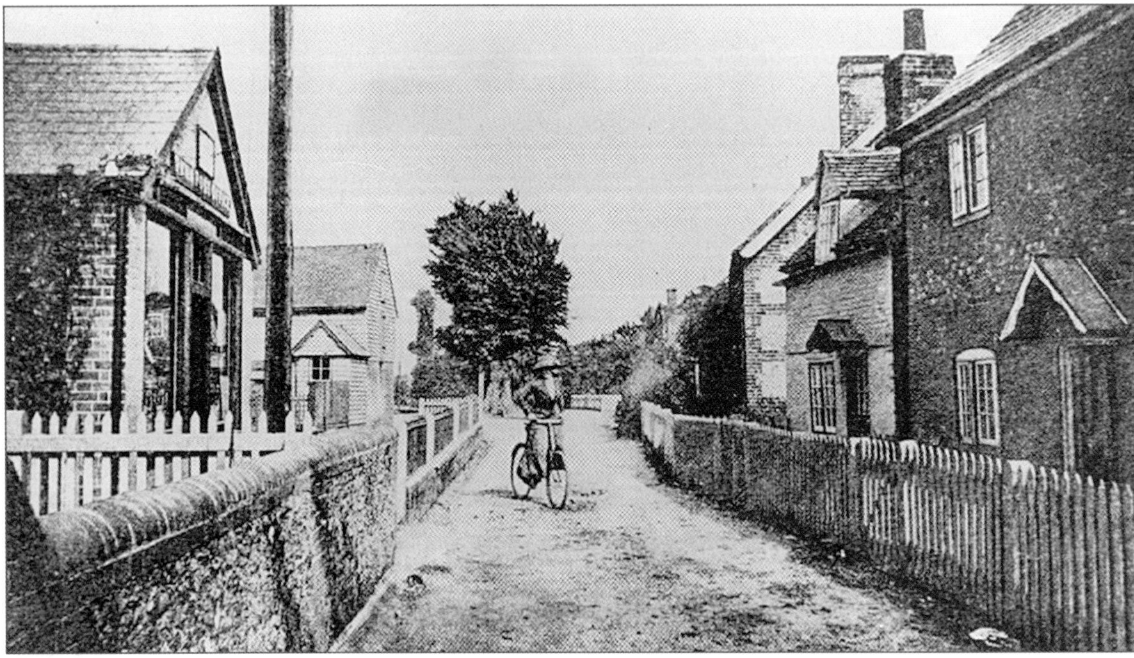

Penn post office, *c.* 1895, was then in Wheeler's, the grocer's shop, which was bought by the Woodbridge family in 1915. The present Cottage Bookshop was then a private house. Before the First World War it became a fish shop and afterwards was briefly Barclays Bank. Between the wars it was mainly used as an extension of Baddeley's general store for gardening equipment, pots and pans and so on. After the Second World War it was shared between an electrical shop and a shoe repairer (Fred Baker), soon joined by the bookshop which opened in 1951. (*Fred Baddeley*)

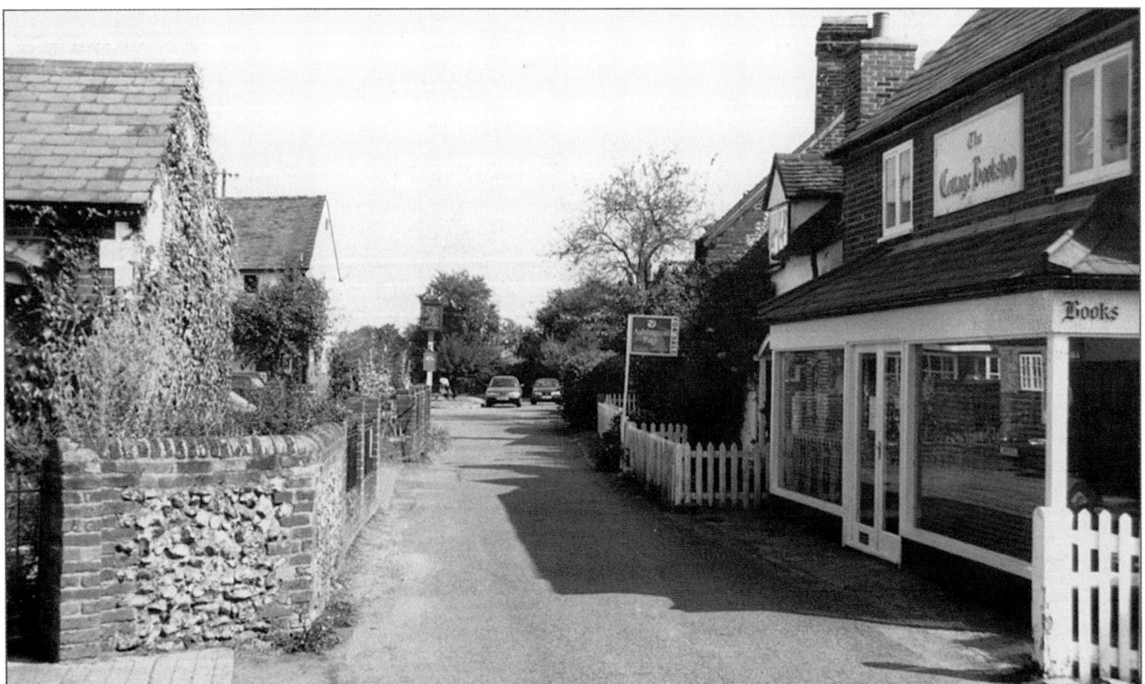

Modern view. (*Eddie Morton*)

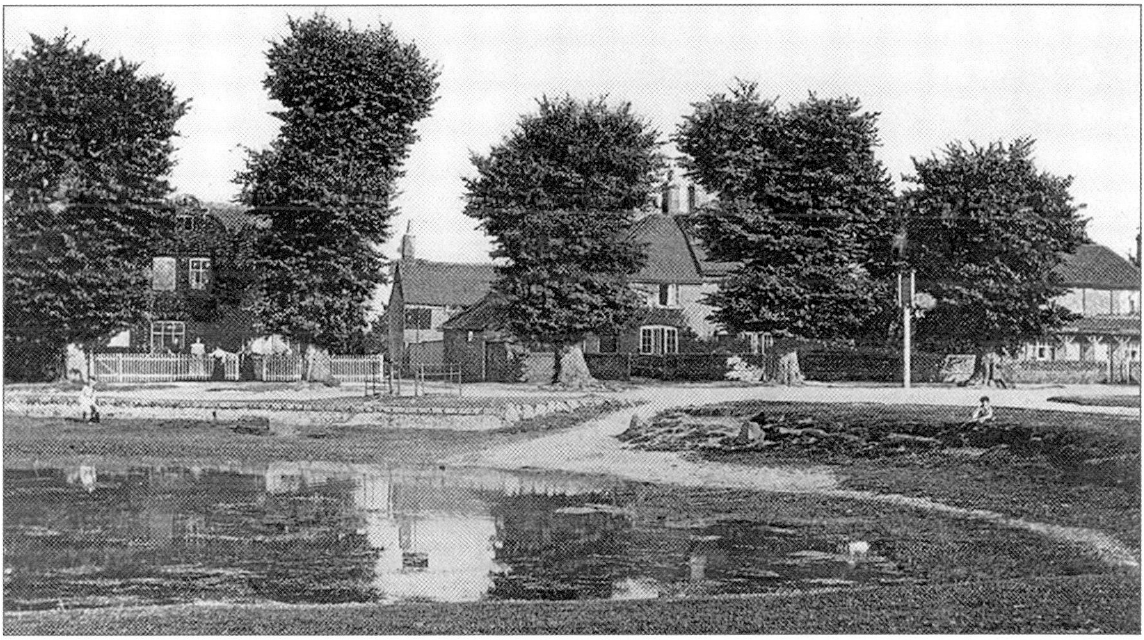

Looking towards the Old Bank House and Red Lion from Widmer Pond, early 1900s. The Old Bank House has a late seventeenth-century brick front on an older house. It was originally a lodge to Puttenham Place, at the entrance to Putts Lane, later two cottages and briefly Barclays Bank in the 1930s. The Red Lion was already a public house in 1753 and is likely to have been one of the only two alehouses recorded in Penn in 1577. The Segraves Manor Court used to meet there on occasions. The boundary between Penn and Tylers Green runs through the pond, which was the main source of drinking and washing water; ducks were kept strictly away. It was known as Great Widmer Pond in 1726 and was stocked with carp, tench and other fish. (*CWPC*)

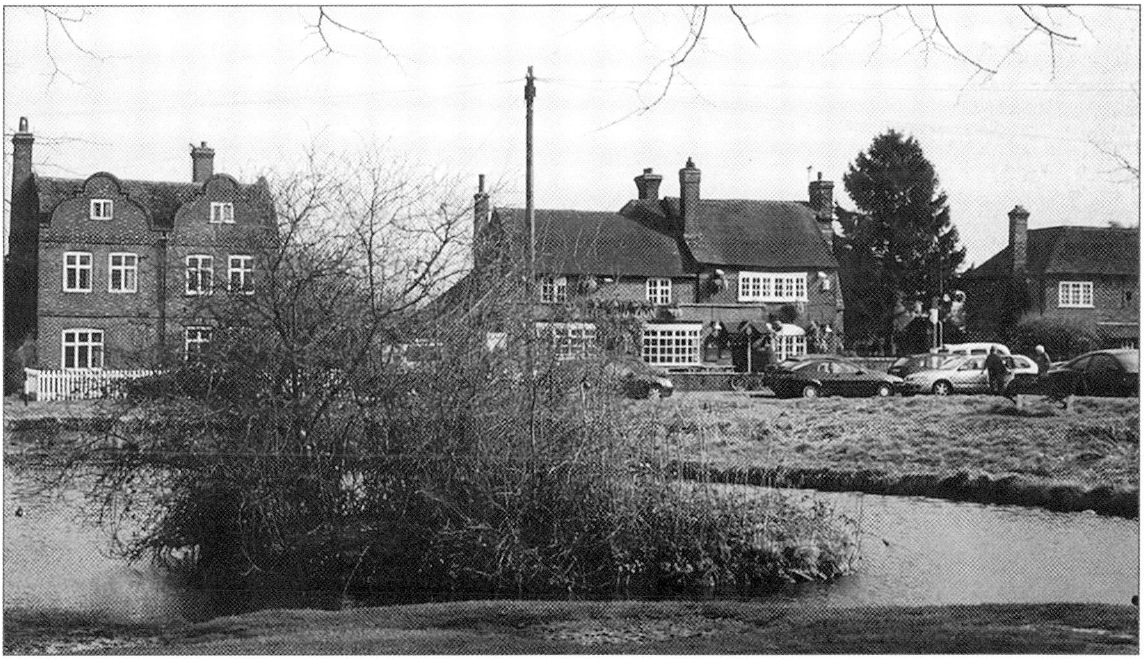

Modern view. (*Liz Tebbutt*)

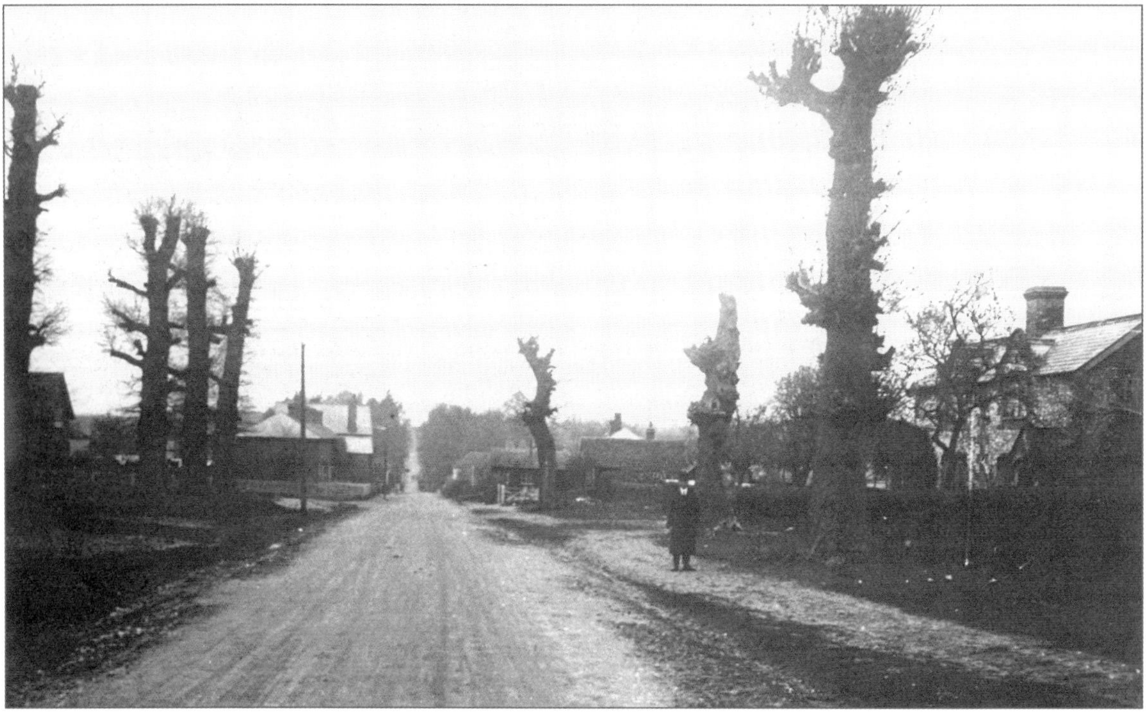

Elm Road looking towards Potters Cross, *c.* 1910. The elm trees, heavily lopped in 1909, gave the road its name. Permission to plant 'elm or other trees' was given in an indenture of 1726 to Daniel Baker, the owner of a large mansion house almost overlooking the pond, who was High Sheriff of Bucks in 1721. The house later became the school for French emigré boys set up by Edmund Burke in 1796. Dutch Elm disease proved fatal in 1977.

From here, the road runs across the former Wycombe Heath up to Hazlemere. It was laid out by the surveyor when the Heath was enclosed in 1855, hence its unexpectedly straight run up the hill to Rushmoor Corner and two marked bends thereafter. (*Wycombe Museum*)

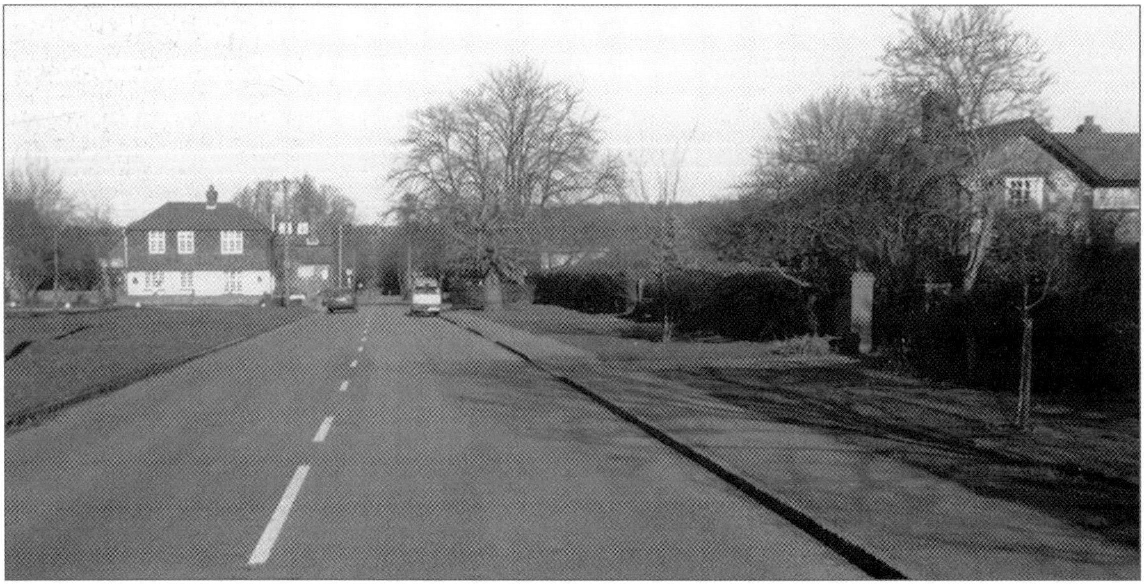

Modern view. (*Eddie Morton*)

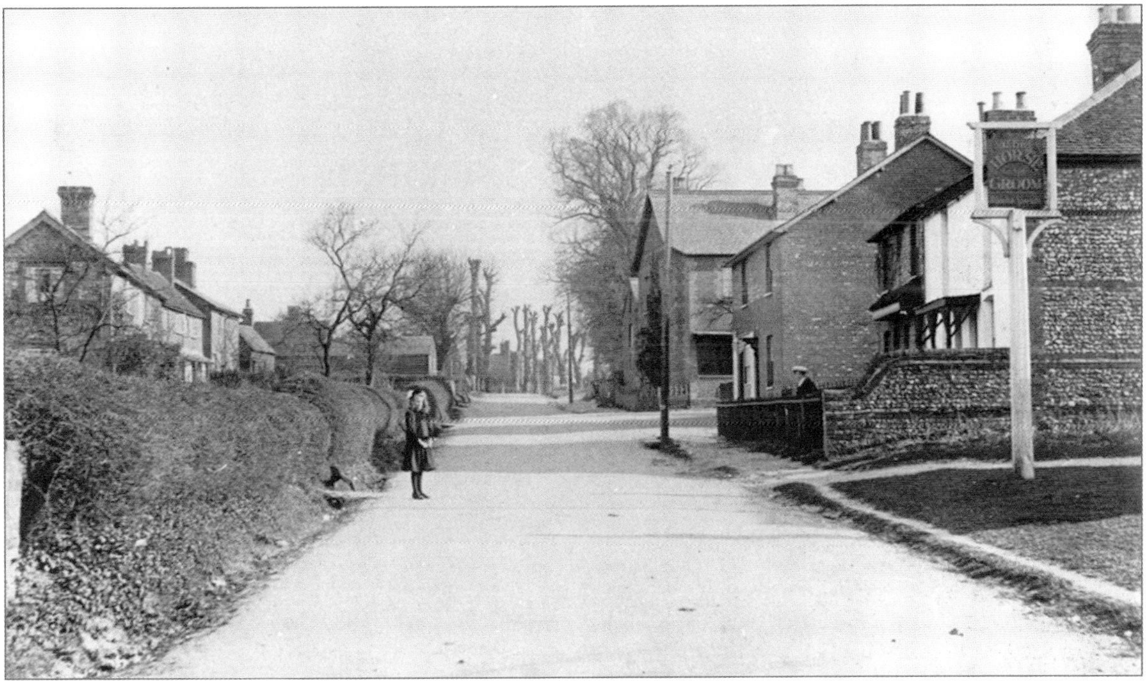

Looking back towards the pollarded elms and Widmer Pond, *c.* 1908. The Horse & Groom is in Tylers Green and its forecourt is in Penn. The Victoria was built in 1868 on the site of an earlier beerhouse called The Travellers' Friend, first licensed in 1830. The Victoria had no bar, just a room. It ceased to be a beerhouse when it was sold in 1906, and was briefly a grocer's shop. (*CWPC*)

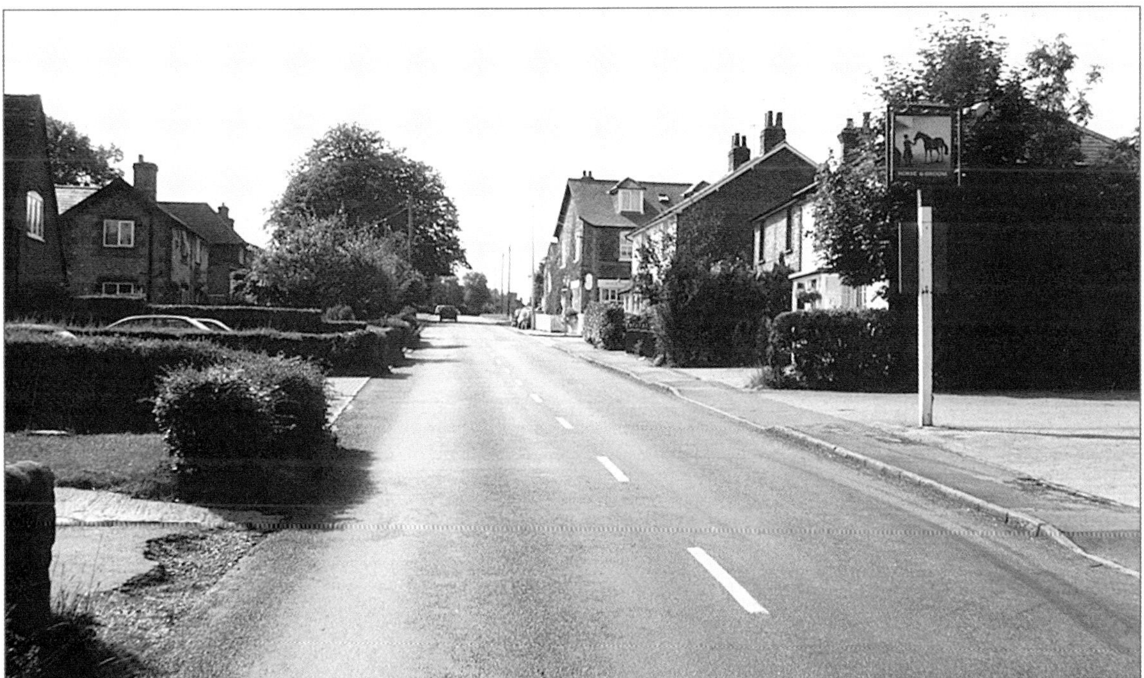

Modern view. (*Eddie Morton*)

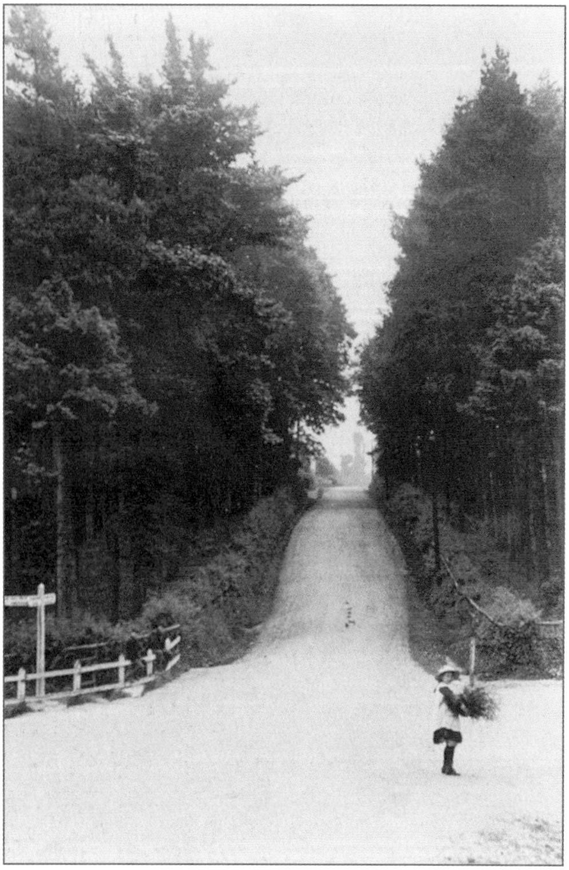

Potters Cross, 1913. The name appears in a deed of 1740. Hollow ways run down through the woods on both sides of the main road, which used to be a track across the common heath. The two ponds, one on each side of the road, were used mainly for horses. (*Eric Britnell*)

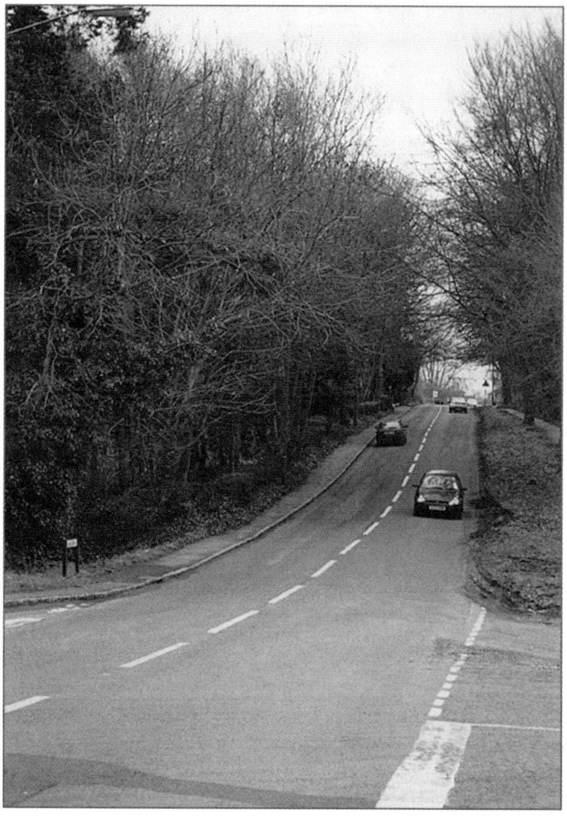

Modern view. (*Liz Tebbutt*)

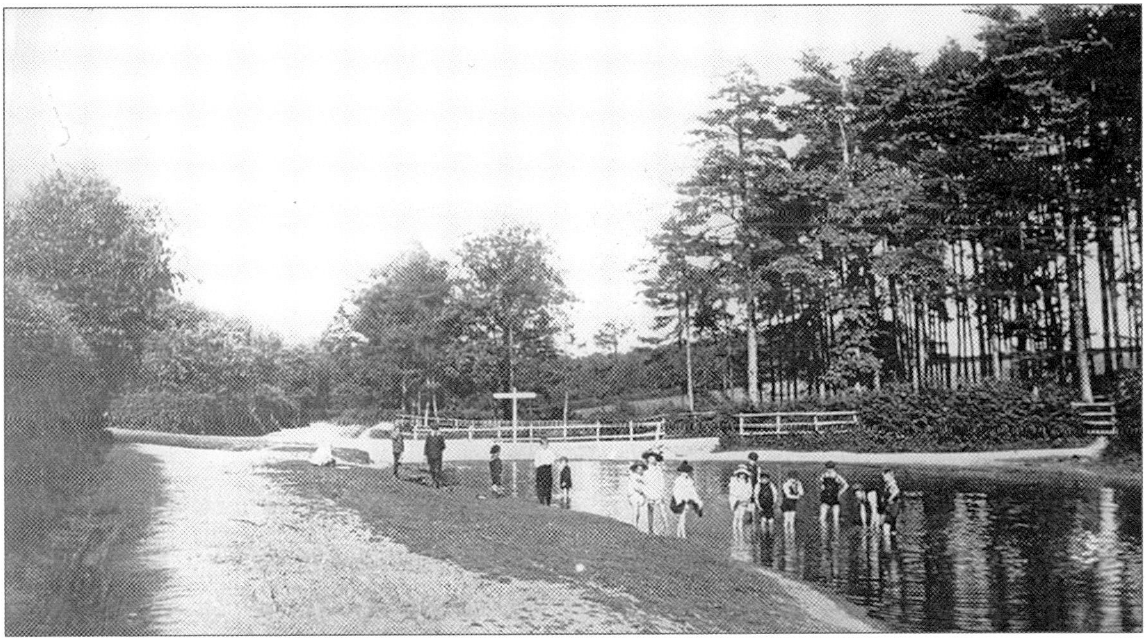

Potters Cross, early 1900s. The photograph looks across the main road towards the road only quite recently named as Common Wood Lane. It had no earlier name because it was a new road set out by the Inclosure Award of 1855, to replace the old track to Penn Street which went through Common Wood. The pond with the children is one of a series of ponds marking the parish boundary between Hazlemere and Beacon Hill. There was a second pond on the other side of the road; it was filled in during the 1950s but has recently been restored. (*CWPC*)

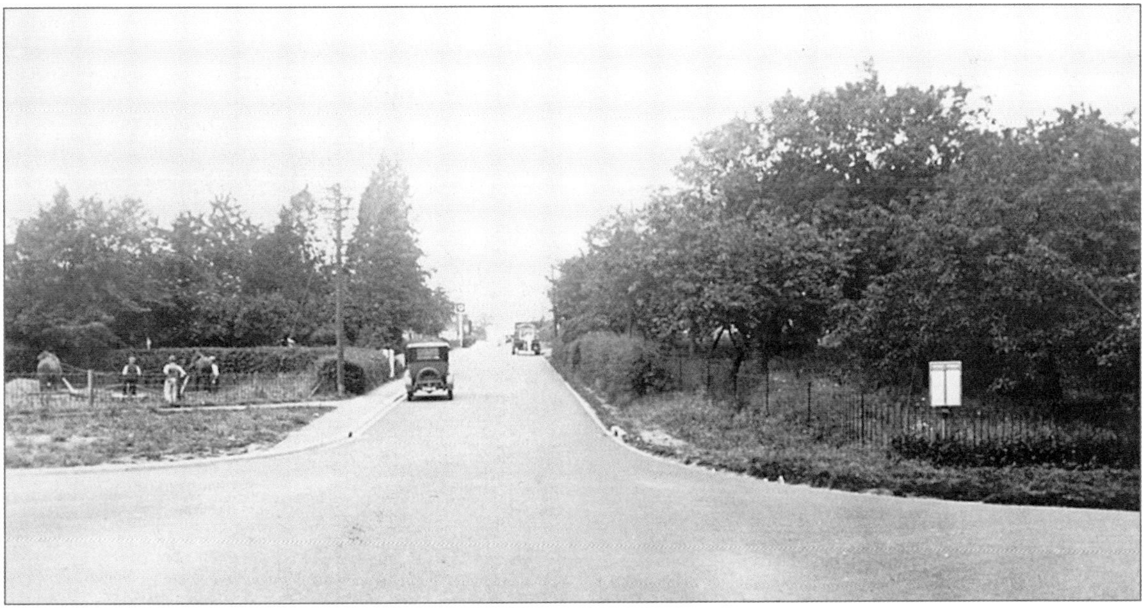

Hazlemere Road, looking up Dog Hill from Potters Cross, 1920s. The Dog pub is on the left. A grocer's shop (now Country Furniture) is on the right at the corner of Back Lane (now Larchlands). The much earlier name for Dog Hill was Rushmere Hill, because it led to Rushmere Pond, another parish boundary marker, which was common land until compulsorily acquired for road widening by the County Council. In 1992, despite strong protest, the pond was sold as a house plot. (*Colin Seabright*)

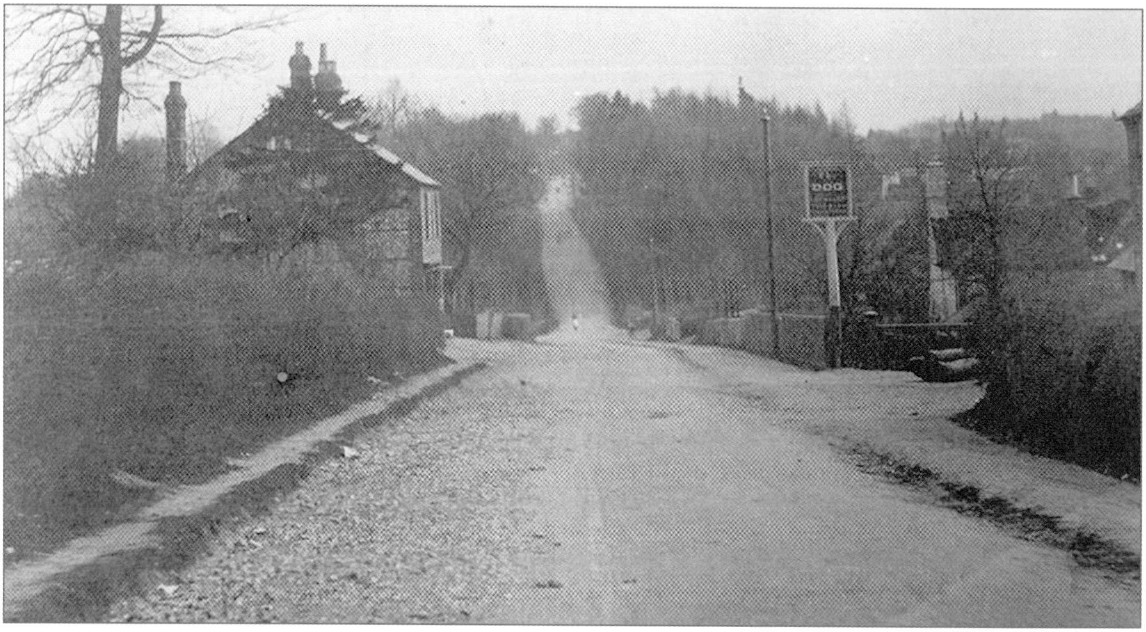

Looking back towards Potters Cross with the Dog on the right, early 1900s. Almost all the older houses on the west side of Hazlemere Road were built on plots of former heathland allotted to private owners by the 1855 Penn Inclosure Award. Both sides of Hazlemere Road are in Penn and a pre-Inclosure memory is of going up the hill through open forest with beautiful beech trees, 'but now cut down and inferior cottages built'. The east side of the road was largely cherry orchards until the 1920s and '30s. (*Eric Hearne*)

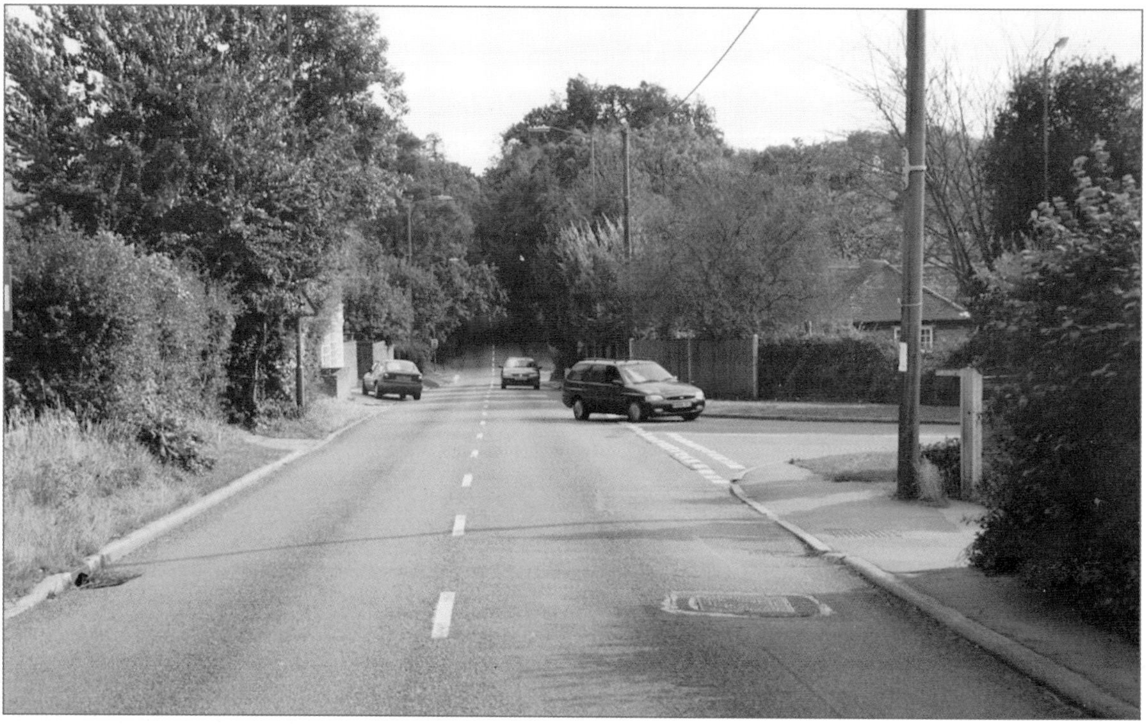

Modern view. (*Eddie Morton*)

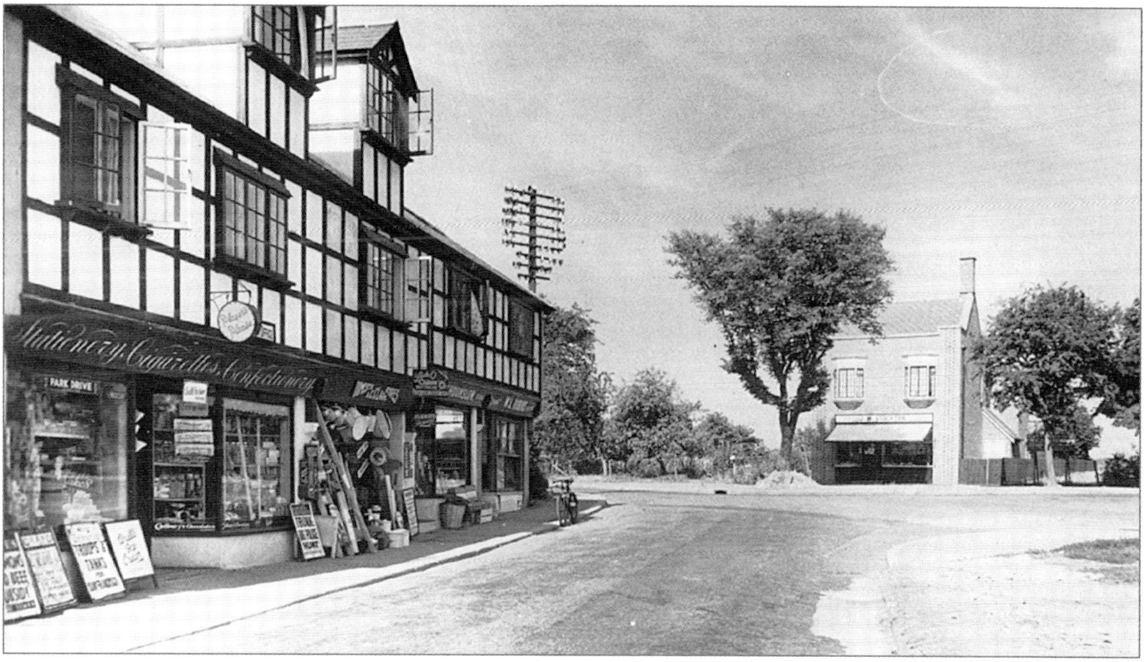

Hazlemere crossroads, with the post office on the left and just one shop, now the butcher's shop, opposite, 1930s. (*Eric Britnell*)

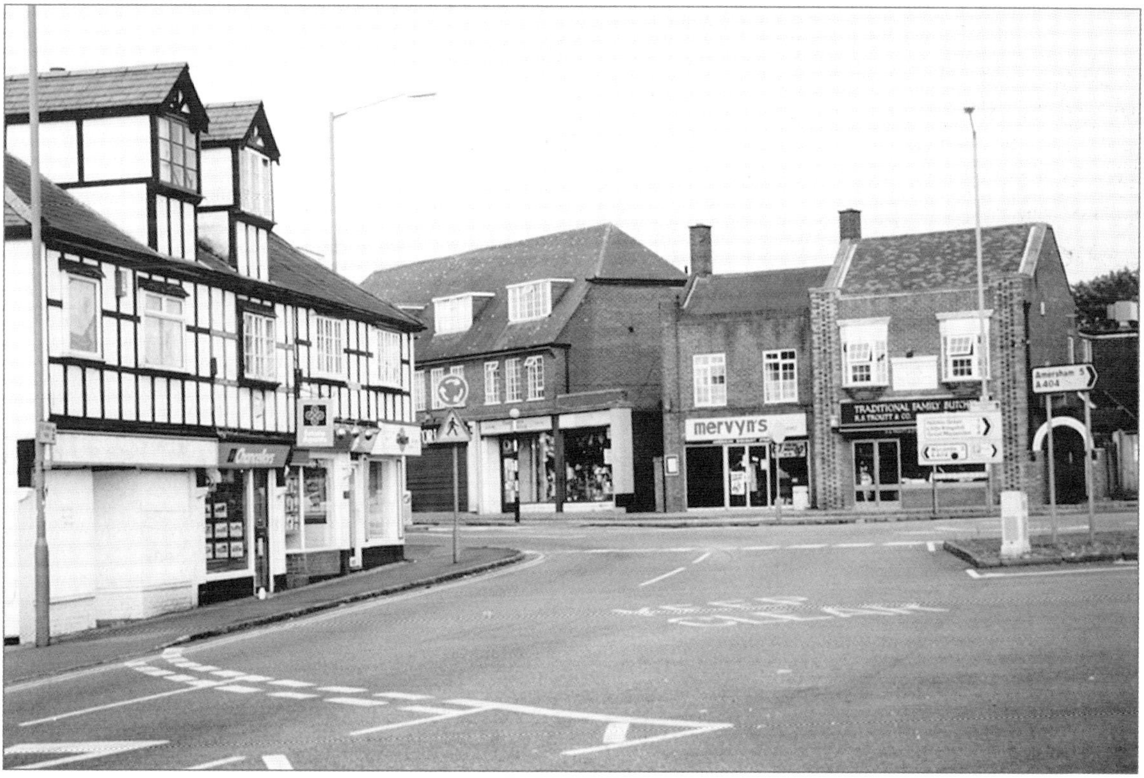

Modern view. (*Eddie Morton*)

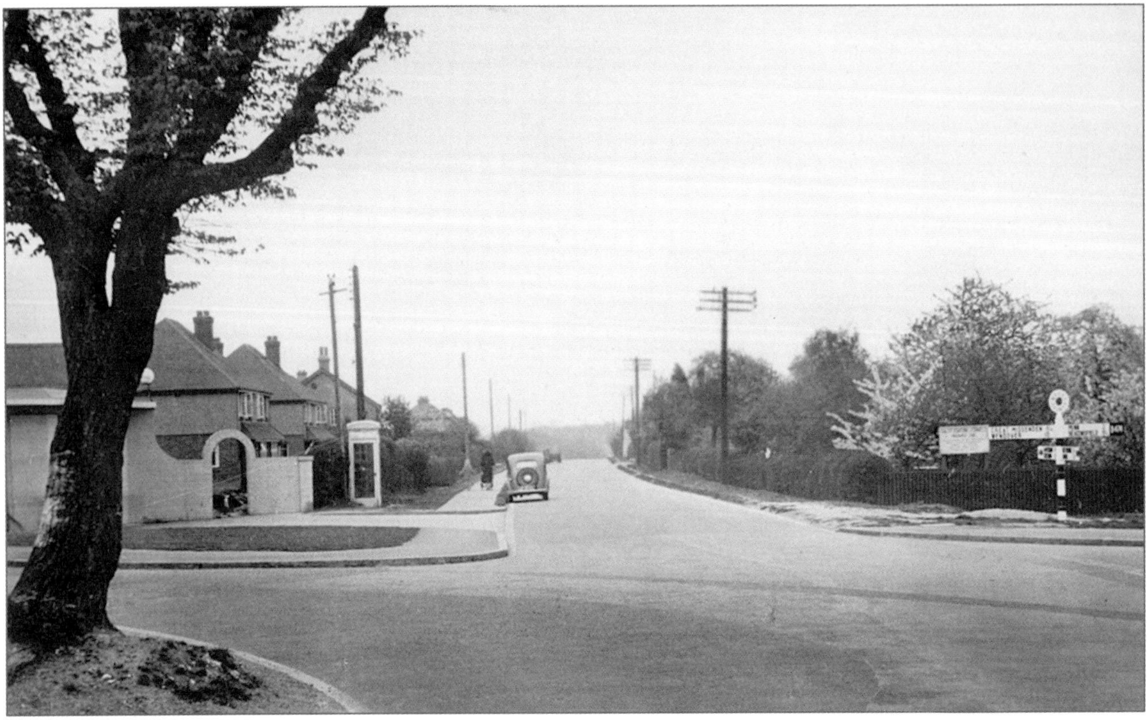

Hazlemere crossroads, looking towards Amersham, 1940s. (*Eric Britnell*)

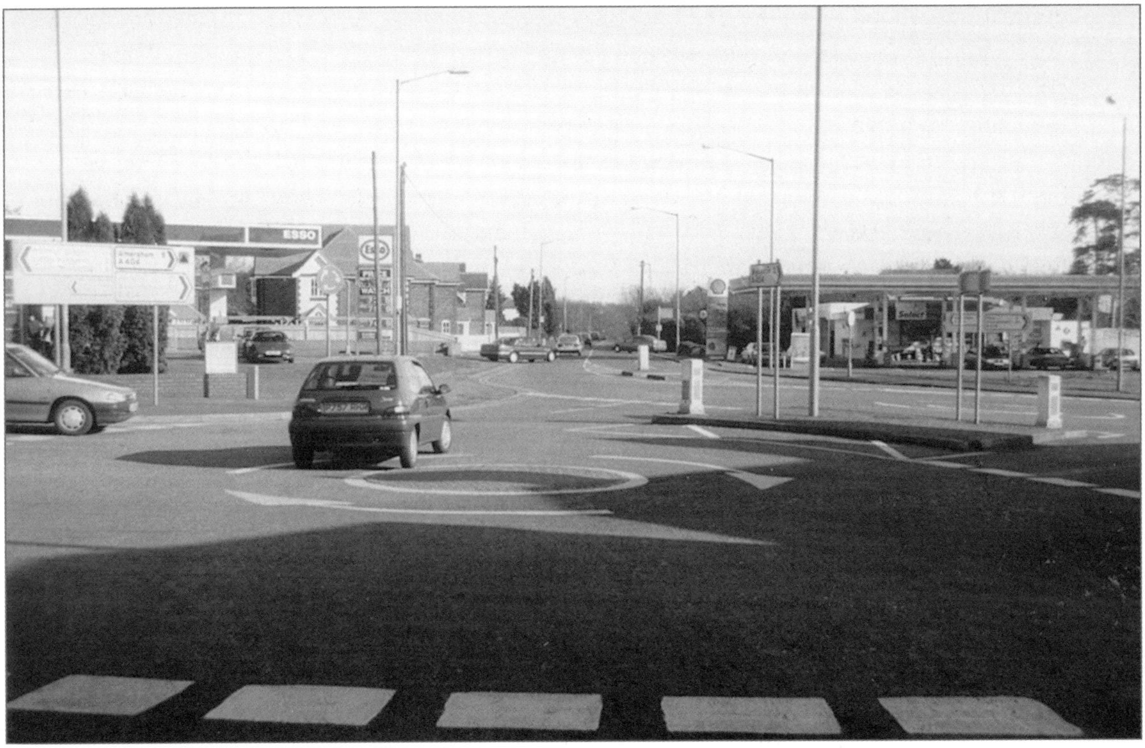

Modern view. (*Eddie Morton*)

CHAPTER TWO

THE PENN ESTATE

The history of Penn during the last two centuries has been dominated by the Penn Estate, owned by successive Earls Howe. At the start of the twentieth century 90 per cent of Penn's 4,000 acres, as well as over 1,000 acres of neighbouring parishes, was owned by the Estate, with over two dozen tenanted farms. The Chairman of the Parish Council for the first fifty years, from its creation in 1894, was the Agent of the Estate and for the next twenty-five was the 6th Earl Howe himself.

The Howes were immensely rich, beneficiaries of a long aristocratic lineage, with properties all over England. They were right at the top of society, living in very grand houses, entertaining royalty and inter-marrying with families like the Duke of Marlborough's. Penn House was a country retreat sometimes lived in by the heir or dowager or visited for the shooting, and for its convenience to London and Windsor.

The prolonged agricultural depression from the 1870s up to the Second World War, and the import of cheaper North American timber, combined to reduce landowning incomes. Together with the increasing severity of estate duties (first introduced in 1894), inflation and social change, such an opulent lifestyle became increasingly impossible to maintain and much land and property was sold in order to make ends meet.

Parts of the Penn Estate were already mortgaged in 1904. In 1906 the first land to be sold was about 100 acres in Knotty Green and Beaconsfield when the Marylebone railway arrived. Death duties had not yet been paid on all this land. In 1907 the 4th Earl sold various treasures from Gopsall Hall in Leicestershire and in 1919 this huge house, where he had once spent £100,000 entertaining Edward VII for ten days, together with an 11,000-acre estate including ten villages, was sold for £400,000.

The 5th Earl succeeded to the estate in 1929. He was England's most famous racing driver in the 1930s, and kept a stable of expensive racing cars. In 1930 he sold Curzon House, his splendid town house in Mayfair. In 1933 Christie's devoted a whole week to successive sales of over 400 lots of silver, furniture and a magnificent collection of 92 Old Masters, including works by Rembrandt, Raphael and Rubens. In 1935 all the remaining property in the south of Penn was put on the market. The largest single sale was in 1940 when over 1,000 acres, the whole northern quarter of the parish, was sold as one lot.

The consequence of these and later sales was a rapid growth in house building, starting with the post-railway development of Knotty Green as a rural outpost of New Beaconsfield. In 1900 the population of Penn was 1,000 and had remained unchanged for the previous century. It had doubled by 1950 and quadrupled by the end of the century, with half the population now living in Knotty Green. The Penn Estate now covers 1,600 acres under a single home farm.

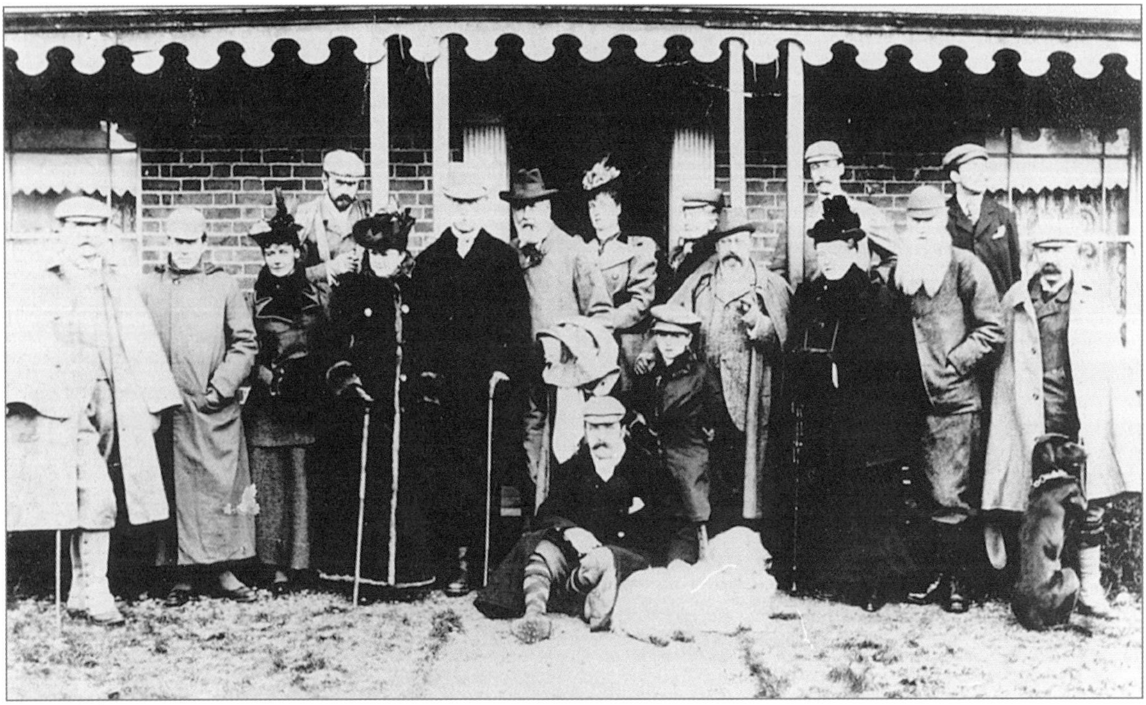

A shooting party outside Penn House Farm in Penn Bottom, 4 January 1894. The Prince of Wales (later Edward VII) is centre right with his hand on the shoulder of the ten-year-old boy, Francis Curzon, who was to be the 5th Earl Howe (1929–64). His father, Viscount Curzon, later the 4th Earl Howe (1900–29) is sitting in front of him. The 3rd Earl (1876–1900) and his wife are centre left, both carrying walking sticks. The bearded man just behind the 3rd Earl is Prince Edward of Saxe Weimar. The shooting book at Penn House notes a day's bag of 11 partridge, 850 pheasants and 2 rabbits. Other photographs record the visits to Penn of the future George V and Queen Mary in 1898, and of Edward VII in 1902, when he brought his mistress, Mrs George Keppel, and stayed at Penn House for five days with a fifteen-strong entourage. A record bag of 1,203 pheasants, 20 partridges, 10 hares and 20 rabbits was recorded for one day. They all went to Penn Street Church on Sunday. (*Evelyn Clark*)

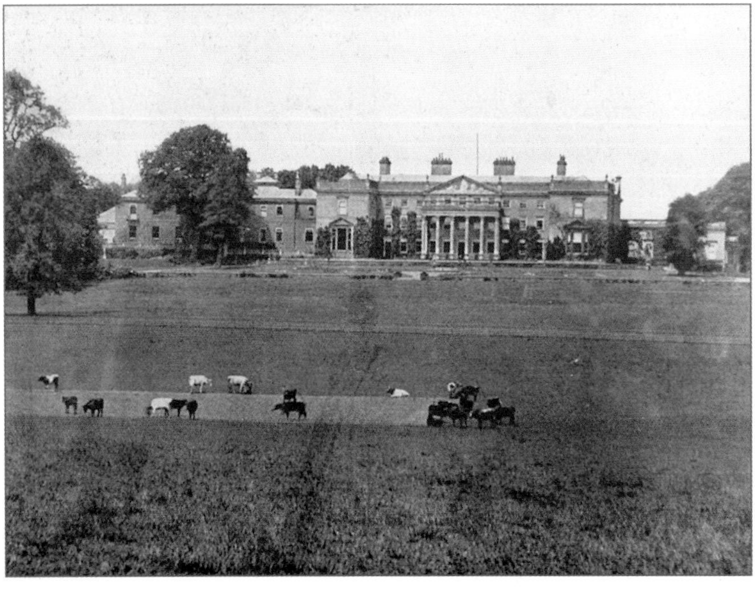

Gopsall Hall at Congerstone, early 1900s. This was the largest estate in Leicestershire after Belvoir, including ten villages. The eighteenth-century house and estate came to the Curzons by marriage to the niece of Charles Jennens, whose vast wealth derived from the Midlands iron industry. He was also a librettist and compiled the text of Handel's *Messiah*. Queen Adelaide, wife of William IV, stayed at Gopsall and Edward VII was a guest of the 4th Earl for ten days. The 6th Earl remembered, as a boy, cycling along the vast corridors. The 4th Earl had to sell the house in 1919 and it was pulled down in the early 1950s. (*PPC*)

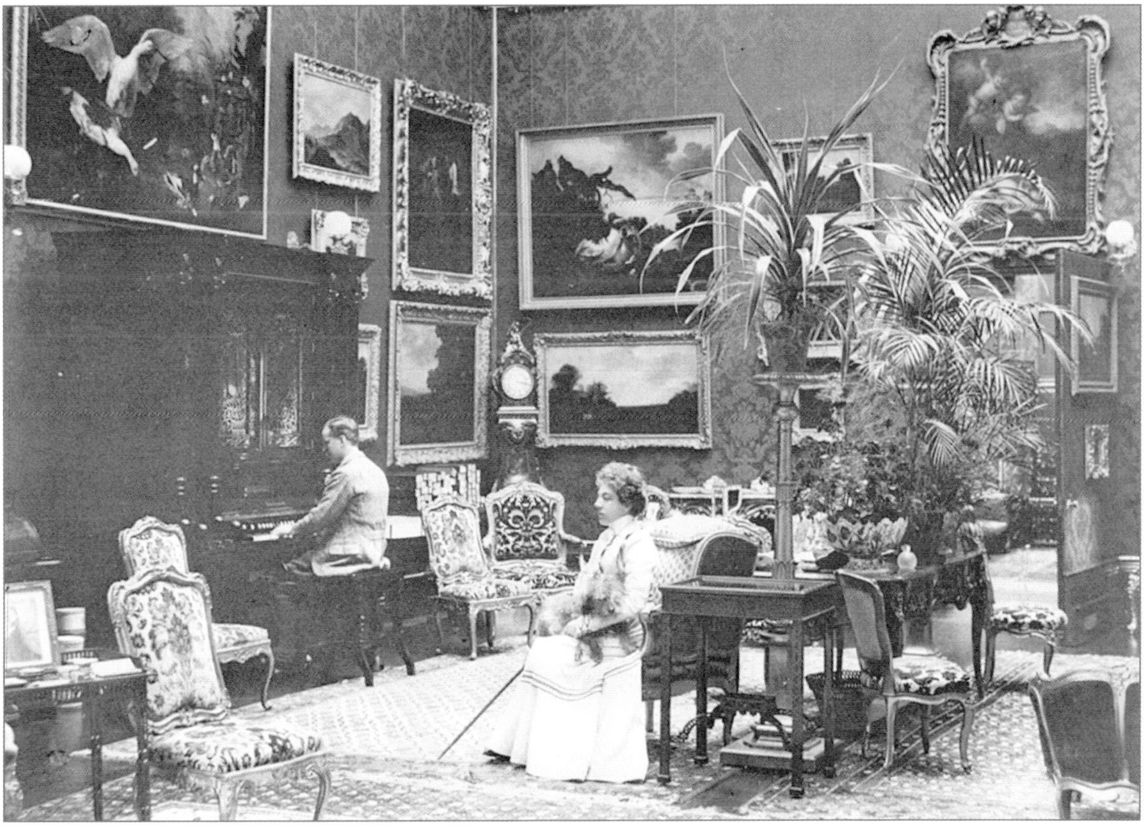

The 4th Earl Howe and his first wife in the Picture Gallery at Gopsall, early 1900s. There was a magnificent collection of family portraits and Old Masters, including works by Hals, Rembrandt, Raphael and Rubens. Ninety-two paintings went on sale at Christie's in 1933 and raised unusually high prices, totalling nearly £20,000. (*Lady Charlotte Dinan*)

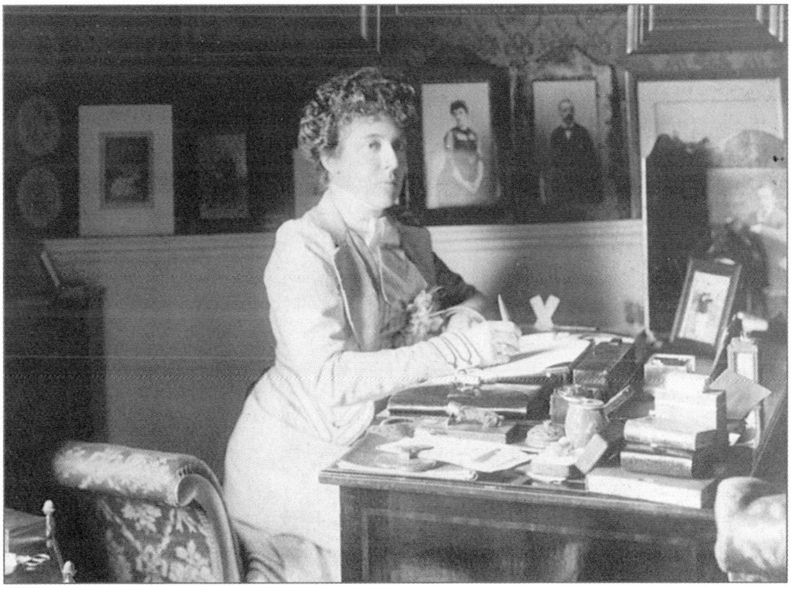

The 4th Earl Howe's first wife at her desk, early 1900s. She was Georgiana Spencer-Churchill (1860–1906), the daughter of the Duke of Marlborough, sister of Randolph and hence aunt of Winston Churchill. She was a woman of considerable character who campaigned on political and defence issues, drove herself around London in her four-in-hand and hunted with the Quorn. In Penn Street churchyard, the gate into Penn Wood is inscribed 'Lady Georgie's Avenue', and there is also a tall monument to her. (*Lady Charlotte Dinan*)

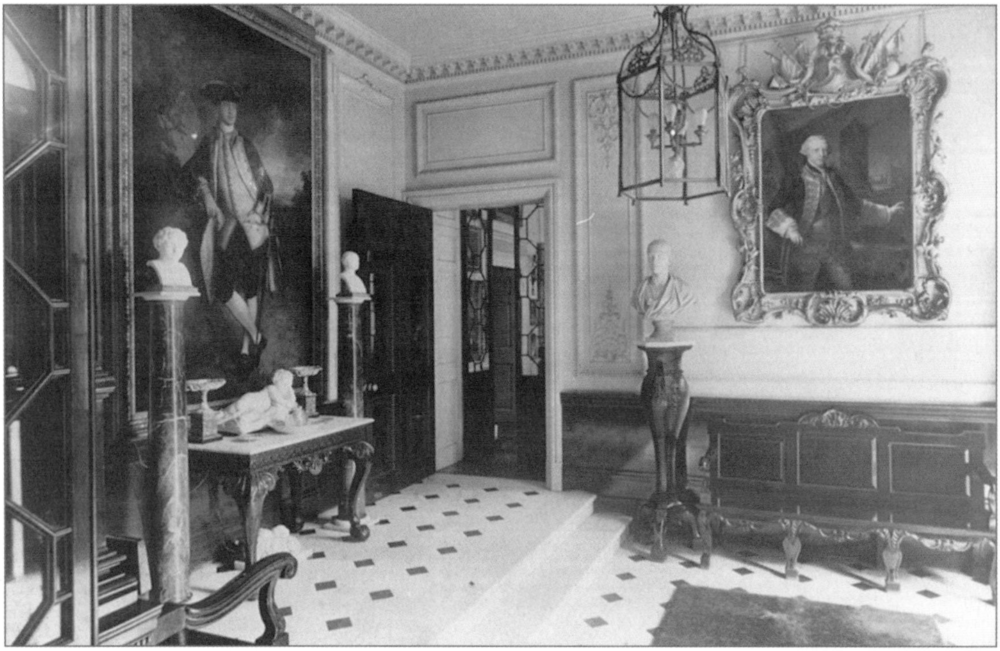

The hall of Curzon House in Curzon Street, Mayfair, early 1900s. The large portrait on the left is a Gainsborough of Admiral Howe (1726–99) when a young Commodore. He became a national hero after a victory against the French on the 'Glorious First of June 1794'. Admiral Howe had no sons. His daughter and heiress married the Curzon heir and the earldom was recreated for their son in 1821. Most of the properties in Curzon Street, including a chapel, belonged to the Howes at one time and Curzon House itself was their own town house. It was let to the future George VI and Queen Elizabeth for some months in 1925. The 5th Earl sold it in 1930. (*Lady Charlotte Dinan*)

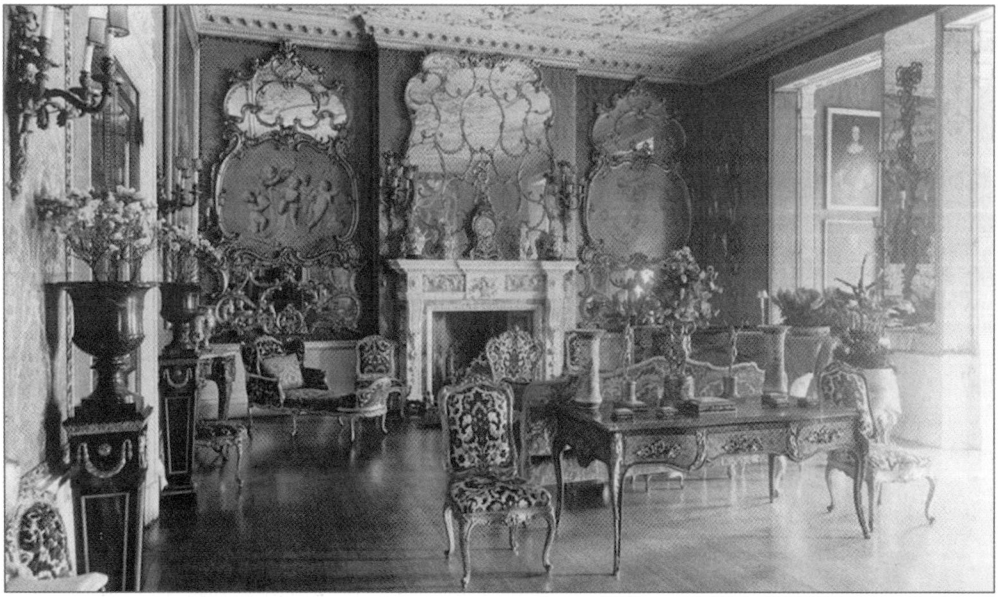

The ballroom in Curzon House, early 1900s. The walls were covered with yellow brocade. The 4th Earl Howe was Lord Chamberlain to Queen Alexandra, wife of Edward VII, as his grandfather had been to Queen Adelaide, and the Royal Family were frequently entertained there. (*Lady Charlotte Dinan*)

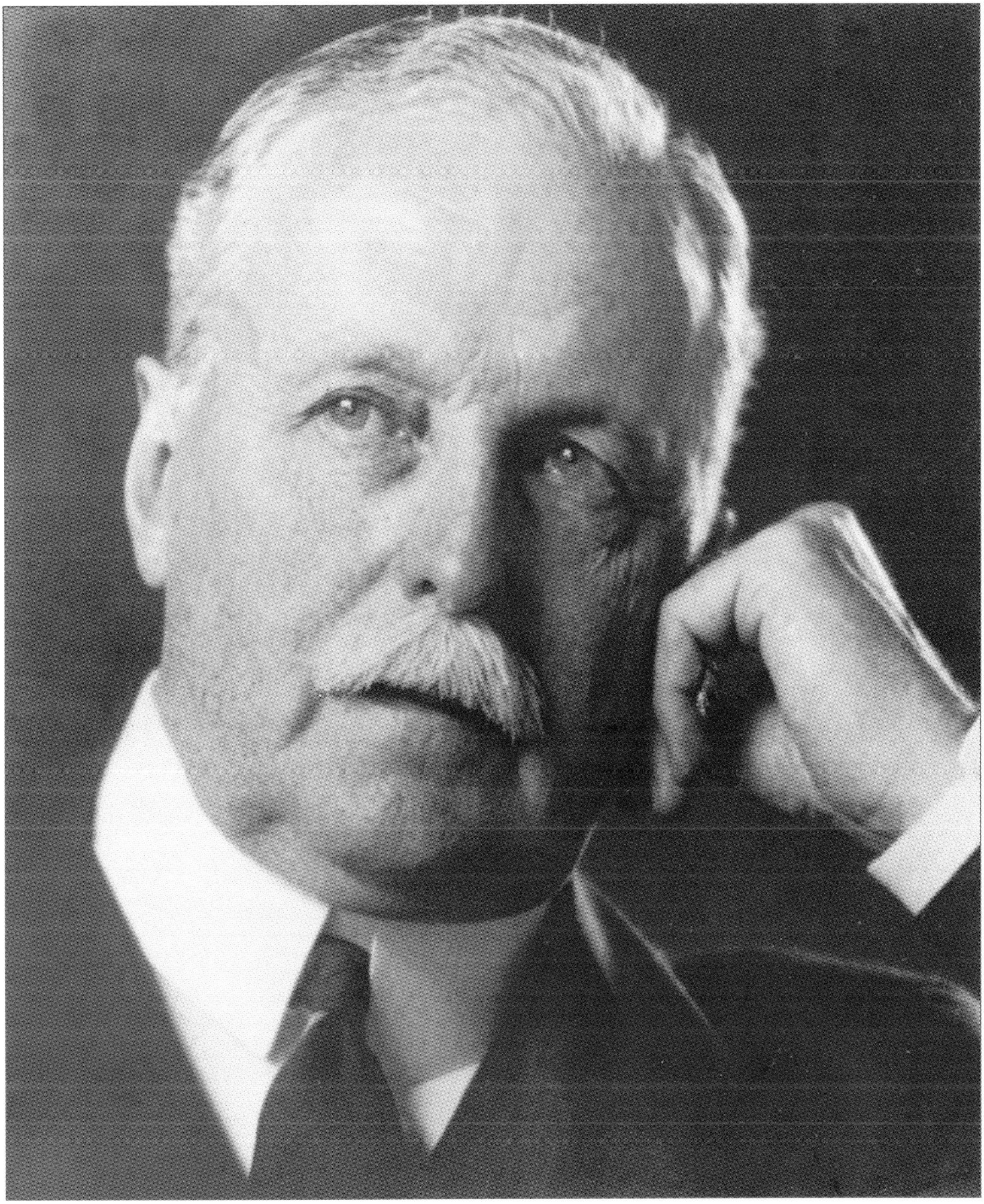

The 4th Earl Howe, aged sixty-five, 1926. In 1920 Gopsall had been sold, his mother was living at Penn House and he was living at Penn House Farm. His second wife, who was American, died in 1925. He died in 1929, survived by his third wife, Lorna, Countess Howe, who won a considerable reputation as a breeder of labradors. (*PPC*)

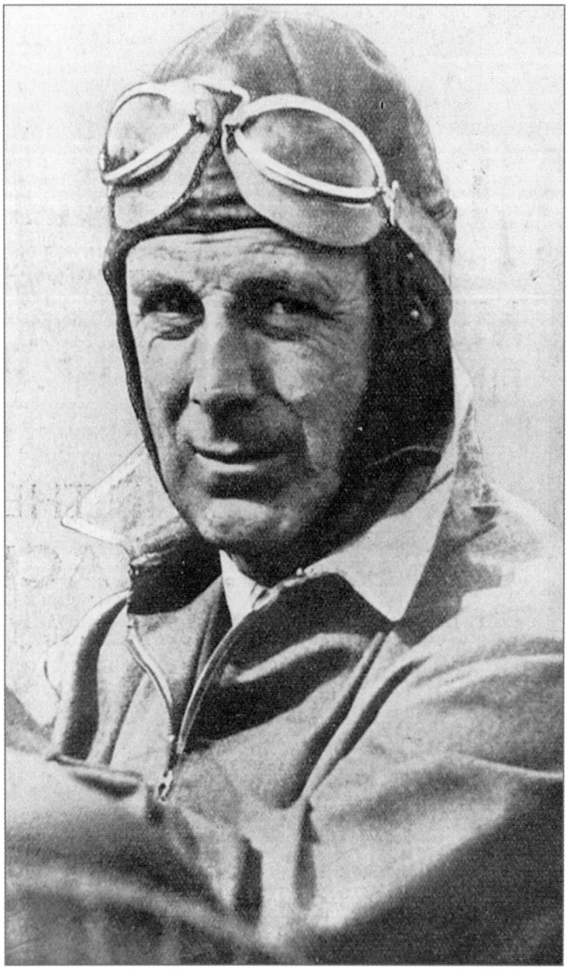

The 5th Earl Howe (1884–1964) in racing helmet, *c.* 1930. He was the only son of the 4th Earl, and through his mother was first cousin to Winston Churchill. He failed the Royal Naval College medical and went instead to Eton and Christ Church, Oxford. Nevertheless he saw active service as a naval Commander in the First World War and was later promoted to Commodore in the RNVR. He was Conservative MP for Battersea from 1918 to 1929. (*PPC*)

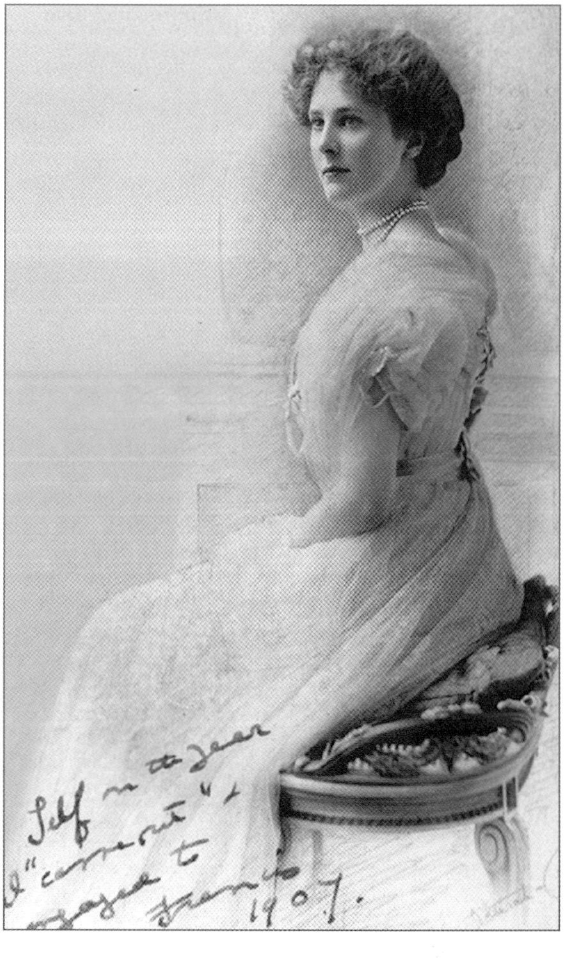

Mary (1887–1962), first wife of the 5th Earl, 1907. She was a Curzon cousin and well-known society beauty, voted one of the six most beautiful women in England for many years. According to a 1930s newspaper report, 'There is no living beauty who can create more of an effect than she, when entering a ballroom or sitting in a box at a theatre.' She later lived at the Knoll, Paul's Hill, Penn, and is buried at Penn Street. (*PPC*)

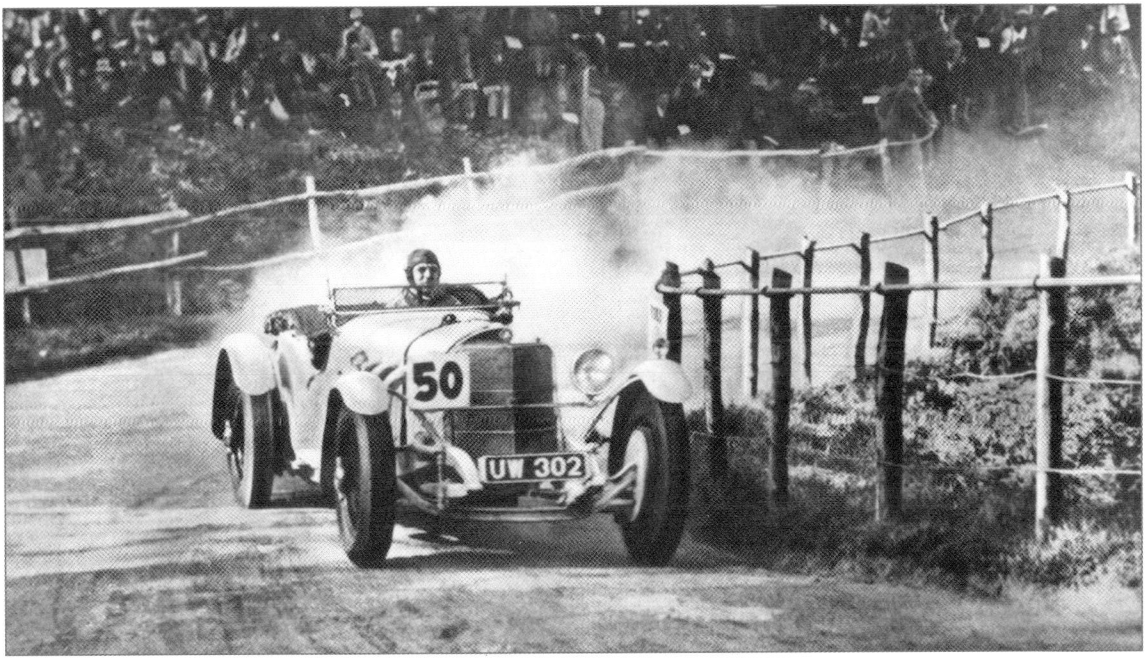

The 5th Earl racing his Mercedes, 1930. In 1924 another page had to be added to his licence book because it was so full of endorsements for speeding. It was at a magistrate's suggestion that he took up racing in 1928 when he was already forty-four. He acquired a succession of expensive cars, including two Bugattis, a Delage, two Mercedes, an Alfa-Romeo, a Maserati and a Ferrari. He was a brave and successful driver, winning at Le Mans in 1931 and many times at Brooklands. His racing colours were blue and silver – car, overalls and umbrella. He carried on racing until the Second World War, despite some serious crashes. (*Lady Charlotte Dinan*)

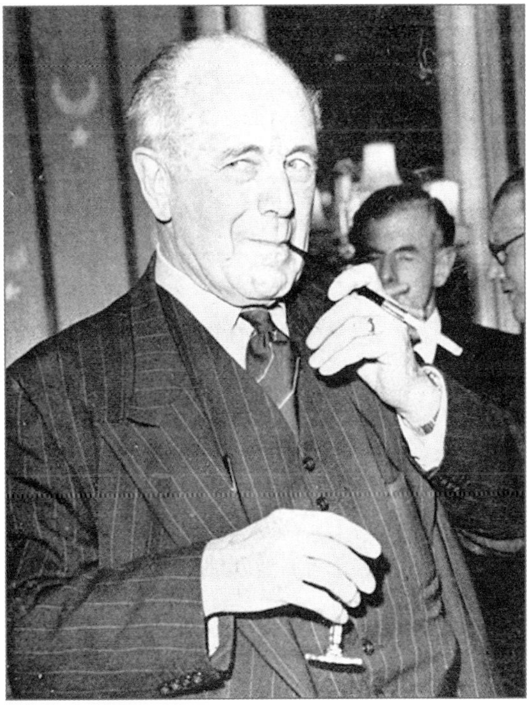

The 5th Earl Howe, *c.* 1960. He maintained a keen interest in motor racing and was President of the British Racing Drivers Club for thirty-six years. He was also Vice-President of the RAC, and an outspoken champion of motorists in the House of Lords. He was President of the RNLI and of the Motor Boat Racing Association. He did not live much at Penn House, which was probably too expensive to run, choosing instead to live at Penn House Farm and later at Hatchits in Paul's Hill. However, he did build a mile-long drive from Horsemoor Lane to Penn House, banked like Brooklands, so that he could practise racing. He was three times married and twice divorced (in 1937 and 1943). He died in 1964. (*PPC*)

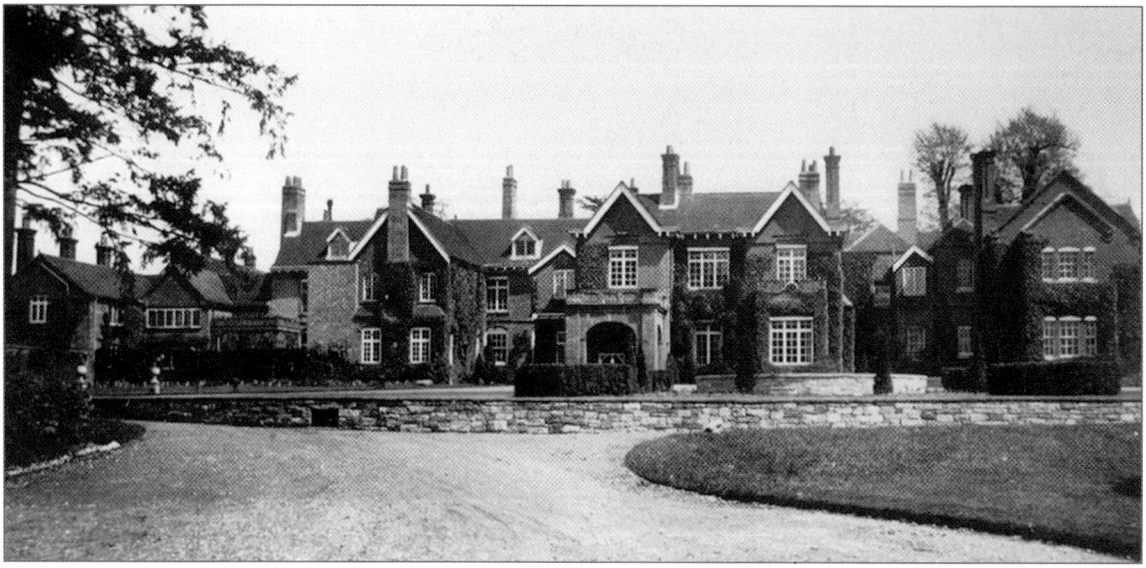

Penn House. A date of 1536 is inscribed on the house, but it is likely that a much earlier predecessor was built in about 1285 on the former heathland to which the de la Penne family moved from their more restricted site at Penbury. The last male Penn heir died in 1731 and the estate was inherited by his sister who was married to a Curzon. The Revd John Middleton, in a letter od 9 August 1802, noted that in 1760 her grandson, Assheton Curzon, pulled down two-thirds of old Penn House and 'fitted up the remainder as a country house to which he might retire occasionally during the sitting of Parliament'. The house is eighteenth-century with more modern additions. Two reception rooms were added in the 1880s to accommodate royal visitors who came to shoot. William IV, Queen Adelaide, Edward VII, George V and Queen Mary visited or stayed in the house. It was used by Emsworth House Preparatory School for fourteen years, between 1940 and 1954. (*PPC*)

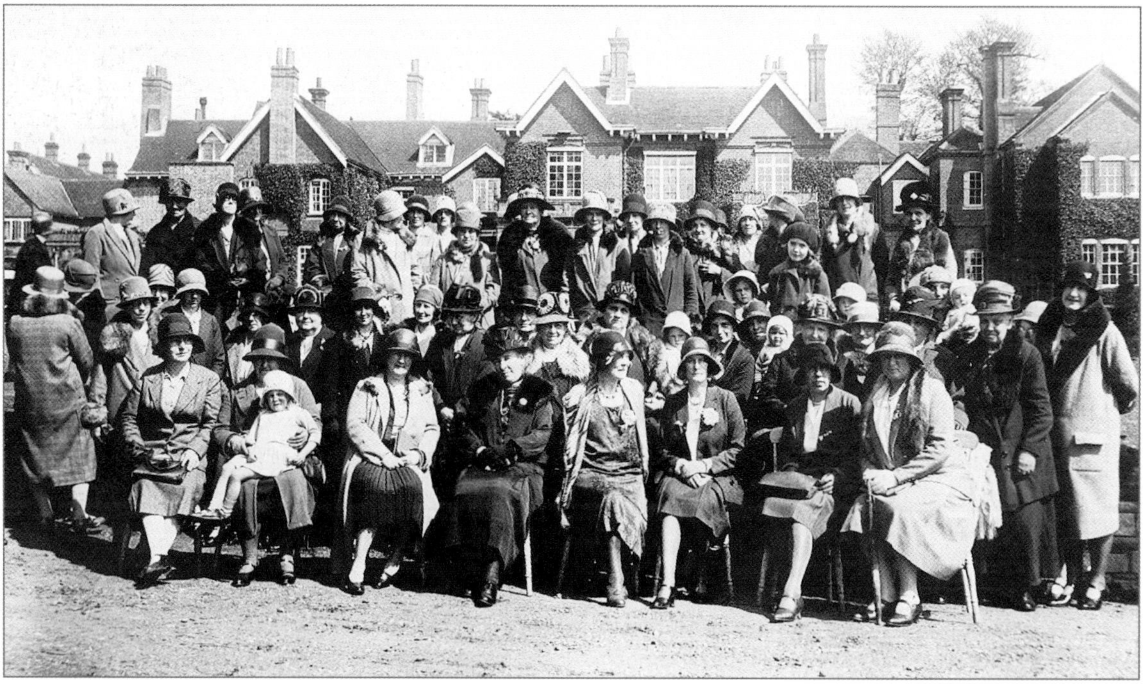

Mid-Bucks Women's Conservative meeting at Penn House, 1930. (*Bucks County Museum*)

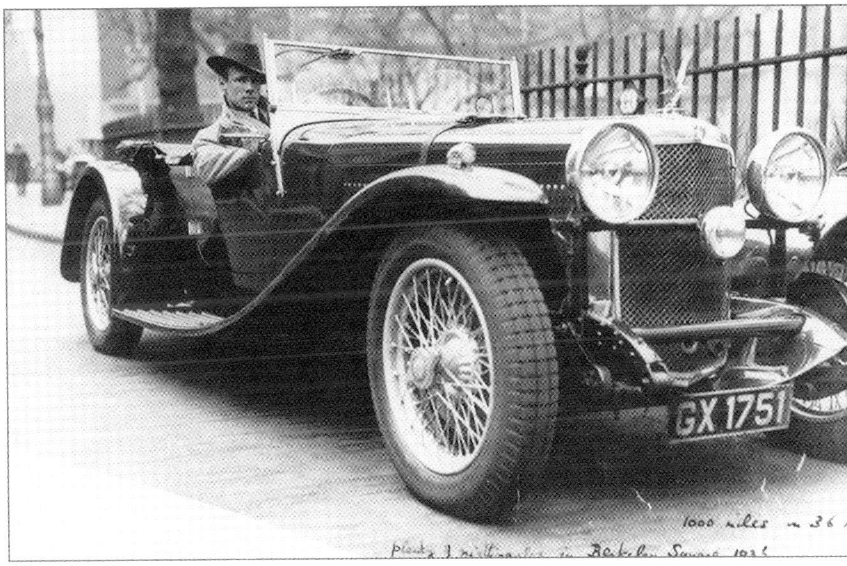

Viscount Curzon in his Alvis Silver Eagle sports car, 1936. He shared his father's love of speed and was president of the British Automobile Racing Club and vice-chairman of the RAC. He campaigned for a 90mph speed limit on motorways, and as a magistrate refused to convict speeding motorists, having himself six speeding convictions. (*Lady Charlotte Dinan*)

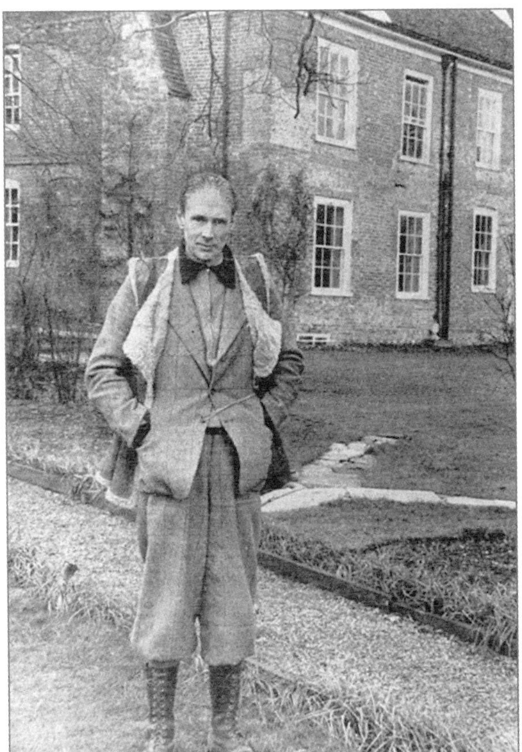

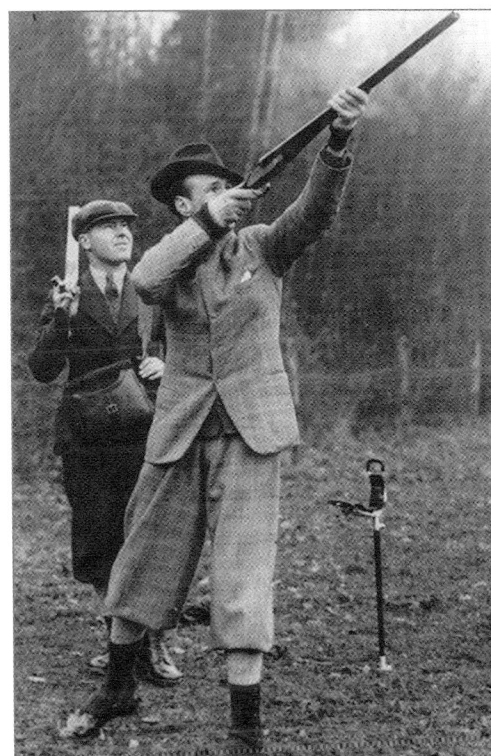

Viscount Curzon outside The Knoll, and shooting at Penn, *c*. 1930. Edward Richard Assheton Penn Curzon, who became the 6th Earl Howe when his father died in 1964, was born in 1908 and was a godson of Edward VII. Eton and Cambridge were followed by the RNVR. He was much involved in local and county affairs, being chairman of Penn Parish Council (1947–73) and of the governors of Curzon C of E School in Penn Street. Later he went on to be a deputy lieutenant, vice-chairman of the County Council and chairman of the County Education Committee. He was made a CBE in 1961. He was divorced in 1943 and remarried in 1946. (*Lady Charlotte Dinan*)

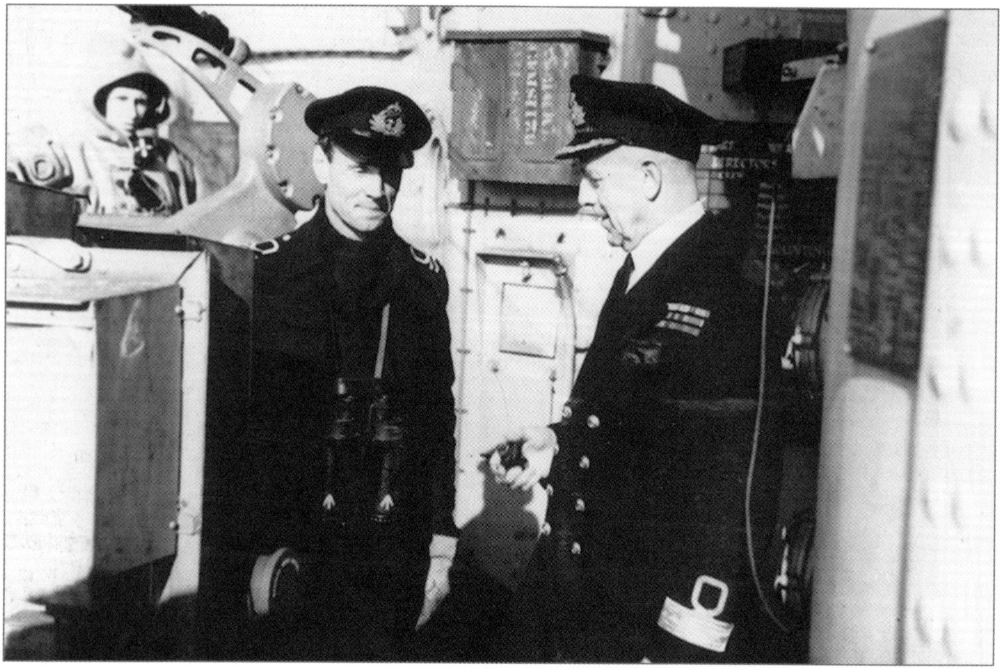

Viscount Curzon as an RNVR Lieutenant with his father, the only Commodore in the RNVR, 1940s. Viscount Curzon served in the RNVR from 1928 to 1946, reaching the rank of Lieutenant Commander, and saw active service in the Atlantic and Pacific. (*Lady Charlotte Dinan*)

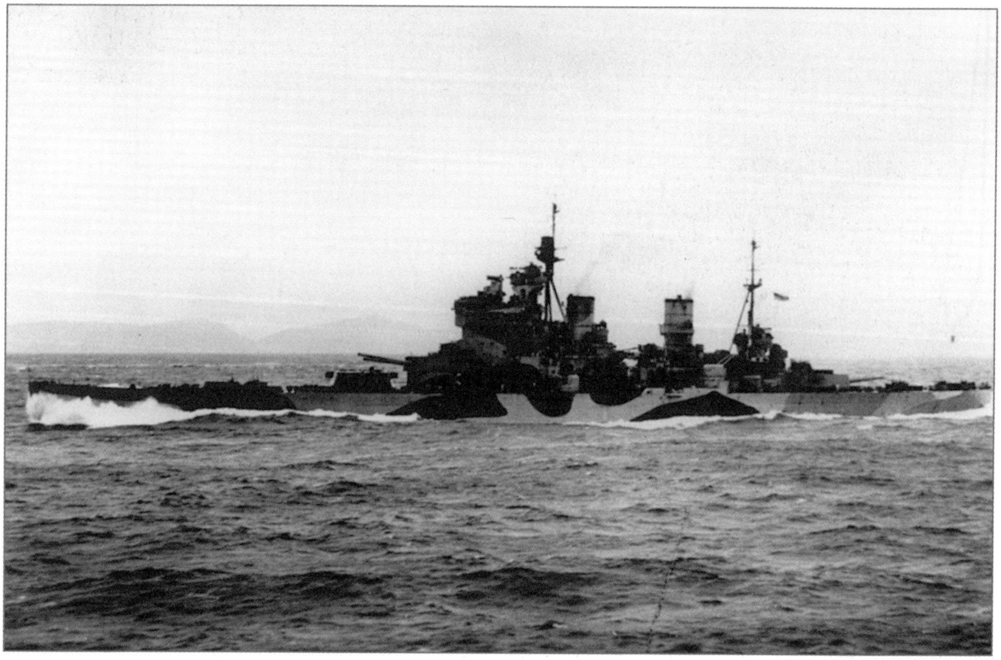

HMS *Howe*, a Royal Navy battleship during the Second World War on which Viscount Curzon served, seen here in the 1940s. A succession of Royal Navy ships have been named after Admiral Howe (1726–99) who won a famous victory over the French off Ushant on the 'Glorious First of June 1794', which is still celebrated by the Royal Navy. (*PPC*)

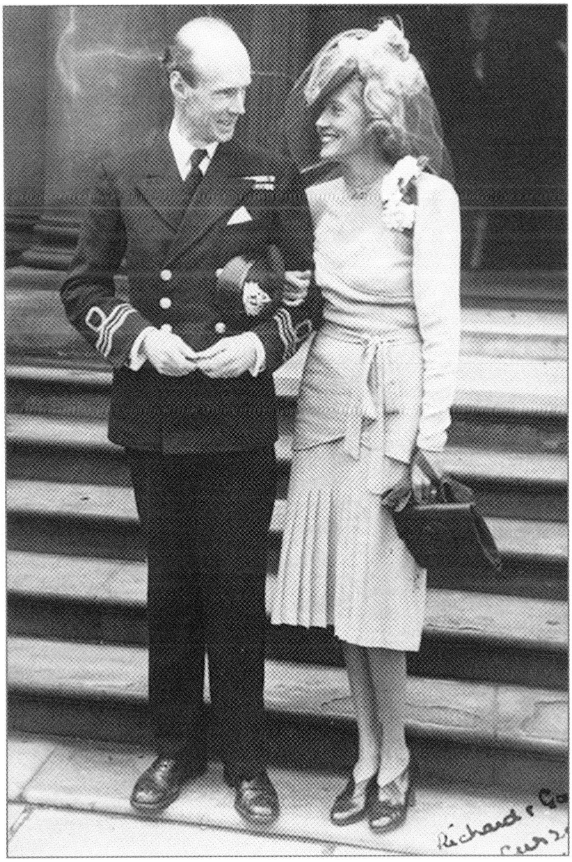

Viscount Curzon on his wedding day, 1946, with his second wife, formerly Gay Wakeling, whom he met when his ship was in harbour in Durban. They lived first in The Knoll, Paul's Hill, Penn, and moved into Penn House when the school left in 1954. (*Lady Charlotte Dinan*)

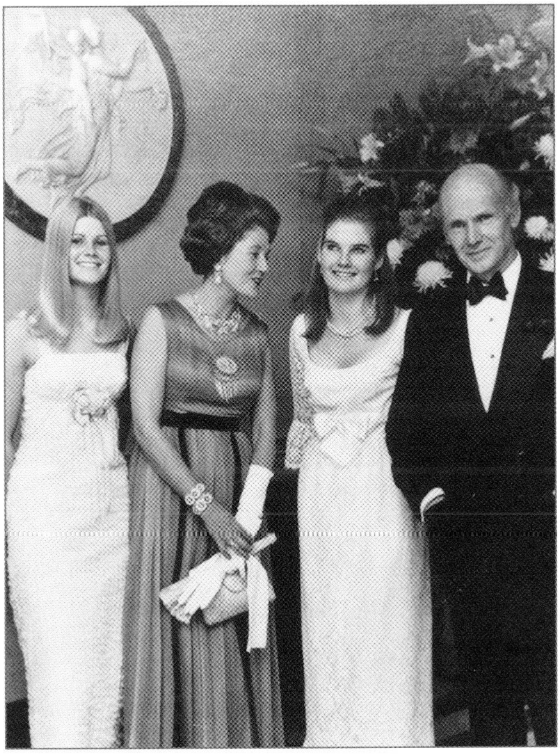

The 'Coming Out' ball at the Dorchester for the 6th Earl Howe's elder daughter, Lady Mary Gaye (between her mother and father), 1965. Her younger sister, on the left, now Lady Charlotte Dinan, still lives in Penn. (*Lady Charlotte Dinan*)

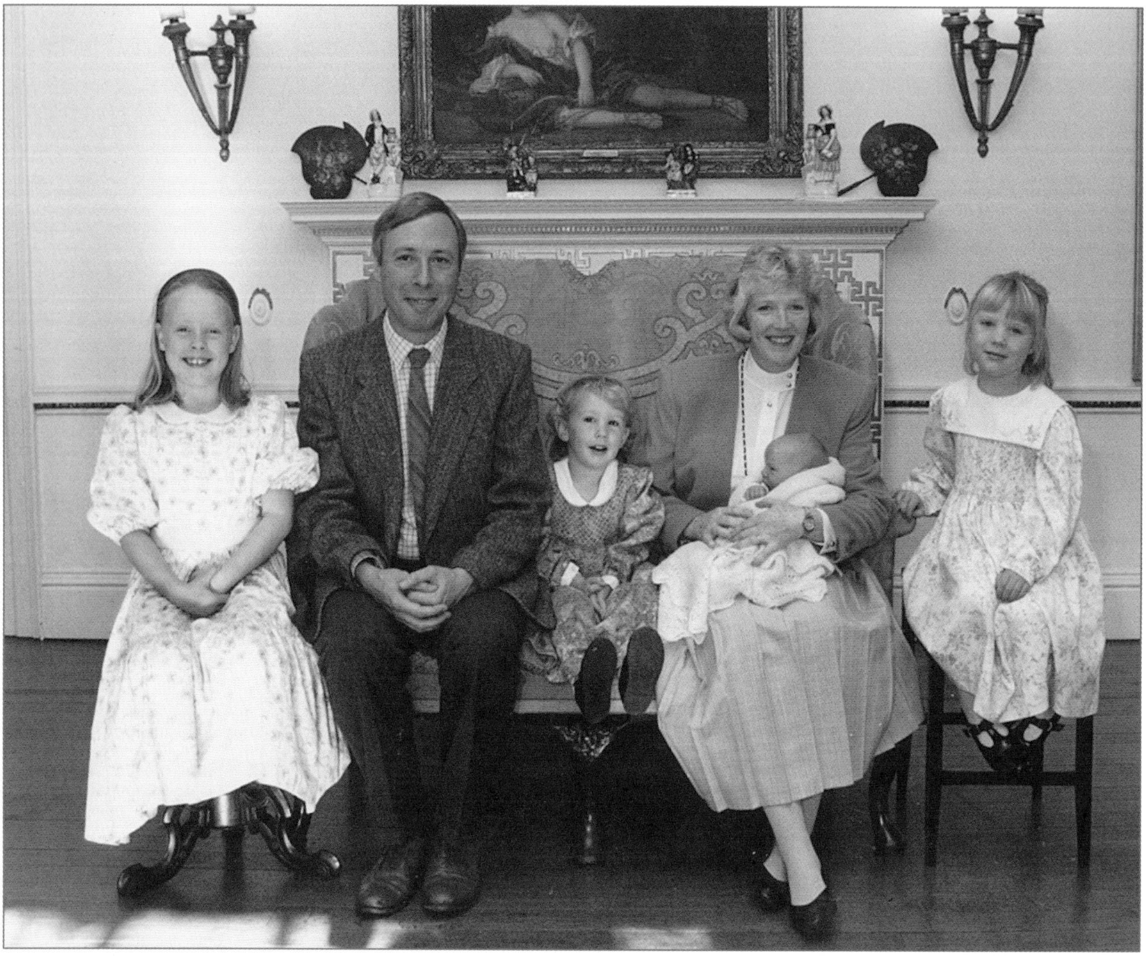

The 7th Earl Howe with his wife Elizabeth and children: from left, Anna, Lucinda, newborn heir Thomas, and Flora, 1994. The 7th Earl is a second cousin of the 6th and was educated at Rugby and Christ Church, Oxford. He was a banker for seventeen years and was appointed a junior minister and government spokesman in the House of Lords on Agriculture, Fisheries and Food (1992) and Defence (1995). He has been the Conservative shadow health minister in the Lords since 1997, and was one of the forty-two Conservative hereditary peers elected to stay on in November 1999. (*Bucks Free Press*)

CHAPTER THREE

KNOTTY GREEN

Knotty Green (*nattuc* in 1222) takes its name from the tussocky grass of the Green. Before the Inclosure of 1855, the Green was much bigger than it is now, about 500 yards long and between 100 and 200 yards wide with half-a-dozen small ponds. It was surrounded by four farms: Baylins (p. 50), Knotty Green (p. 12), Egham's (p. 54), Gomm's (later Hutching's), and a handful of cottages (see military map of 1800 on p. 48).

In 1841 there were fourteen families with seventy-three inhabitants. There were no shops, schools or churches, but the Red Lion was already established. There were three shoemakers and a young lacemaker; the rest were agricultural or ordinary labourers, apart from one married couple of independent means.

Beaconsfield station opened on 2 April 1906 and two months later, at the Railway Hotel, the Penn Estate auctioned 105 acres in 121 lots of varying size. They were to be sold for a 'perpetual yearly rent' rather than capital. Tithe rent was payable to the Vicar and a contribution was required for making new roads. The plots varied from ¼ to 7 acres and were divided into five classes on which a minimum value of building was specified – country cottages, £200; superior country cottages, £250; moderate-sized houses, £300 and £400; superior country residences, £750. Water mains had just been put in along the Penn Road, gas was close by and the railway hotel advertised large stable accommodation.

The immediate post-railway development, which increased the population of the parish as a whole by nearly 50 per cent in five years, was confined to Penn Road and Forty Green Road. There was still an obvious 'parting of the parishes' between Beaconsfield and Penn, where the boundary stream ran under the Penn Road and where Beaconsfield's pavement and new houses stopped abruptly. Electricity had arrived by 1915. The development of the former fields of Seeleys Farm took place after the Second World War from the late 1940s to the early 1970s. The first street lights appeared in 1959. The population is now just over 2,000.

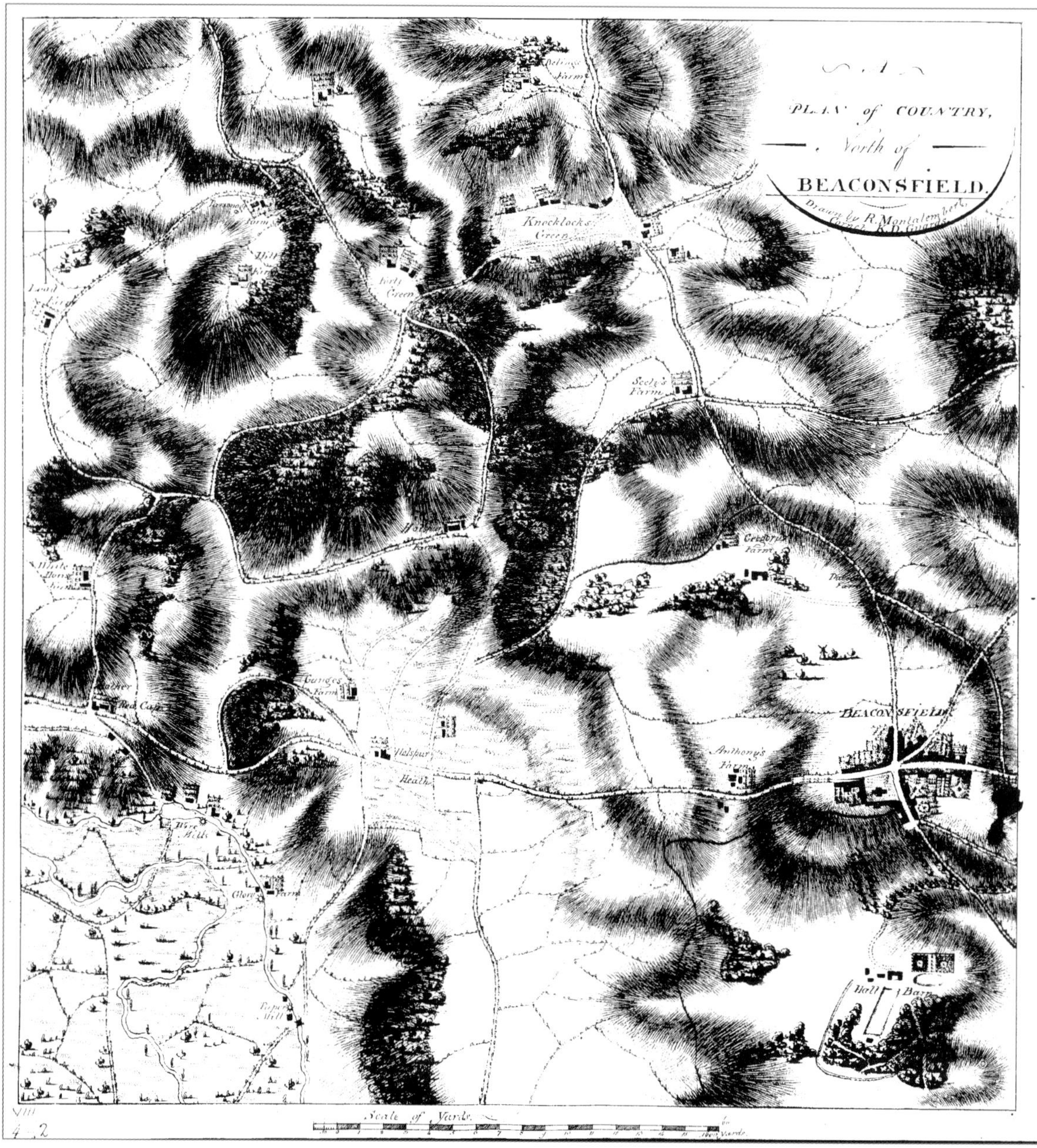

Military map, 1800. The Royal Military College, the predecessor to the Staff College at Camberley, was first established in the High Street of High Wycombe in 1799, and for the next fourteen years the surrounding countryside was the scene of their training exercises. There was not yet an Ordnance Survey and the army was responsible for mapping. The first task was to make good maps of the local area and these were mostly completed in 1800. Waterloo was won on the hilly fields of the Chilterns as much as on the playing fields of Eton. (*Map Room, British Library*)

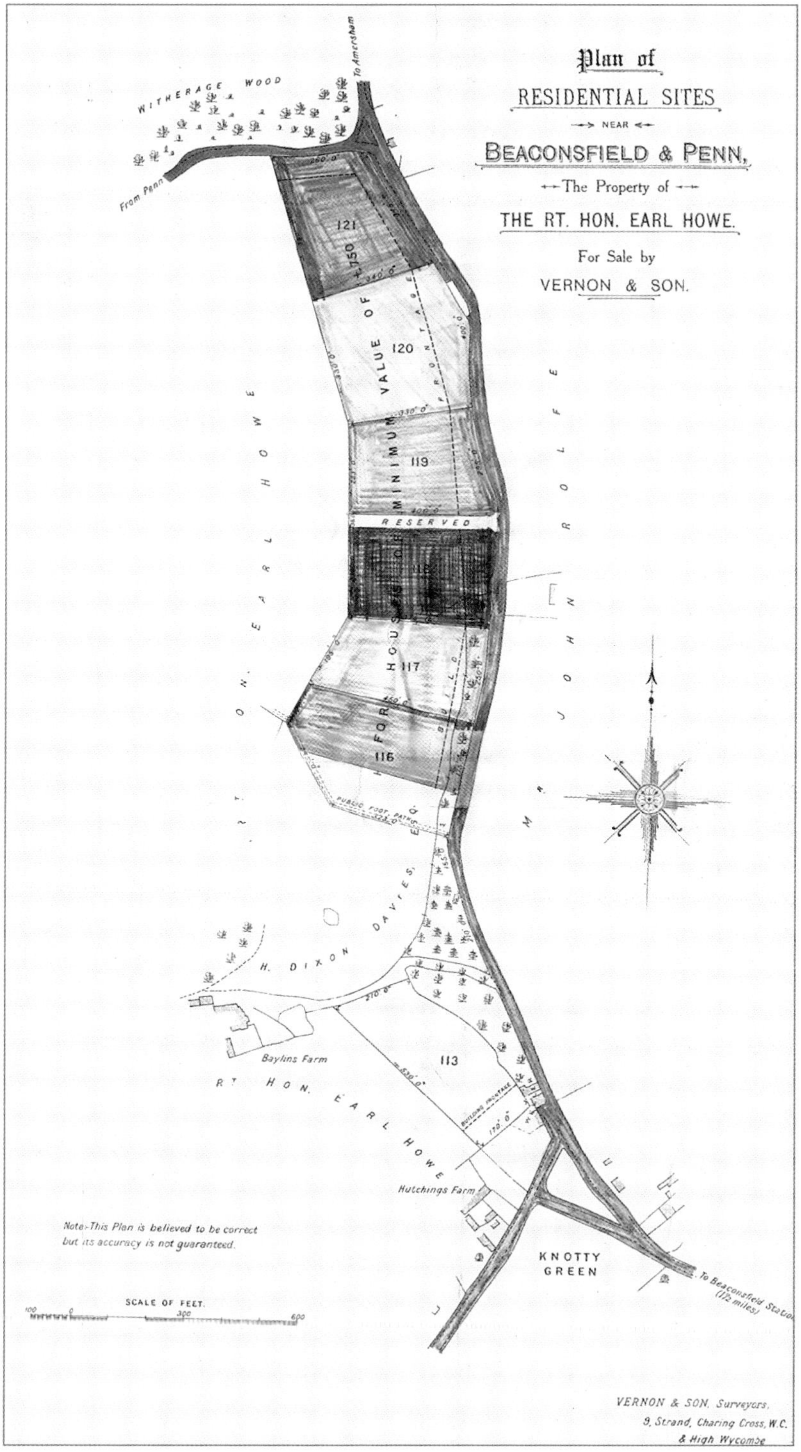

Plan of residential sites, 1906. The plan illustrates some of the (most desirable) £750 plots. Earl Howe's architect or surveyor had to certify that the required standard had been reached for each plot that was auctioned and only one house could be built on each plot. (*David Wooster*)

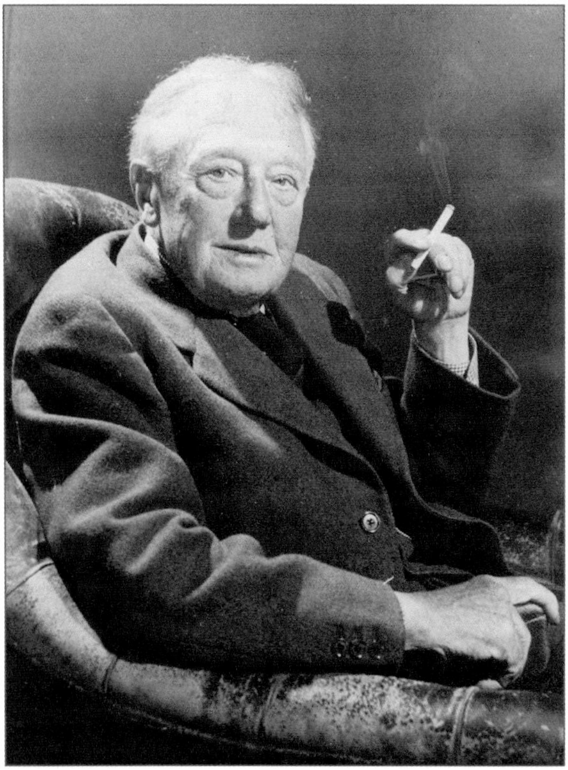

Sir Ambrose Heal (1872–1959), great-grandson of the founder of Heal & Son, who purchased Baylins Farm from the Penn Estate in 1920. He converted it into a private house, employing well-known architects Edwin Forbes and Sir Edward Maufe. He was knighted in 1933. (*Oliver Heal*)

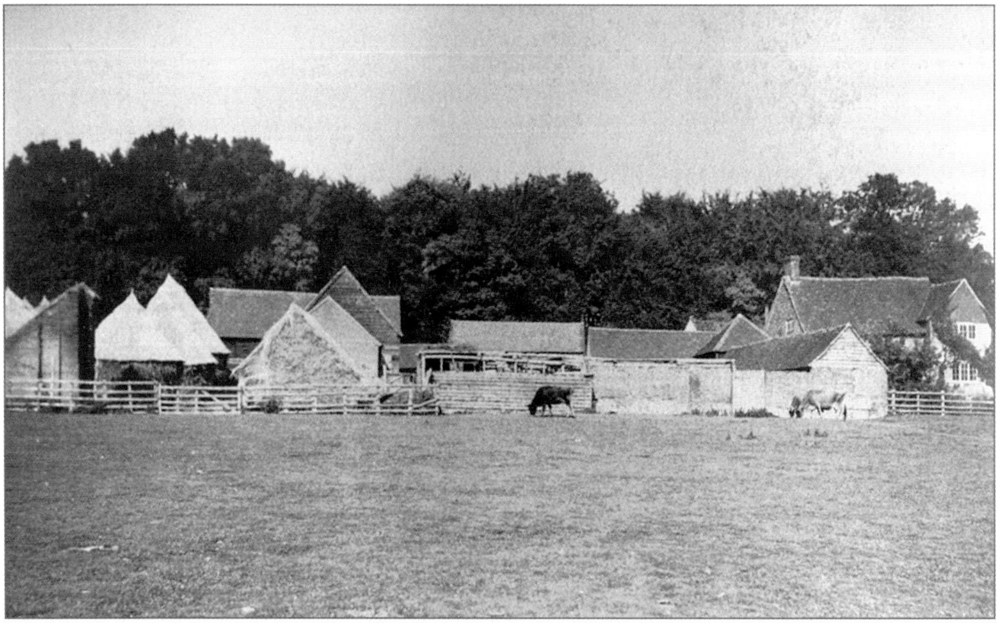

Baylins Farm and outbuildings, 1920. This photograph shows Baylins as a working farm of about 150 acres. The earliest reference to Baylins is in 1325, when John Belynges was a tenant of Segrave Manor and the fourth highest taxpayer in Penn. His name may refer to the bell-shaped edge of the common land, now marked by the two tracks off the Penn Road, which meet the 'handle' leading up to Baylins (see plan on p. 49). (*Oliver Heal*)

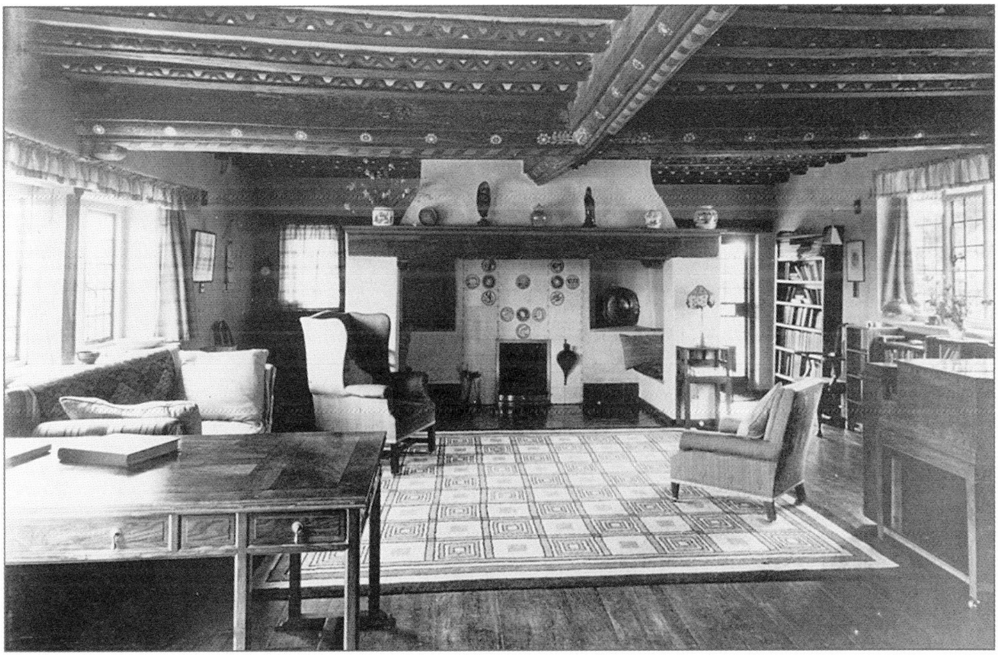

Baylins Farm sitting room, 1921. The house is grander than an ordinary farmhouse and was built in the late fifteenth or early sixteenth century as a late medieval hall house, open to the roof. The original arched hall trusses and curved braces dominate the first floor. A first floor and brick chimney-stacks were put in, probably at the end of Elizabeth's reign. The huge beams supporting the first floor can be seen in this photograph, bowed with weight and age, with brightly coloured stencil decorations by Macdonald Gill to lighten and enliven the room. It is a listed building. (*Oliver Heal*)

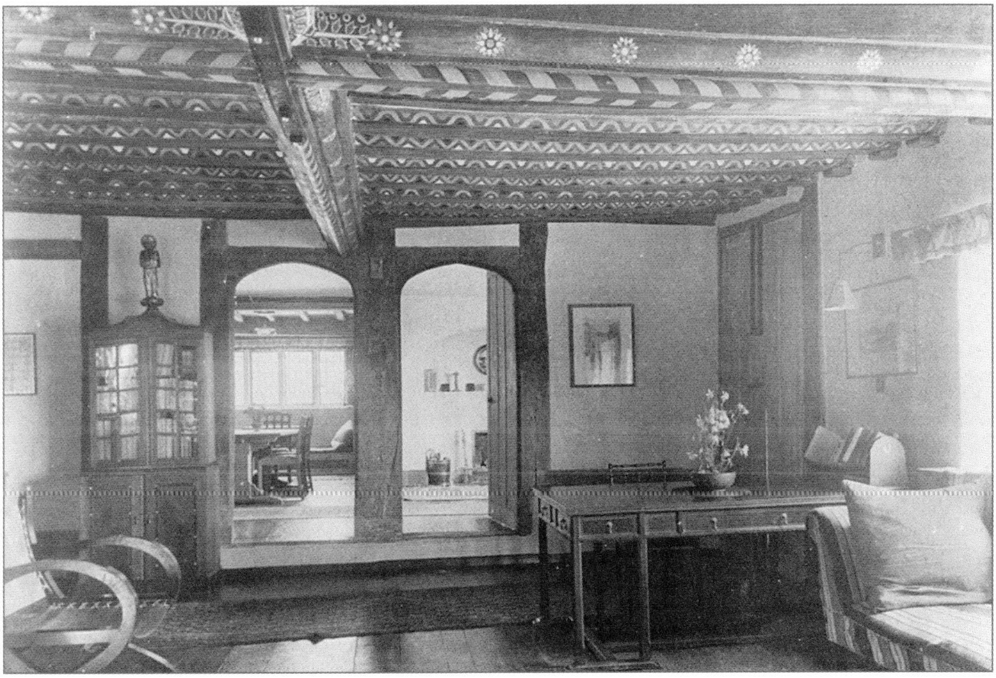

Looking through from sitting room to dining room, 1921. (*Oliver Heal*)

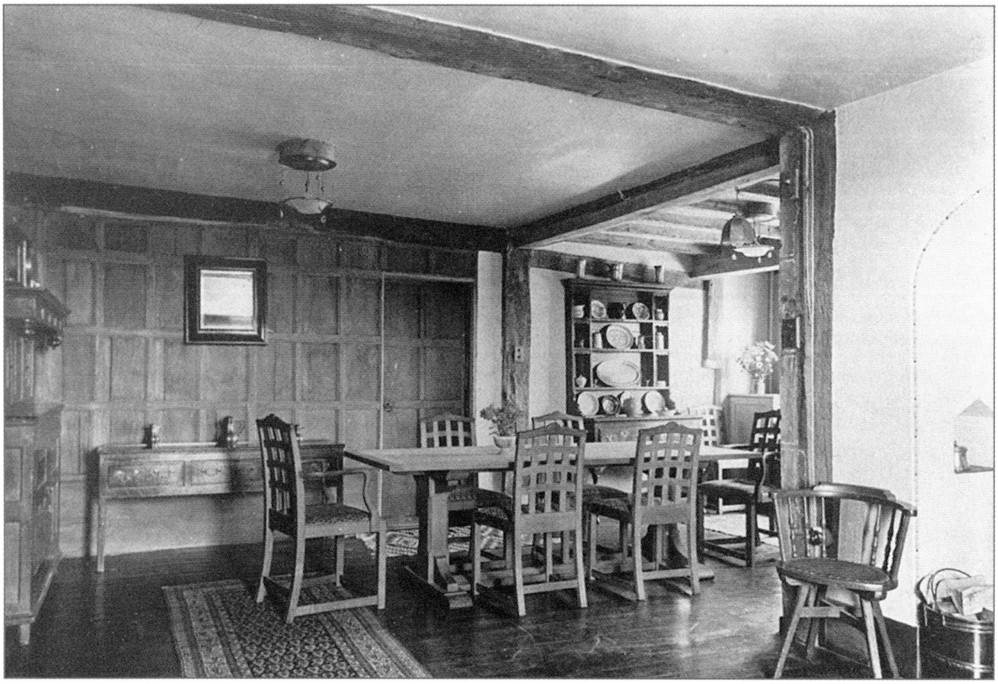

The dining room, 1921. This photograph shows the fine sixteenth- and seventeenth-century oak panelling with the oak chairs and table designed by Sir Ambrose Heal himself. He maintained that the good work of today had no less a claim than the good work of the past. (*Oliver Heal*)

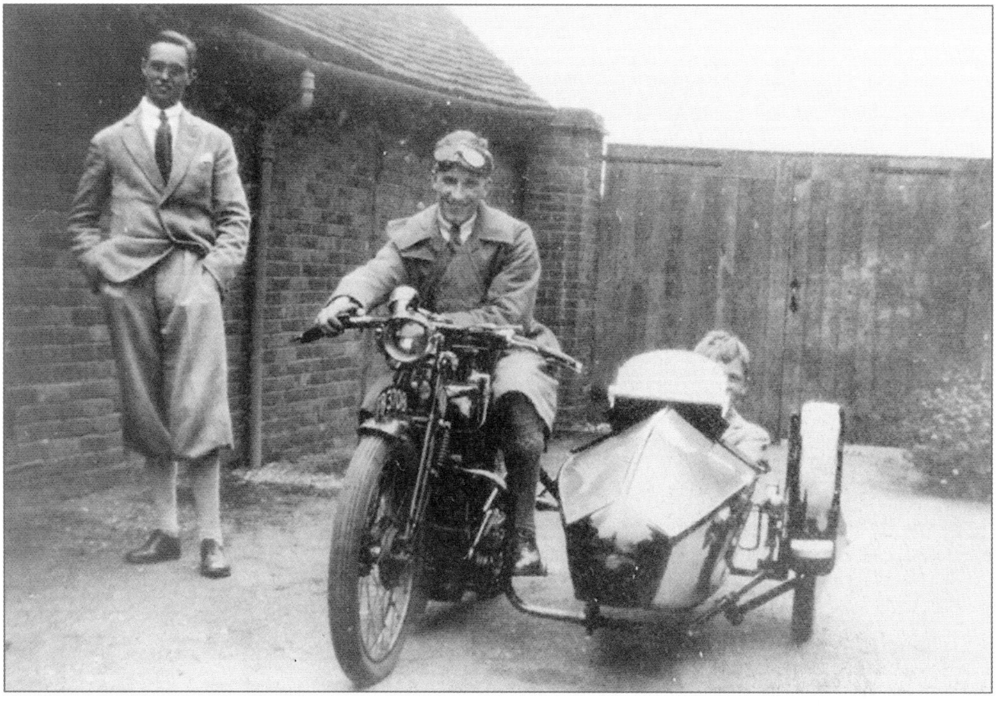

Young members of the Heal family in the plus fours of the time, with their motorbike and side-car, *c*. 1930. (*Oliver Heal*)

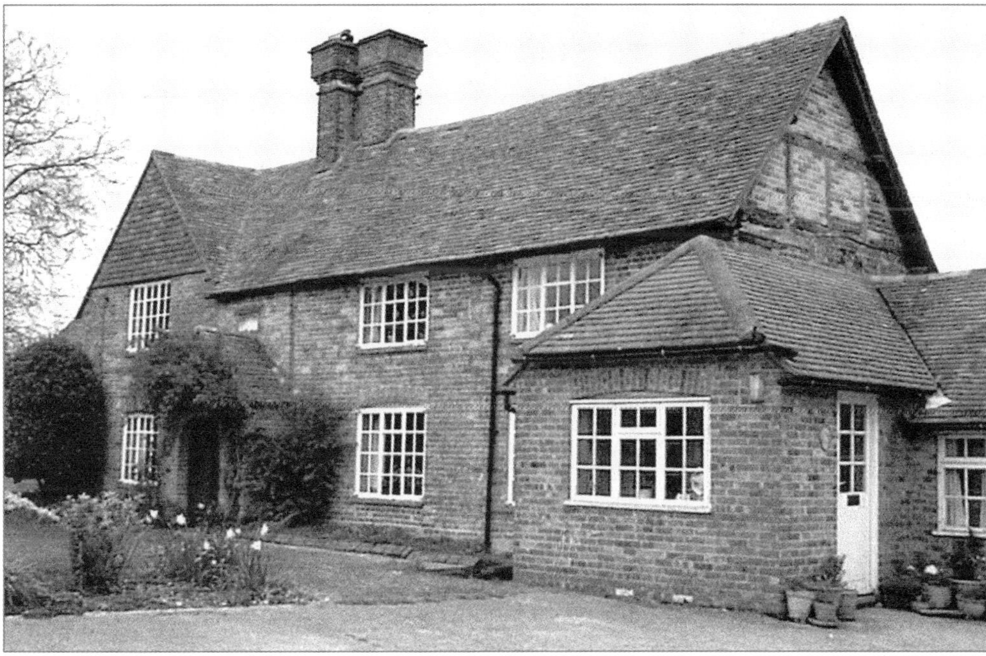

Segraves Farm is a listed building. It was built in the sixteenth and seventeenth centuries, but has re-used older timber from a medieval predecessor. In the early seventeenth century it was described as 'an old awncyen farme house'! It is likely to have been a medieval hunting lodge belonging to Segraves Manor, since it stands at the centre of a 150-acre deer park bounded by a deep ditch and external bank, much of which survives today. (*Bill Bundy*)

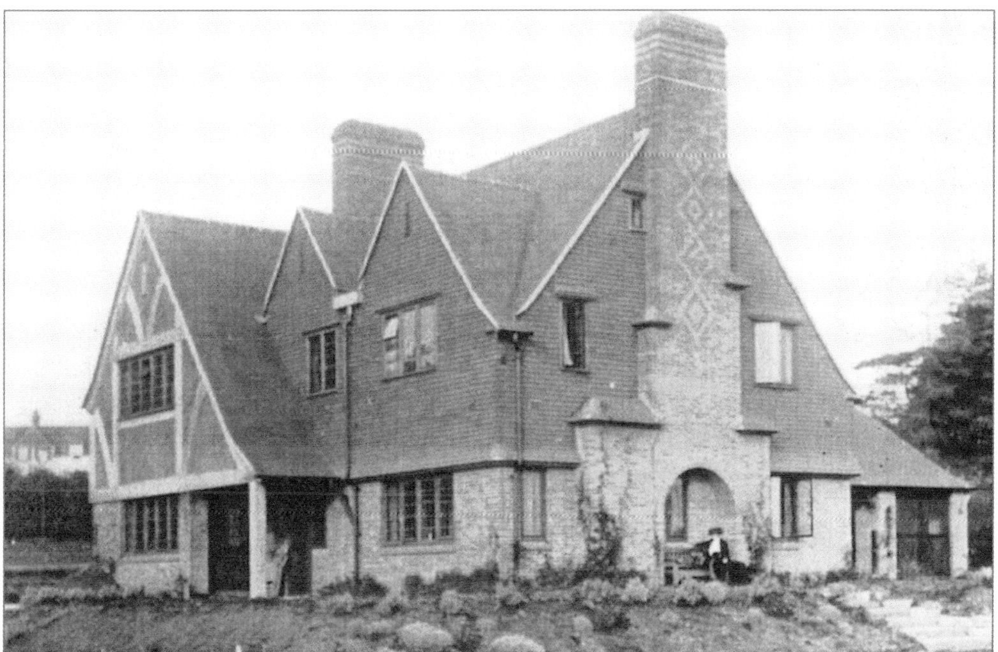

Davidge House, 1914. This was one of the first houses to be built after the railway arrived in 1906 and was named after Davidge Meadow on which it was built. (*David Lamb*)

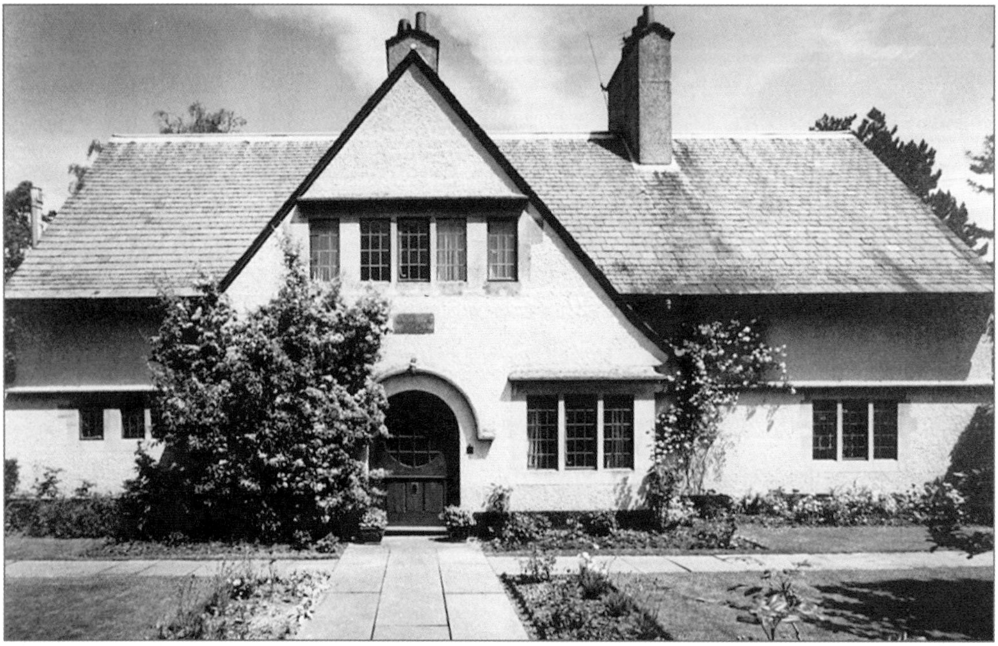

Holly Mount in Penn Road, 1994. A listed building designed by C.F.A. Voysey in 1907, it is a fine example of the Arts and Crafts style of architecture of that period. (*Martin Charles*)

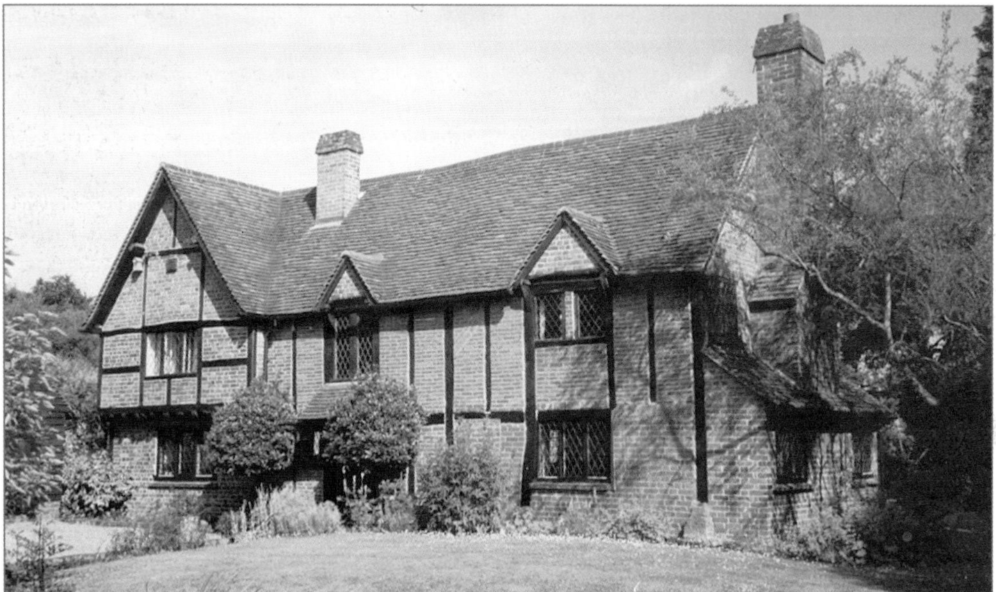

Egham's Farm, 1990. This is a timber-framed listed building of the late sixteenth or early seventeenth century. It was one of the four farms on the edge of the Green and was purchased by Thomas Weedon in 1779, and known as Weedon's Farm. In 1885 it was sold by the Weedons to Earl Howe and is shown as Egham's Farm on the 1897 map. Tenant farmers held the farm of 70 to 80 acres – members of the Perfect family between 1841 and 1891 and Hubert and Eric Hine by 1903 until 1930, when it ceased to be a farm. In 1929 the farm was sold by the Penn Estate to a Mr Farquharson. (*Research and photograph by Joan Whiteside*)

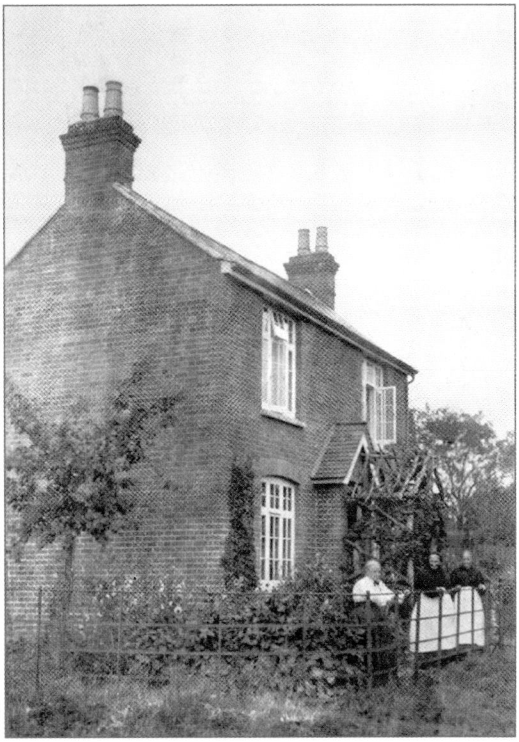

Whitethorn Cottage, off Forty Green Road, *c.* 1900. Emma Perfect (in a white blouse), 'Aunty' in the centre and Rhoda Ellen Perfect (aged about twelve). (*Geoffrey Green*)

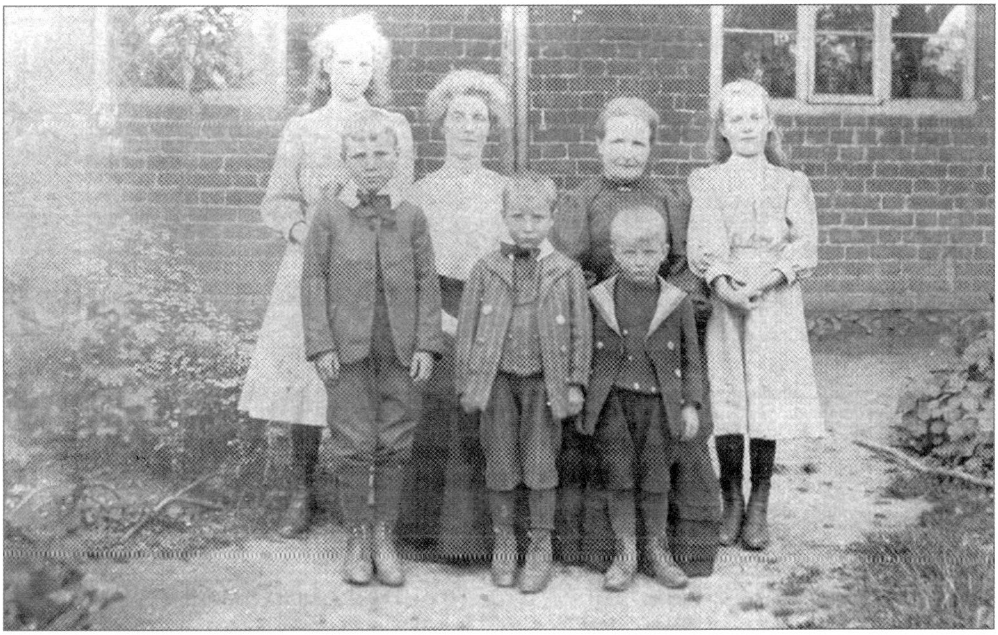

The Allen family outside what is now Dutch Cottage, *c.* 1913. It was then two cottages. George Allen was a shepherd. There were nine children eventually. Back row, left to right: Ada (Bates), Sarah (Curtin), Mrs Ellen Allen, Clara Jane (Green). Front row: Frederick, William James (Jack), Stanley. Sarah Curtin lived in Forty Green for most of her life and died, aged 100, in 1988. (*Geoffrey Green*)

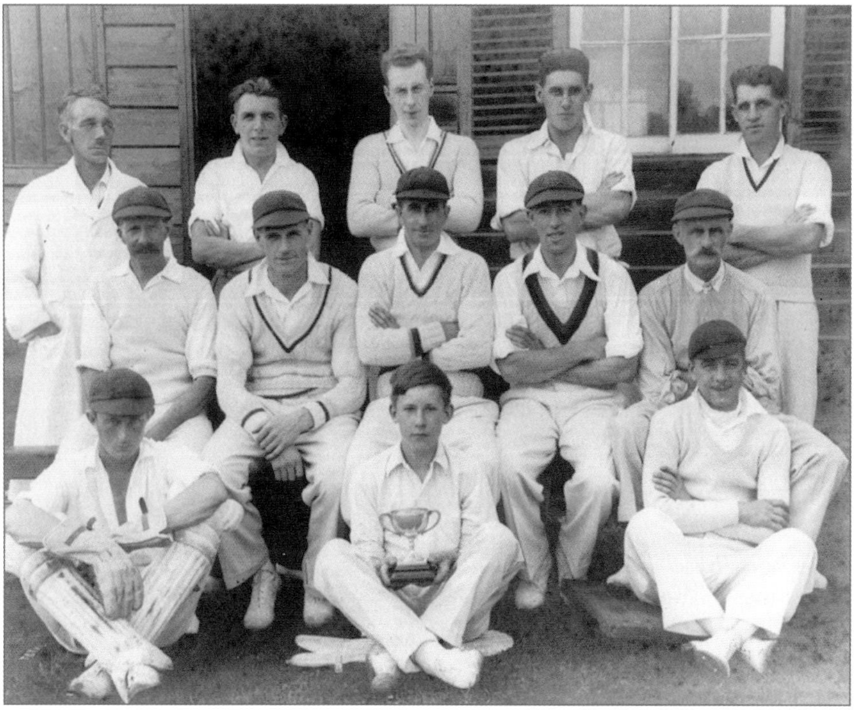

Knotty Green Cricket Club, winners of the President's Trophy, 1935. Back row, left to right: R. Bolton (umpire), T. Bates, S. Whapshot, G. Holden, F. Long. Middle row: B. Scales, J. Strickland (vice-captain), D. Hallett (captain), A.R. Hobbs, A.E. Perkins. Front row: G. Perkins, D. Pratchet (scorer), H. Chapples. There may have been some rough village cricket on the Green before the railway came in 1906, but the population was then very small. In 1896 Mr Brookes was taken on as grazing tenant for the Recreation Ground. In January 1908 there were complaints that Mrs Brookes' pigs were rooting up the turf, and in August she successfully applied for a reduction in rent to £1 10*s* p.a., 'as the ground is used a good deal more than formerly for cricket'. Mr Hubert Hine of Eghams Farm took over as tenant in 1910. His son Eric remembered cutting the grass with a horse-drawn machine. (*Knotty Green Cricket Club*)

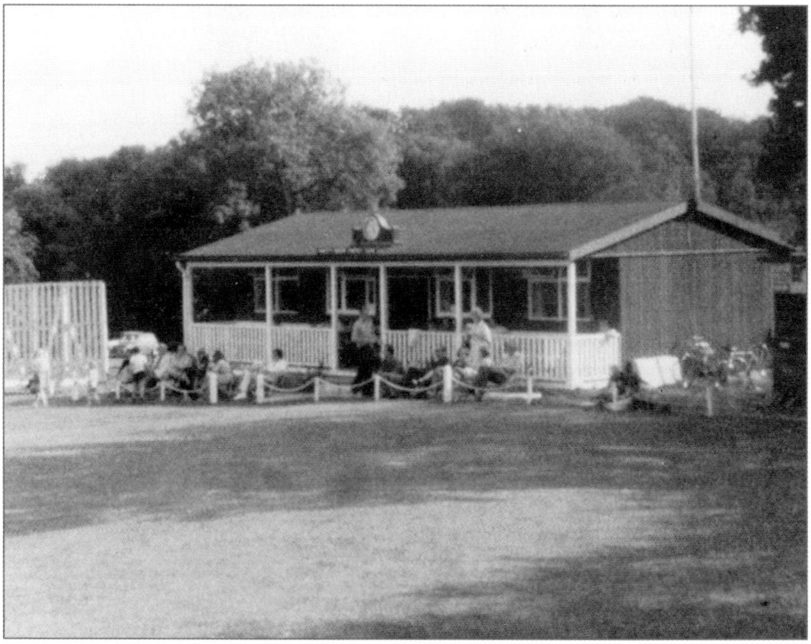

Knotty Green Cricket Club Pavilion, *c.* 1970. Earl Howe opened it in 1960. The cost of £2,132 was raised by a £700 local subscription and grants from the Parish, District and County Councils. The builder was Mr T. Bates who appears in the 1935 team above. In 1920 Captain H. Barr Davies was allowed to erect a club room for a nominal rent, despite some local opposition. This earlier club room was an old 10ft by 8ft shed on stilts, and committee meetings and teas were held at the back of the Red Lion. During the Second World War the only six surviving members joined forces with six members from Rotax, a branch of Lucas in Beaconsfield, then making armaments, to keep the Club going. The surviving Minute Books of the Club run from 1934, but an earlier one is missing. (*Knotty Green Cricket Club*)

CHAPTER FOUR

FORTY GREEN

Forty Green takes its name from the dominant topographical feature, i.e. the jutting out island of land encircled by Ridings Lane (Old English *for*, as in forehead and Old English *eg*, island, as in Dorney).

In 1841 the hamlet was a little bigger than Knotty Green with eighty inhabitants in fifteen families. The men were nearly all working on the local farms. In 1955 there were five families of Perfects, three of Bates and the Allens of Hill Farm, all with descendants still living locally. The cottages mostly lined the northern edge of the large, open, triangular green which had several ponds. Unlike other hamlets of the parish, Forty Green lost all its former common land in 1855, when the green was enclosed.

Older inhabitants remember a village before the Second World War of about twenty-four families, mostly related, with one small combined baker and shop opposite the Royal Standard. In 1955 there were about forty houses before a further twenty-five were built in Gomms Wood Close. The present population is about 220 in eighty-five houses.

Two well-known authors are connected with Forty Green. Alison Uttley (1884–1976), whose books still weave magic for children with Tim Rabbit, Sam Pig and Little Red Fox, lived in Beaconsfield but often walked in Forty Green which she loved greatly. In her book *Buckinghamshire* (1950), she starts her journey around the county in the cherry and apple orchards of Forty Green and walks up the lane to Penn. She is buried in Penn churchyard. Terry Pratchett (b. 1948), famous for his Discworld fantasy novels, lived in Brindle Lane, Forty Green, as a young boy in the 1950s.

Mains water arrived before 1926 and, as in many places, some of the old villagers refused to have anything to do with it. Electricity came to Brindle Lane in 1957 and gas in 1965, though earlier along the Forty Green Road. 'Dirty Dennis' was still making a two-weekly call, to empty cesspits, until about 1970.

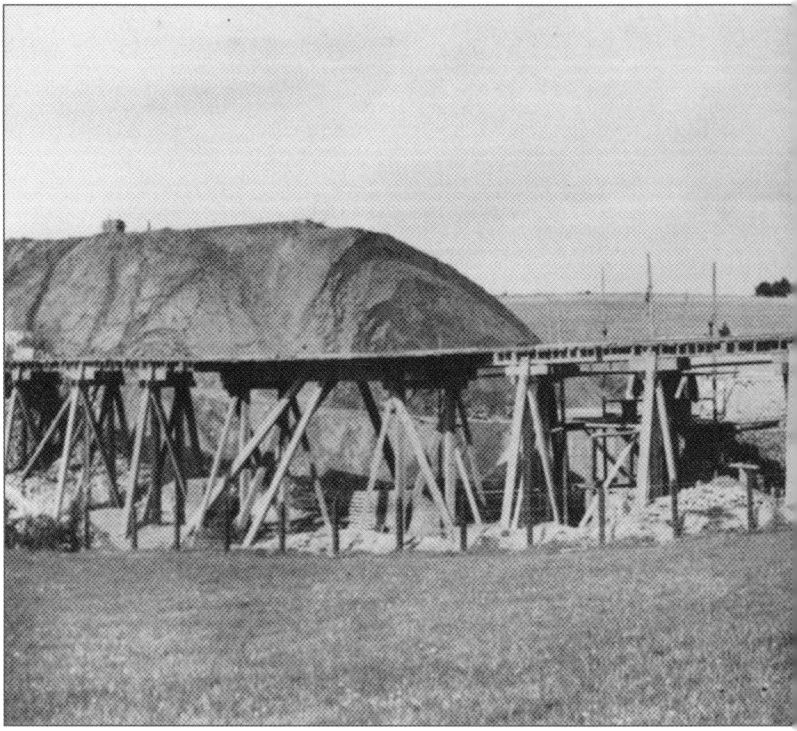

Construction of the railway bridge over Holtspur Lane (R1, on the map on p. 4), 1905. This photograph was taken from the hillside to the south-east of the bridge. The top of Hogback Wood can be seen to the right and the rounded hill which gave Forty Green its name (p. 57) can still be seen through the gap in the embankment. The brickwork of the bridge itself has just been started. Earth for the huge embankment was brought up on the temporary railway from cuttings further down the line.

Job Wooster (1850–1927) from Seeley's Farm is standing in the foreground. He was brought up on Knotty Green Farm, and started at Seeley's with his father in 1868. (*David Wooster*)

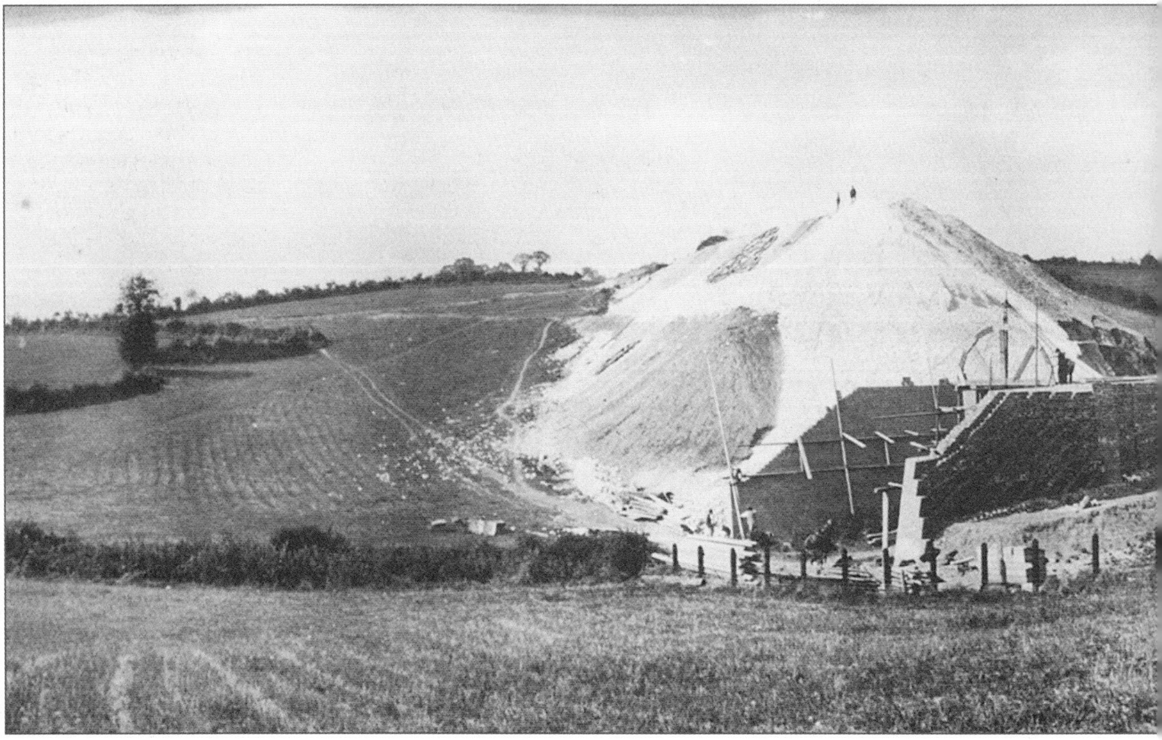

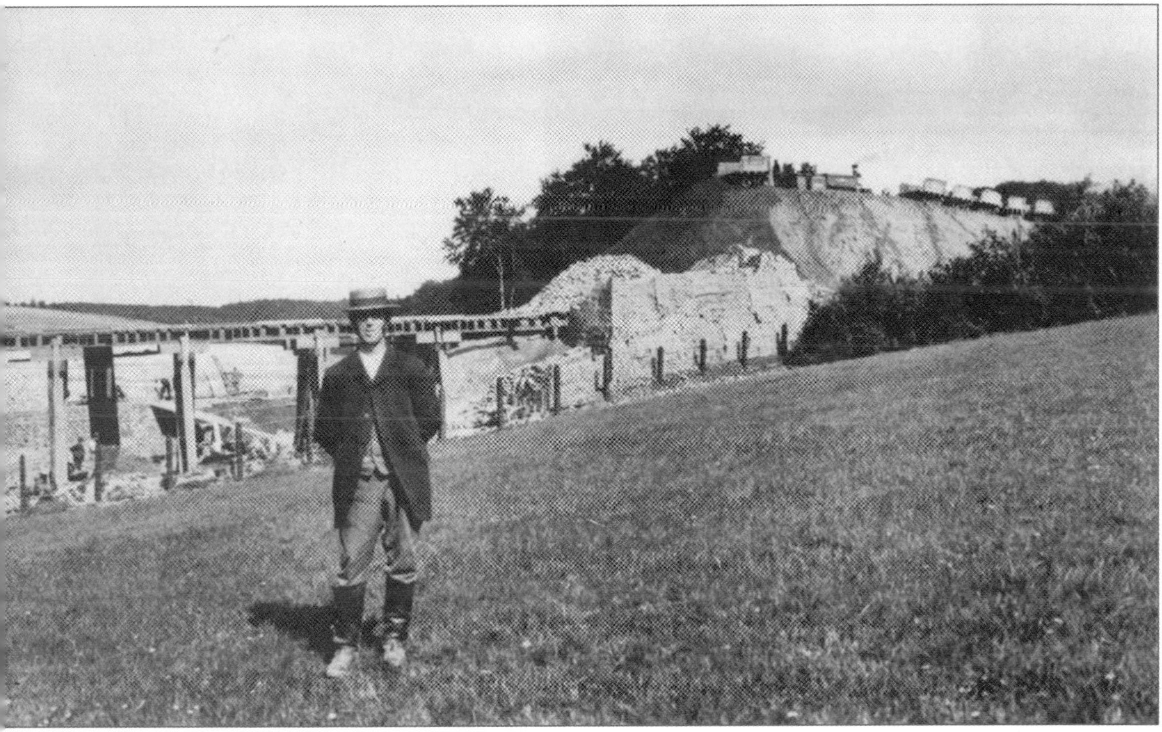

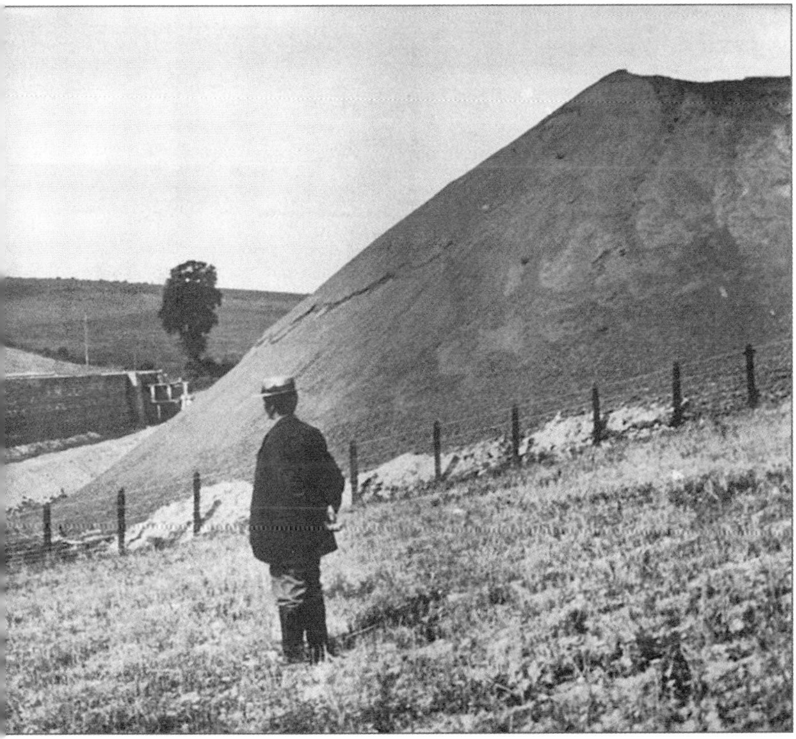

Construction of the railway bridge over Ridings Lane (R3 on the map on p. 4), 1905. This photograph is also taken from the south-east. This bridge was not so easy to identify, but the hedge pattern and tracks seen in this photograph to the south-west correspond exactly to those both on the ground and on the map at Ridings Lane, as does the height, shape and angle of the tunnel. Job Wooster is again viewing the operation. Two thousand men, including some from Forty Green, were employed on the very difficult hilly stretch between Gerrards Cross and High Wycombe, which involved deep cuttings, high embankments, a big tunnel under White House Farm and a long brick viaduct at Loudwater. The decorative brickwork around each arch is a different pattern for each bridge. (*David Wooster*)

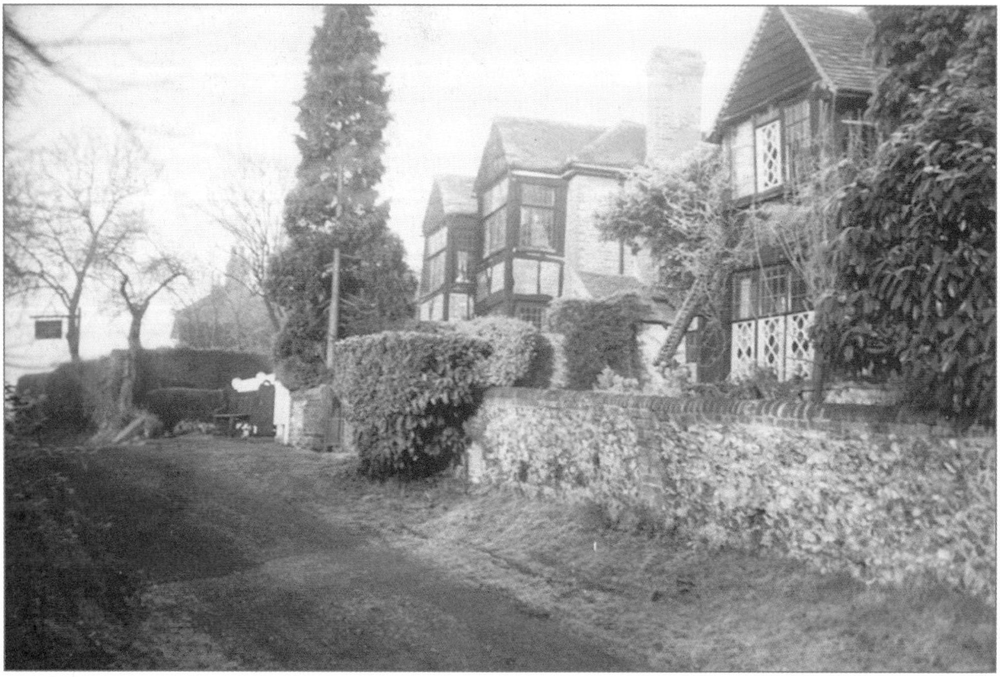

The Royal Standard of England, 1950s. This well-known public house started life as a beer house soon after the 1830 Beer Act. In 1847 it was called the Britannia, in 1852 it was the Ship, and by 1872 the Royal Standard. The 1875 map shows it as the Royal Standard of England. The landlord between 1891 and 1905 was James Perfect (1835–1915) who still has great-grandchildren living in Forty Green. He reputedly lost his licence in 1905 for keeping the pub open after licensing hours for the men building the railway. Landlord Edmund Allison arrived in 1915 and together with his daughter, Mrs Hylda Holderness, and her husband, transformed the pub and made it the centre of village life. (*Kay Mellor*)

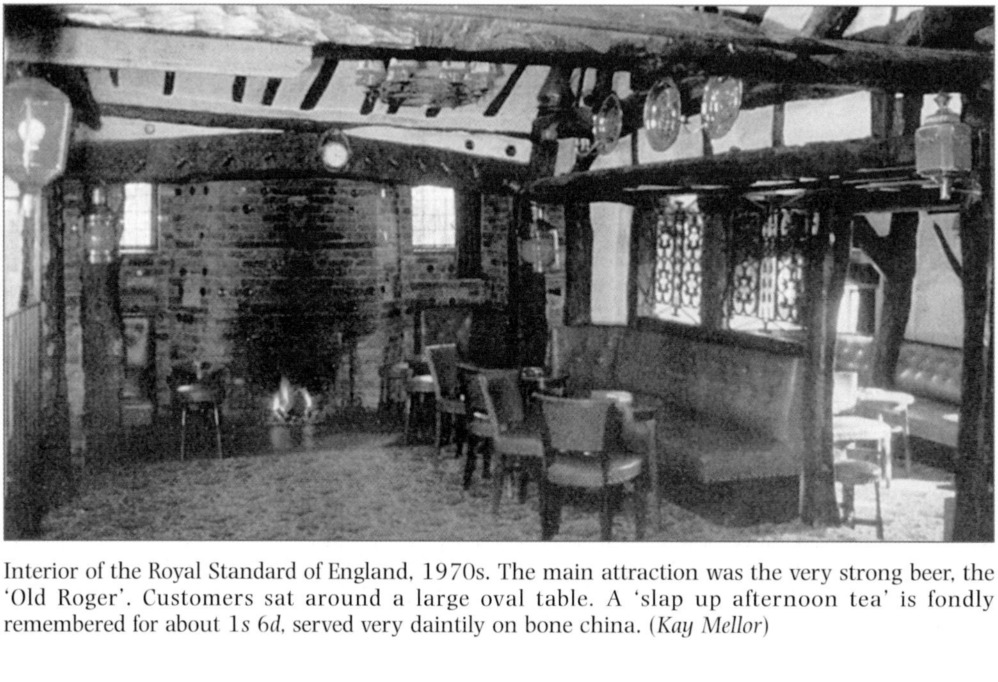

Interior of the Royal Standard of England, 1970s. The main attraction was the very strong beer, the 'Old Roger'. Customers sat around a large oval table. A 'slap up afternoon tea' is fondly remembered for about 1*s* 6*d*, served very daintily on bone china. (*Kay Mellor*)

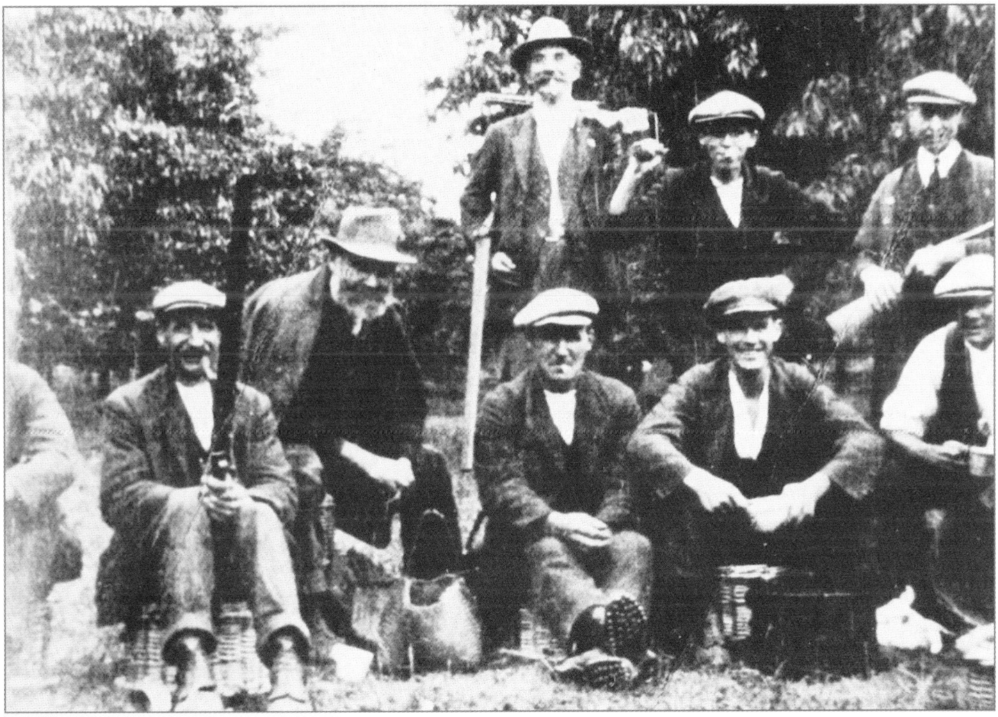

'Cherry starvers' working for farmer George Pitcher, *c.* 1930. Their job was to starve the birds by scaring them away from the cherries with their guns. Standing, left to right: -?-, -?-, Victor Curtin. Seated: George Allen (1890–1959), Walter Allen, Fred Allen, -?-, -?-. (*County Museum*)

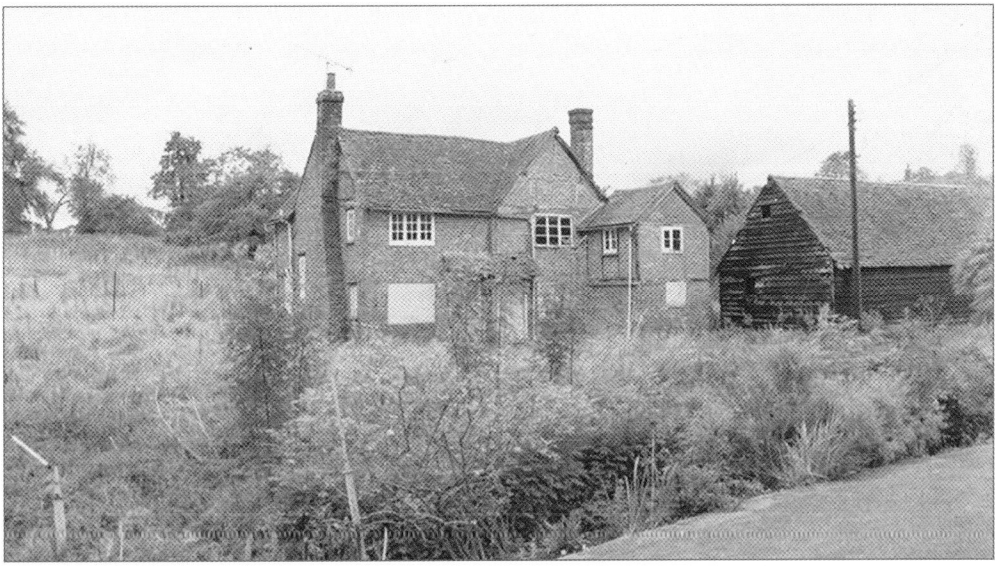

Hill Farm Cottage, 1993. This is the only listed building in Forty Green now that boundary changes have taken Holtspur Bottom Farmhouse out of the parish of Penn. It is a late sixteenth- or early seventeenth-century timber-framed building which has been recently enlarged and modernised. Hill Farm was about ¼ mile away. It was shown on the 1875 map and the last mention of it was in 1880. It is not shown on a map of 1897. In its later stages it seems to have been a collection of cottages occupied by Allens, Bates and Perfects. (*PPC*)

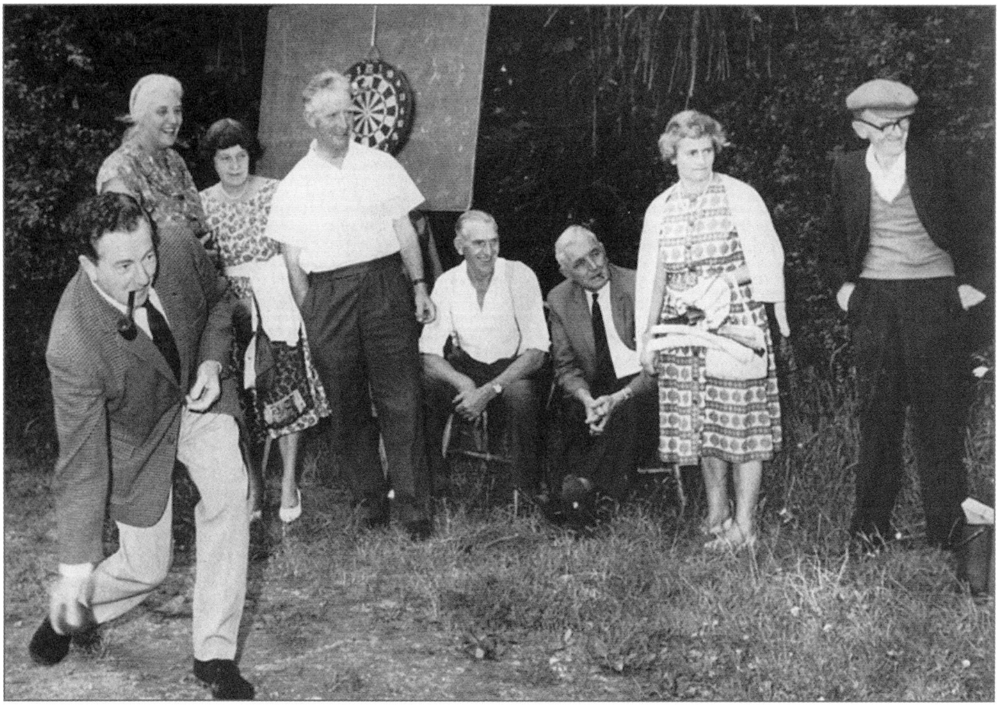

Rupert Davies, TV star of Maigret, playing bowls in a WI fête held in 'The Dip' opposite Gomm Wood Close, *c.* 1960. Left to right: Rupert Davies, Florence Jackson, Mrs Craft, Jack Allen, Arthur Bates, Tom Bates, Margery Bates, Tom Jackson. (*Mr and Mrs G. Feast*)

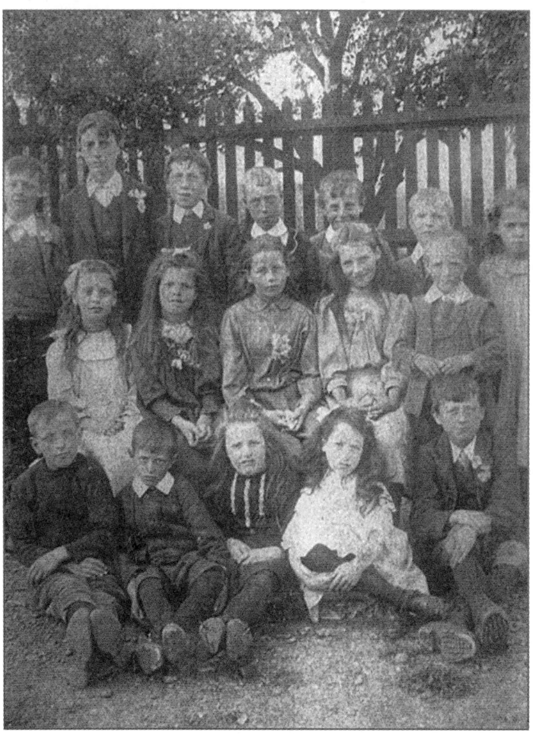

Local schoolchildren at Penn School opposite Penn Church, *c.* 1912. The Forty Green children used to walk just over a mile up Pauls Hill. In her book *Buckinghamshire* (1950), Alison Uttley wrote lyrically about the natural beauties of her walk up the lane with little Joy Allen. Centre, far left, Florence Allen; fourth from left, with tilted head, Clara Jane Allen. (*Geoffrey Green*)

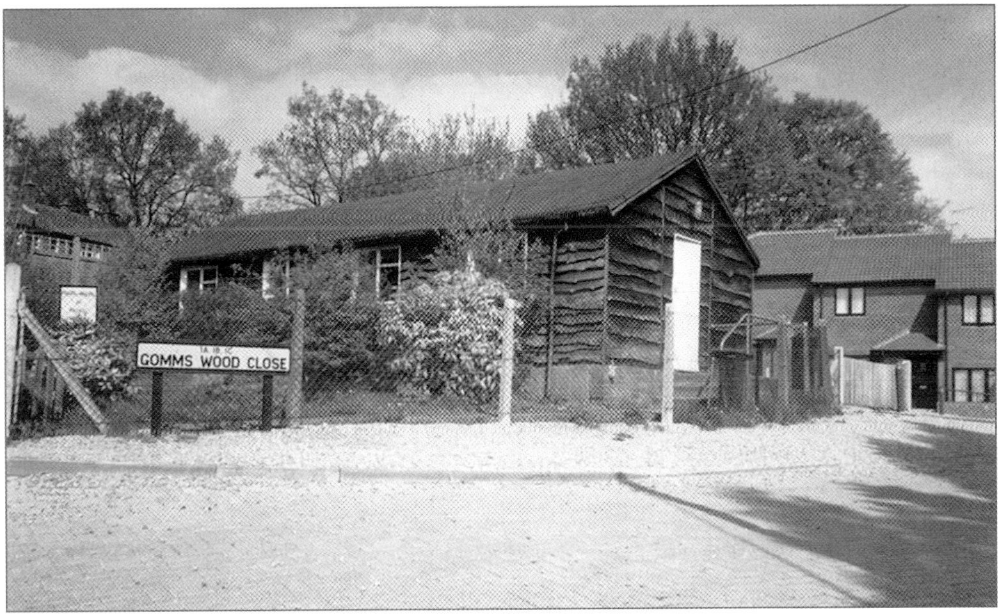

Old WI hut, Forty Green, 1998. Early meetings were held in the summer house of the Royal Standard where Mr and Mrs Holderness were the landlords. The WI's first great achievement was to get the WI hut put up in 1955, on District Council land for which a peppercorn rent of £1 p.a. was paid. It was made out of two second-hand wooden sheds. Money was raised by all sorts of events and by private subscription, with the help of local celebrities such as Alison Uttley, Stanley Holloway and Rupert Davies. (*PPC*)

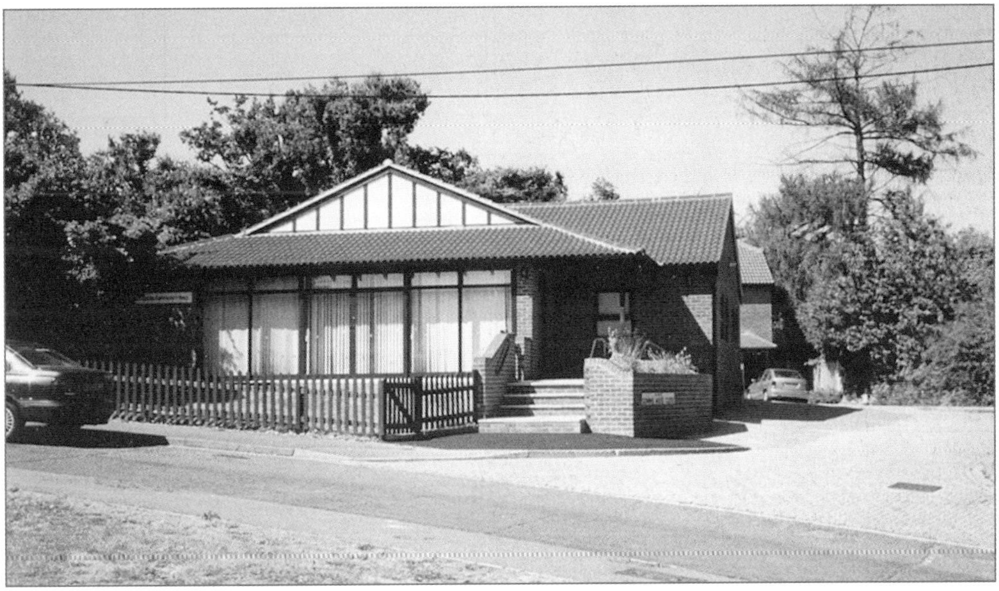

New Community Hall, 1998. In 1994 surveys showed that the old WI hut was beyond sensible repair after forty years' good service. A new brick hall was likely to cost £75,000, of which £25,000 would need to be raised locally. There were only thirty-two WI members of average age 70, but, bravely, they decided to go ahead. The WI was dissolved and a new Trust formed. The final cost was £110,000. There were generous grants and some £20,000 was raised by local events and subscriptions. The new hall was opened by Earl Howe on 24 October 1998. (*PPC*)

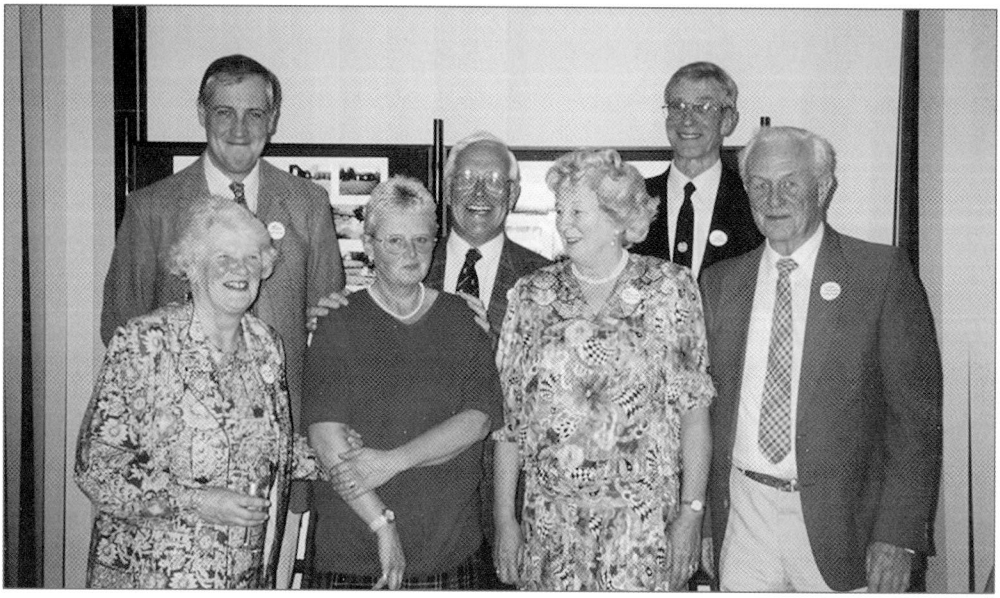

Building Committee of the new Community Hall, 1998. Back row, left to right: Nigel Spicer (legal advisor), Colin Jones (treasurer), Geoff Feast (PPC). Front row: Pat Colley (WI and chair), Sue Garrett (secretary), Kay Mellor (WI founder member). Gerry Fenner (PPC). Howard Williams (building advisor) is not in the photograph.

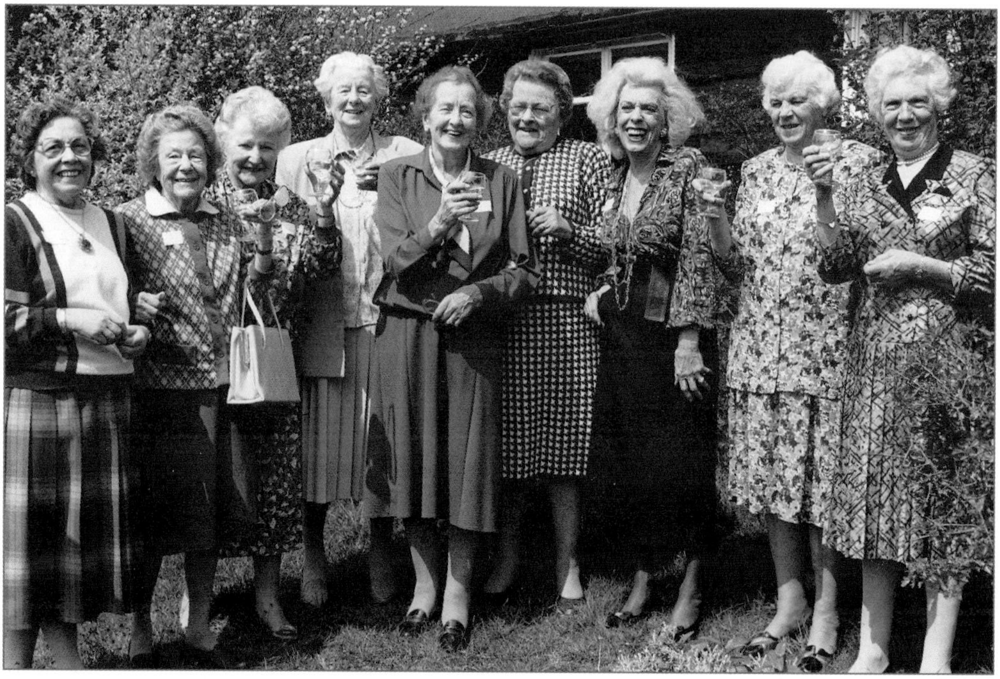

All the former presidents at the fortieth anniversary of Forty Green WI, 1990. Left to right: Hilda Ball, Day Tytherleigh, Bunty Pennefeather, Mary Waugh, Meylor Parker, Pam Peppiatt, Lorna Stoneham (the first president), Betty Brown, Eileen Boyles. The Forty Green WI was formed in 1950 by Mrs Lorna Stoneham and Mrs Hylda Holderness, with members from both Forty Green and Knotty Green. (*PPC*)

CHAPTER FIVE

WINCHMORE HILL

Historically Winchmore Hill was a divided village, both between the two parishes of Amersham and Penn and between Buckinghamshire and Hertfordshire. This was because, until 1844, the Coleshill part of Amersham parish, together with the northern part of Beaconsfield, was a detached part of Hertfordshire, sometimes known as Little Hertfordshire. This old county boundary made a sharp angle at the crossroads and gave the name 'the angled boundary hill' to the hamlet (Old English *wincel*, angle and Old English *maer*, boundary). A member of a local jury in 1223 was William de la Wenche. Part of Marrods Bottom (Old English *maere rod*, boundary cross) marks the same county boundary.

The population in 1912 was about 300 and growing by about a house a year. Almost all were employed locally in chairmaking (sixty-nine in five factories), farming (twelve in Fagnall & Glory Farms), and the pottery by the Potters Arms (five). From 1897 villagers pressed for a school, and almost succeeded in 1910 when seventy-six of the seventy-seven ratepayers signed a petition on behalf of their 134 eligible children. They failed because they did not want a C of E school – 'the inhabitants are practically all non-conformist' – and because Winchmore Hill was then shared between the three parishes of Coleshill (newly formed in 1894), Amersham and Penn. The parishes all met at a point at the crossroads by The Plough, and children used to try to stand in all three parishes at the same time. In 1955, in response to a proposal to remedy this untidy arrangement by placing the whole village in Coleshill, there was a postal vote in favour of Penn by 72 per cent of those who responded. A Local Inquiry also decided in favour of Penn. The combined population in 1954 was 569 (Coleshill 310, Amersham 157, Penn 102), with chairmaking and agriculture still the main industries. The population is now 618.

Despite grazing horses and the many dells, pits and ponds which still covered the common in 1895, the Winchmore Hill Cricket Club played cricket on it and was allowed to mark and level off a pitch. In later years both the cricket and football clubs played in the Park of Penn House. After the flattering vote of 1955 to join Penn considerable, though unsuccessful, efforts were made to find a suitable sports ground. The final solution was to fill in all the ponds and dells and bulldoze the common flat. This was done between 1958 and 1963. Water mains arrived from Coleshill in 1911, at first as a single standpipe used by the whole village. Electricity came in the mid-1920s, earlier than it might have done because it was en route for Penn House. Street lighting appeared in 1957, the mains sewer replaced the 'Honey Wagon' in 1989 and gas arrived in 1990. In 1930 strong protest was made to the County Council's proposed erection of a smallpox hospital at Marrods Bottom.

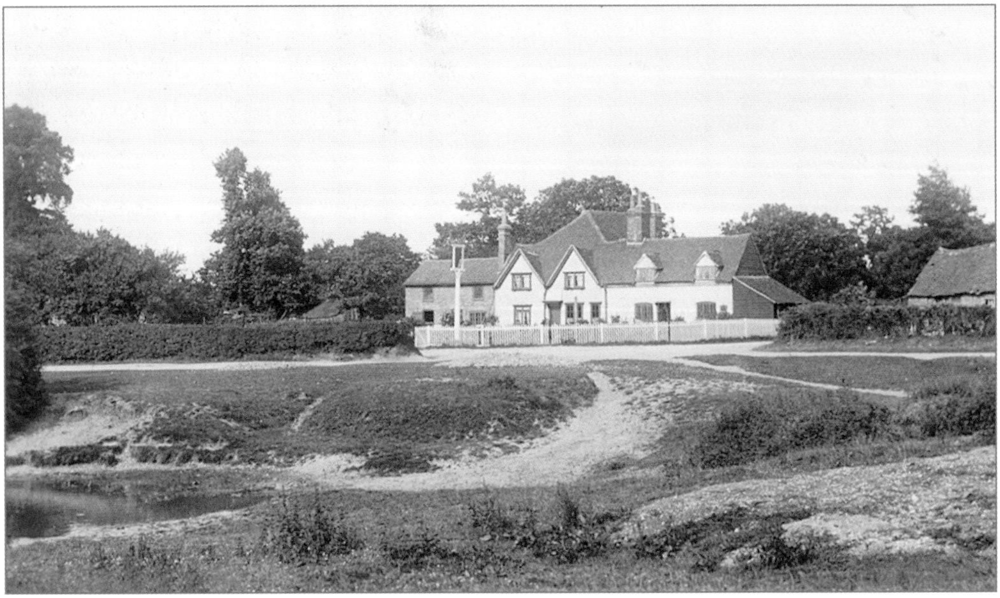

The Plough and the 'Pit', c. 1918. The Plough stands on the former Coleshill side and the point of the hedge of the garden opposite, in the centre of the picture, is where the three parishes met. Horses were allowed to graze on the common, which was twice its present size, running right up to The Hill, until the Amersham Inclosure Award of 1816 allowed cottages to be built on that half. *(Colin Seabright)*

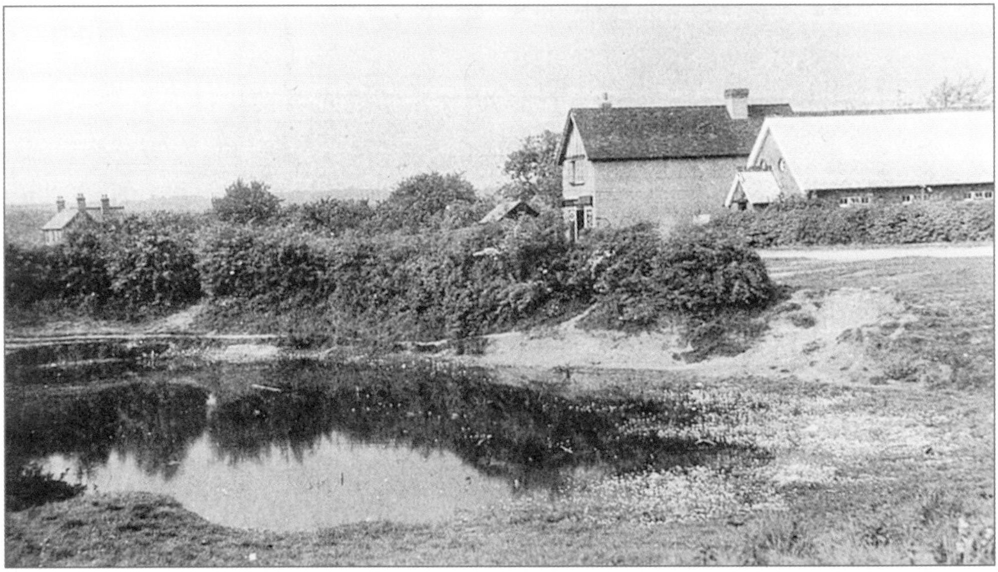

The Memorial Hall and the 'Pit', 1921. The Hall was opened on 27 November 1921 as a memorial to those who died in the First World War. It stands on the former Amersham side of the boundary which ran along the edge of the present common. The house on the left was a general store opened by Sid Wingrove in about 1921 and closed in the late 1950s. There was a butcher's shop at the top of Coleshill Lane, and a sweet shop in 3 The Row, on The Hill.

There was a very big and deep pit, described in 1903 as 'an old gravel pit', though it was more likely clay. Edward Payne, aged eight, was drowned in the 'Pit' as it was called, when he fell through the ice on Boxing Day 1915. It was filled in during 1958. *(Colin Seabright)*

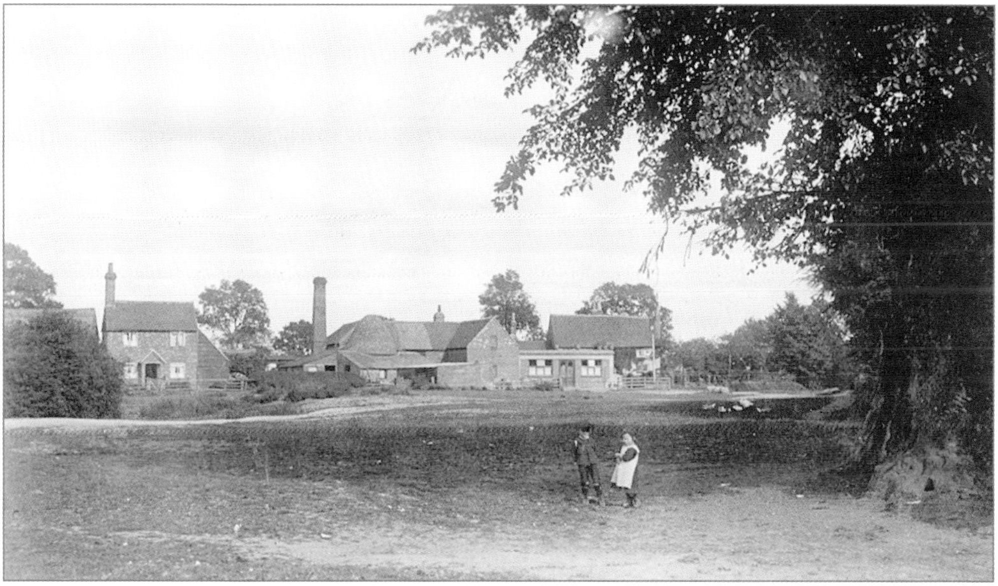

Potters Arms and Pottery, *c.* 1912. This view continues that in the photograph of the Plough (facing page) and shows the Pottery, which was presumably the cause of the many pits and dells on the Common. There were also a dozen former clay pits behind it, along the Coleshill road. It stood on the former Coleshill side and a potter is first recorded there in 1785. It remained a working factory until after the First World War. In 1912 it employed five men. The Potters Arms was first licensed as a beer house in 1830, following the 1830 Beer Act. There was a small pit or pond on the common in front of it. (*Colin Seabright*)

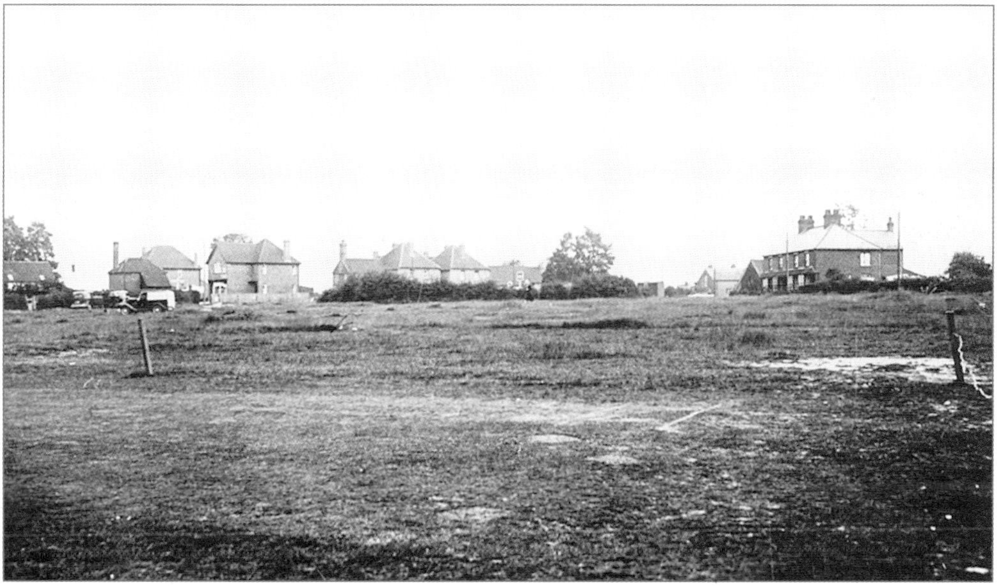

The Common and Royal Cottages, 1940s. The Pottery next to the Potters Arms has been replaced by houses, as have the old single-storey sheds near the crossroads. Royal Cottages, on the right, were built in about 1919 and take their name from Royal Pond or The Ryle which used to lie between the cottages and the track leading to Dell Orchard and Horsemoor Lane. The pond was not deep and children used to skate on it. It was used as a rubbish tip until filled in by the Parish Council in 1958. (*Colin Seabright*)

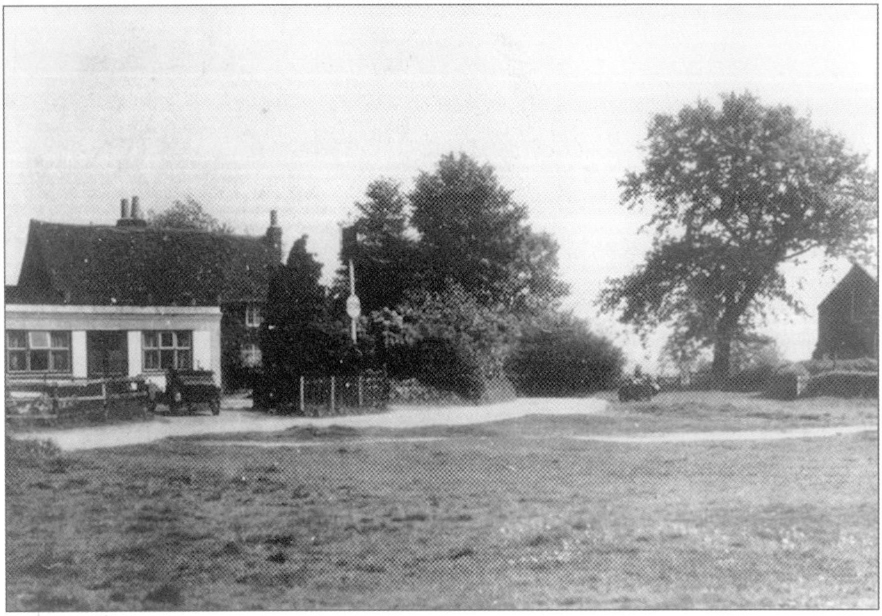

Fagnall Lane with the Potters Arms and the Methodist chapel, *c.* 1918. The only cottages down the lane were Fagnall and Glory Farm Cottages. The first Wesleyan Society was established in 1818 and met in Glory Farm, led by Thomas Bovingdon. The chapel was built in 1861, at a cost of £160, and enlarged in 1885. More recently it was sold to the C of E and became St Andrew's Church for a few years until 1984. It was pulled down in 1991 and rebuilt as a house. (*Maureen Seymour*)

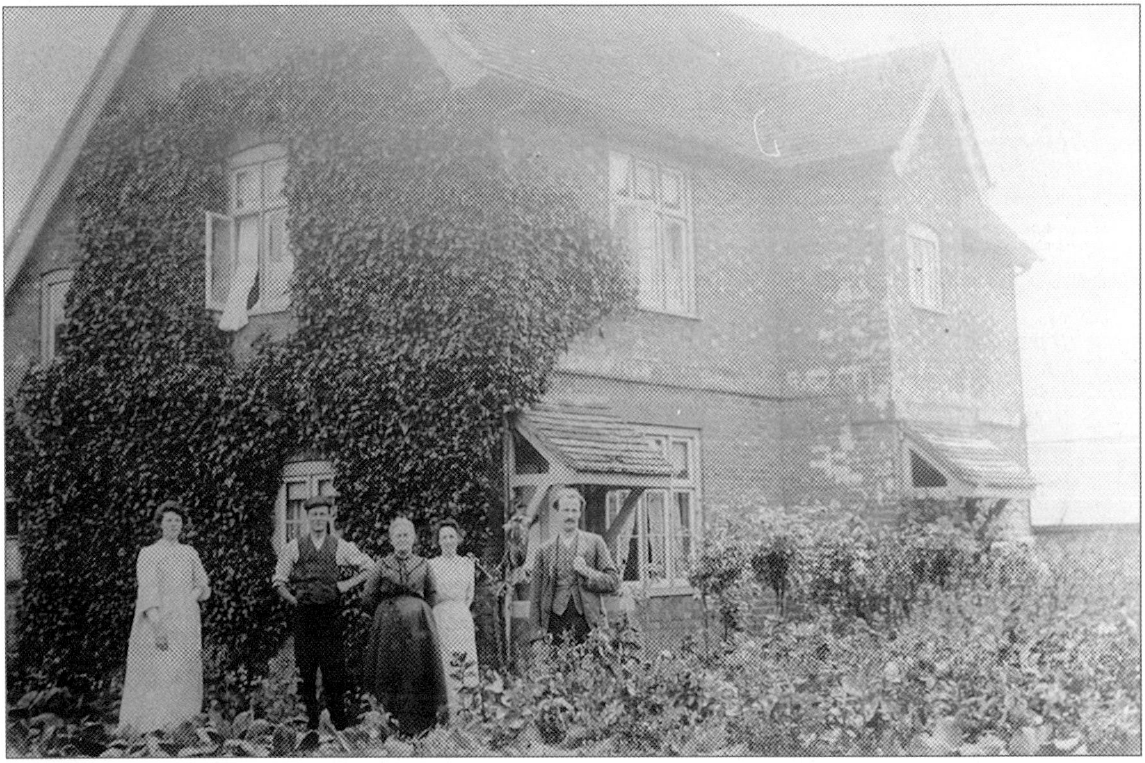

Winchmore Hill Farm and the Hatch family, *c.* 1901. The farm was next to the Methodist chapel opposite the Potters Arms, and the farmyard stretched from Royal Pond back to Horsemoor Lane. It was pulled down after the Second World War. Left to right: Olive, Albert, Sarah Jane (widow of William), Marian, Arthur. William Hatch died in 1901 and his two sons, Albert and Arthur, took over the tenancy of the farm from the Penn Estate, afterwards moving to Fagnall Farm. (*Maureen Seymour*)

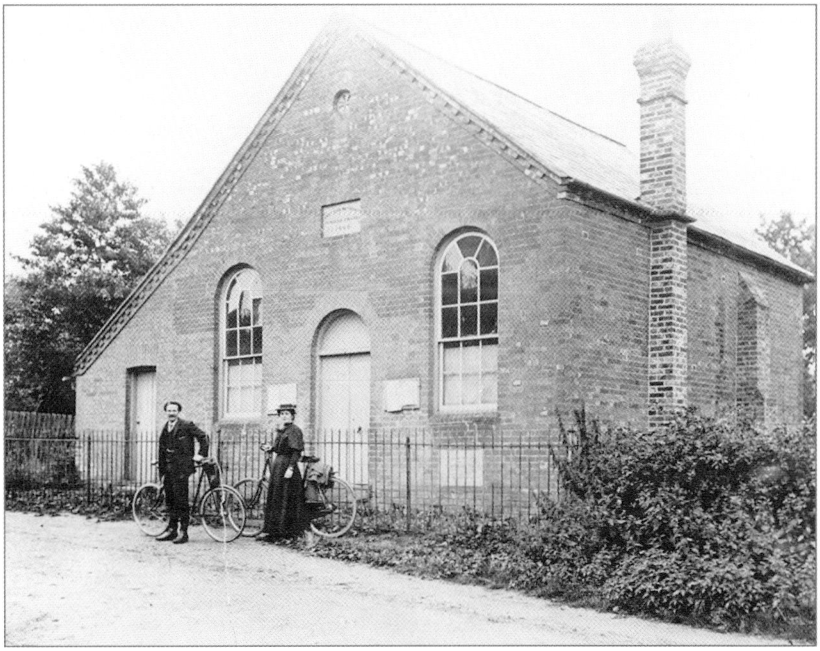

Arthur and Elizabeth Hatch (née Cox) outside the Wesleyan Methodist chapel on The Hill, *c.* 1905. He was a farmer at Winchmore Hill Farm and later at Fagnall Farm. This chapel was built by the Primitive Methodists in 1860, just inside Amersham parish. A schoolroom was added in 1953 and a porch in 1960. In 1860 its leading members were from all three parishes and included a gentleman, four potters, two blacksmiths, two carpenters, two labourers, one shoemaker, one cordwainer and one chairmaker. In 1912 it was claimed that practically all families in Winchmore Hill were non-conformists. (*Maureen Seymour*)

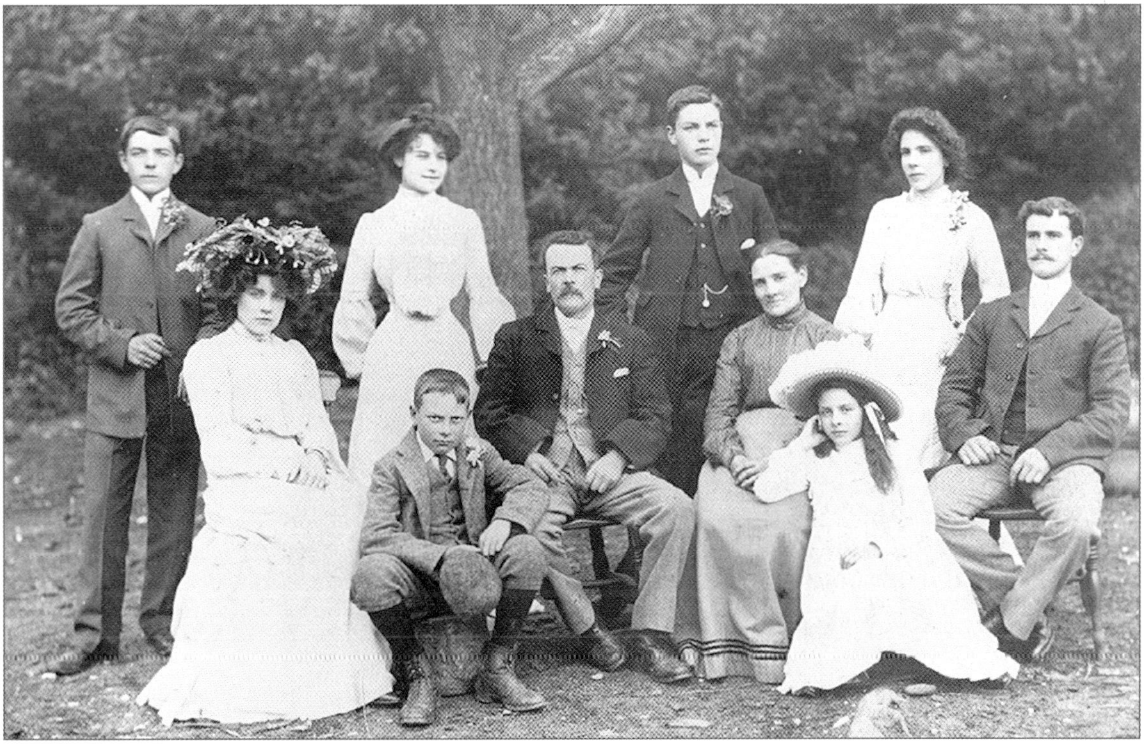

The Pursey family behind The Plough on the eve of Rosetta Pursey's marriage to George Sawyer, 1903. Back row, left to right: Arthur, Florence, Thomas, Rosetta. Centre row: Kate, Thomas (father), Emma (mother), William. Front row: Frank, Sarah. Thomas Pursey (1853–1919) was landlord of The Plough following his father George. Frank Pursey (the boy) was landlord until about 1953. (*Maureen Seymour*)

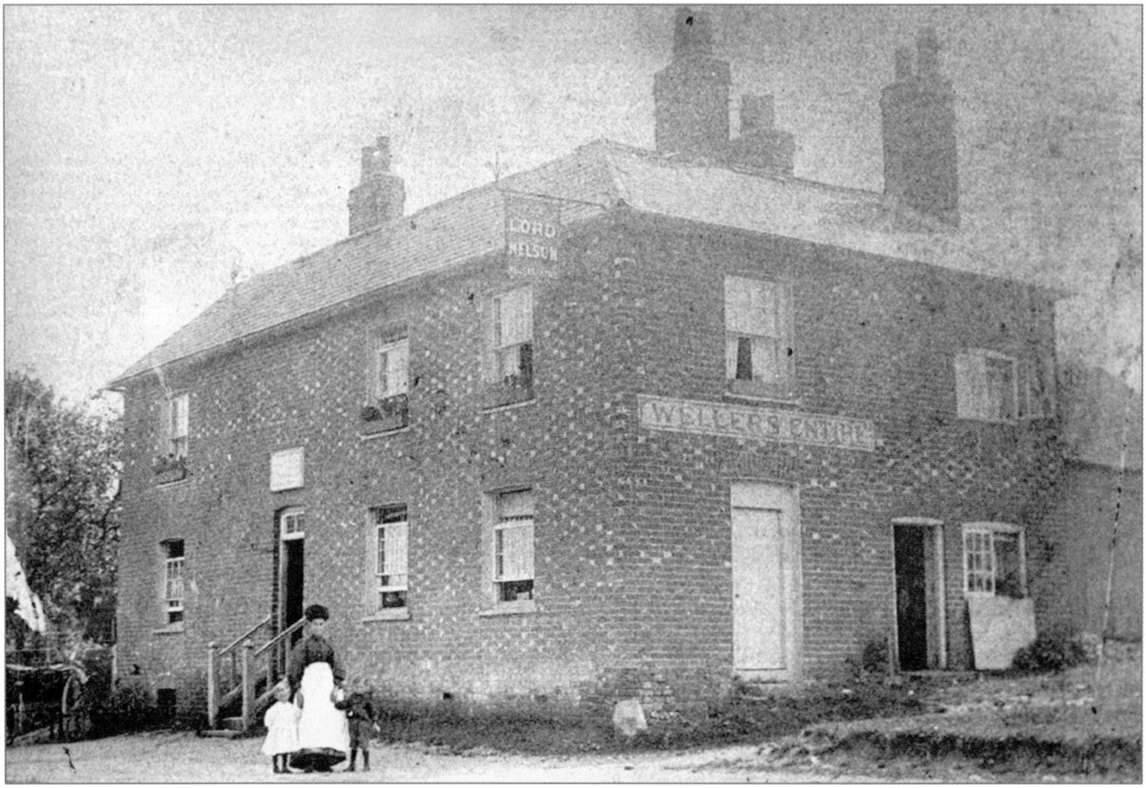

The Lord Nelson, *c.* 1909. Fred Payne (aged four), his brother Ted (aged two) and their mother. It was Ted who drowned in 1915 while skating on the 'Pit' on the common. This pub used to stand right on the edge of Whielden Lane on the corner of the Common. In 1852 it was called The Harrow, having been first licensed as a beer house in 1830. It closed in 1937, and was pulled down to make way for Nelson Close in 1960. (*Fred Payne*)

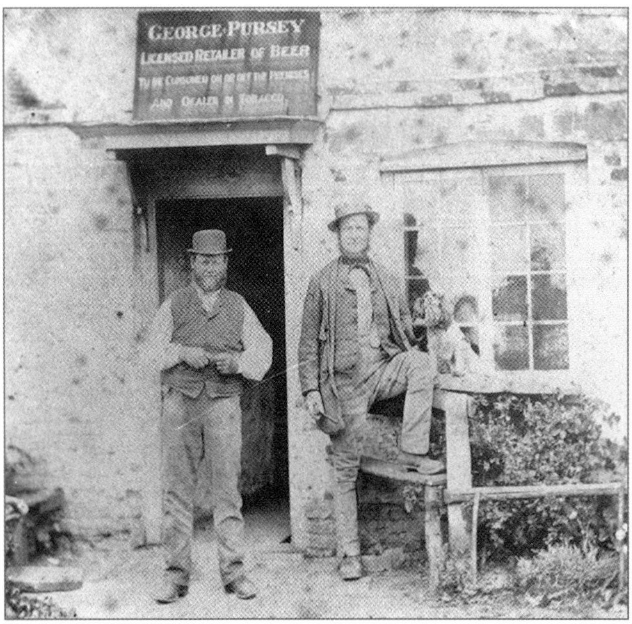

The landlord of The Plough, *c.* 1880. This is the second oldest photograph in the book. George Pursey (1832–1911), the landlord, is standing in the doorway. The building dates from about 1619, but was first licensed as a beer house in 1830. George was succeeded by his son Thomas (1853–1919) and grandson Frank who retired in 1953, nearly completing a Pursey family century at The Plough. George Pursey also had a saw pit and 'turn shop' behind the pub, making chair seats and legs for his factory on The Hill. He also sold meat from The Plough. Barbara Windsor's ownership of the pub, from 1986 to 1996, raised its profile considerably. (*Maureen Seymour*)

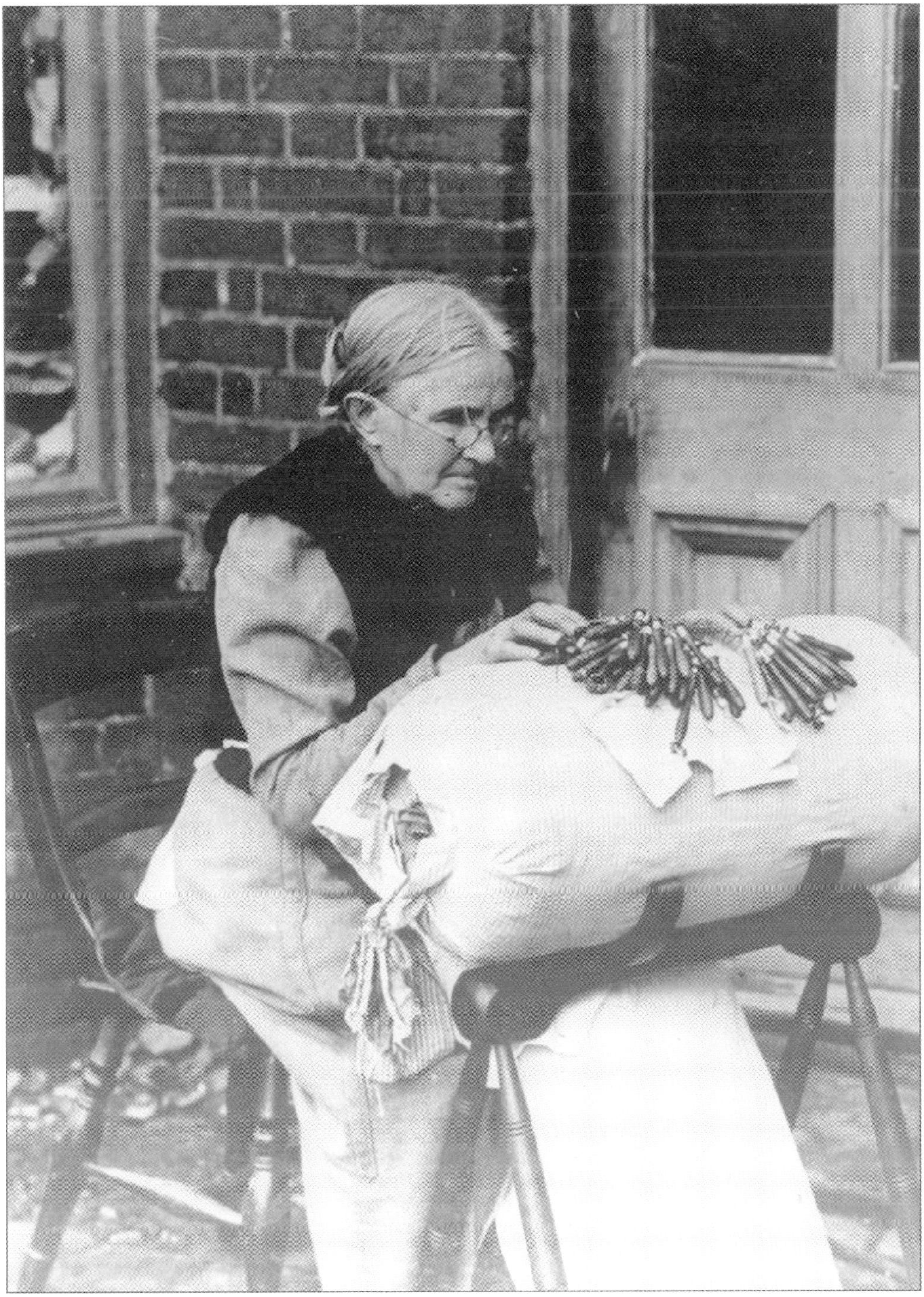

Probably Mrs Annie Rogers, of Ivy Cottage, one of the last in a 400-year-old cottage industry making Buckinghamshire Lace, *c.* 1918. When she was a young girl there were three lace dealers and forty-six lacemakers in Penn parish. Queen Adelaide ordered some of their lace when she visited Penn in 1833. There was a lace school for children in the Old Parish Room, near Penn Church. (*Fred Payne*)

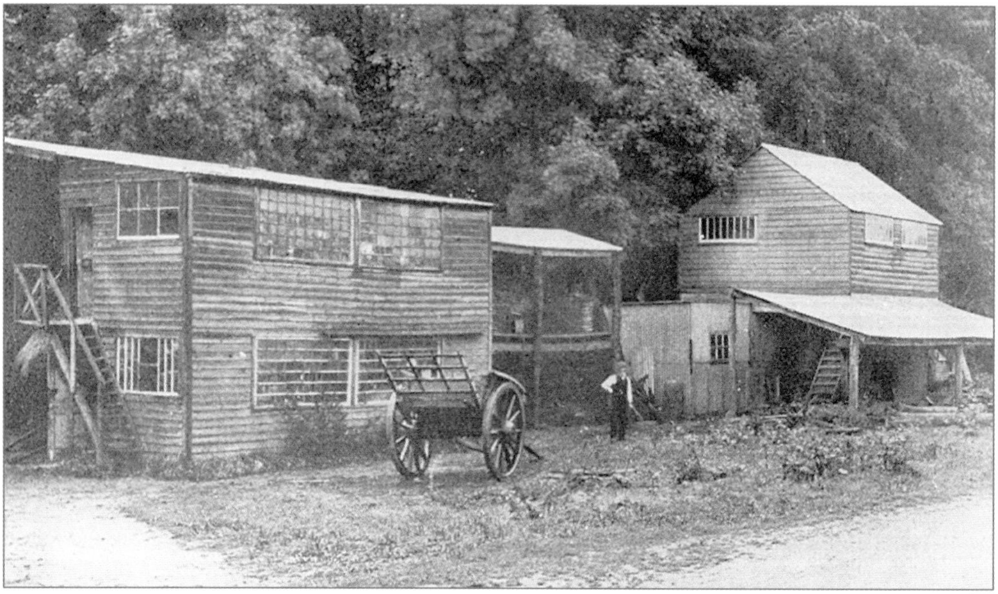

Joseph Hatch's chair factory at Whielden Gate in Whielden Lane, *c.* 1910. It is now a picnic area. Fred Payne of Winchmore Hill worked here as a boy collecting wood for turning. The wood behind the factory is still called Turner's Wood. The factory was owned by Squire Drake of Shardeloes. Whielden (curving valley) Gate was so called because it was an entrance point to the 4,000-acre Wycombe Heath, which was not enclosed until the nineteenth century. The gates were to prevent cattle straying. (*Fred Payne*)

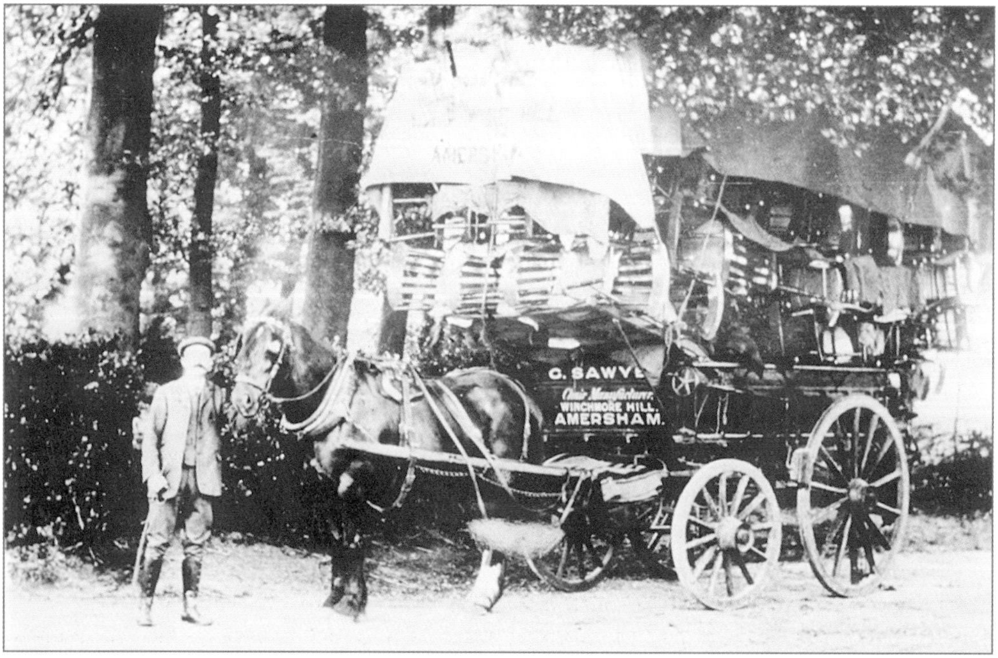

George Sawyer with a load of chairs for London, *c.* 1914. They were made in his Coleshill Lane factory which he opened in 1905. A report of 1912 says there were three chair factories in the village employing twenty-four, twelve and two men and boys respectively. There were two other chair factories close by. The photograph was taken by A.W. Dennis. (*Colin Seabright*)

Chapter Six

Penn Street

This hamlet stands on part of the former Wycombe Heath and was probably first established in the late thirteenth century to service the new manor house of the Penn family when they moved from Penbury. The houses line the road and the oldest goes back to the late fifteenth century. Six others are seventeenth- and eighteenth-century listed buildings, and a Conservation Area covers most of the village. The road itself is very old. The Saxon word *straet* was one which was often used for a road which had survived from the Roman period, and the main highway between Wycombe and Amersham ran through the village until the turnpike road was built in 1768.

In 1849 the church was built and Penn Street was combined with Holmer Green to become an independent ecclesiastical parish, although Penn Street remains a part of the civil parish of Penn.

A century ago there were thirty-five households, almost all in small cottages and nearly half working directly for Earl Howe, who also had about twelve living-in servants. Chairmaking occupied five households. The brickmaker, potter and lace dealer of the nineteenth century had disappeared, but there was a postmaster, policeman, baker, coalmerchant, wheelwright/undertaker and two carpenters.

The common was uneven, with a large dell at one end and two ponds at the other, and was still used for grazing horses. The Widdowson family had enclosed a tennis court. Penn Street Cricket Club was well established by 1895, and had started the manicuring process when they were given permission to level their pitch. They won the local league in 1908, and celebrated the 1918 Armistice with a Gentlemen *v*. Ladies match.

The 15 ft deep dell was gradually filled in with soil from the new cottages opposite (1907), mud from pond clearance (1911), earth from road widening and unauthorized local rubbish. It was finally bulldozed flat after the removal of the last vestiges of the army camp which had taken over the common during the Second World War. The cricketers acquired their extra bite into the wood at that time.

Mains water arrived in 1936 and electricity in 1939, when the church lost its oil lamps. Mains gas and drainage arrived only recently, in 1990 and 1991. The present population is about 230 in ninety-two households.

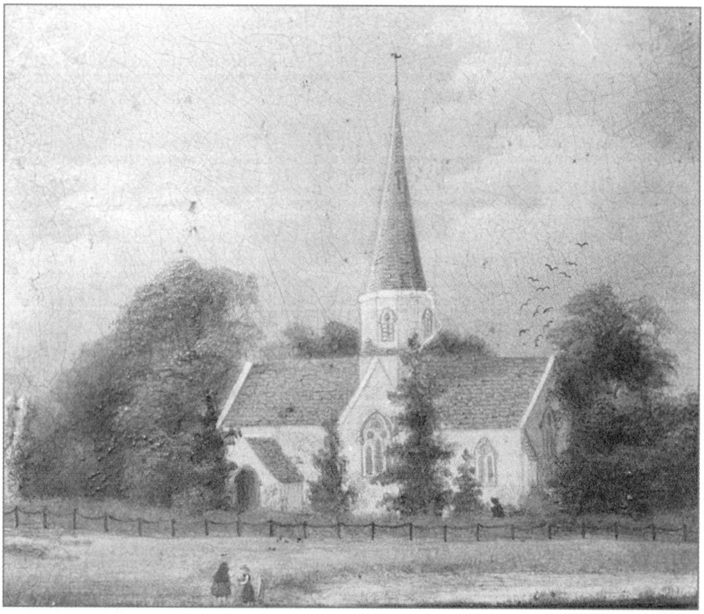

A painting of Holy Trinity, Penn Street, with its 75 ft wooden spire, 1850s. The church was endowed and built by the 1st Earl Howe, at a cost of £10,000, in memory of his first wife. Its location was apparently suggested by Queen Adelaide. It was completed in 1849, built by the Earl's tradesmen and tenants over two years, under the architect Benjamin Ferrey. Both Queen Adelaide (who gave the altar window) and Edward VII worshipped there. The 3rd, 4th and 6th Earls and their wives are buried in the churchyard. Primitive Methodists held open-air meetings on the common in 1835, and a licence for a dissenting meeting house was granted in 1847. (*Alice Timms*)

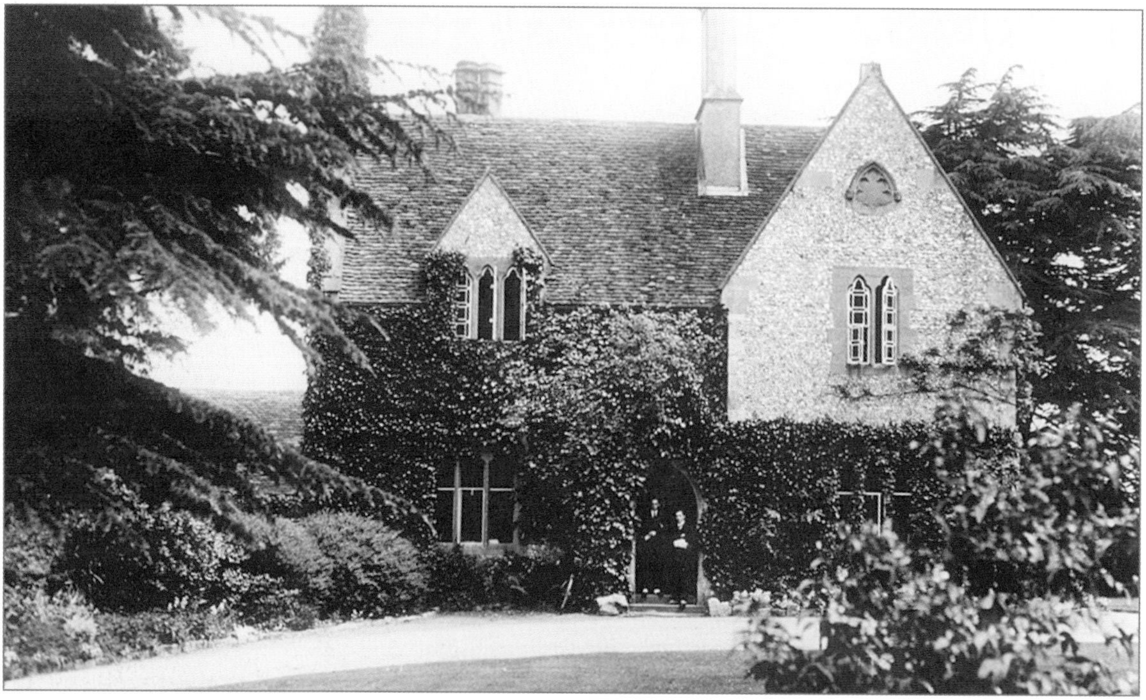

The Vicarage, *c.* 1915. This was also designed by Benjamin Ferrey (Pugin's biographer) and built in 1850 at a cost of £7,000. The first vicar, Edward Bickersteth, went on to be vicar of Aylesbury, Archdeacon of Buckingham and Dean of Lichfield, where his statue can be seen. David Niven lived here between 1920 and 1922, as a ten to twelve year old, one of a dozen boys (who included two Persian princes and the young third Sir Philip Rose) in the crammer run by the Revd Arthur Browning. Niven's autobiography remembers a very pleasant interlude in Penn Street, despite the vicar – who was 'a magnificent looking grandson of Robert Browning with clear blue eyes and white, wavy hair. He was uniformly adored by the parents and loathed by the boys, without exception, as an evil-tempered, vain old tyrant!' (*Colin Seabright*)

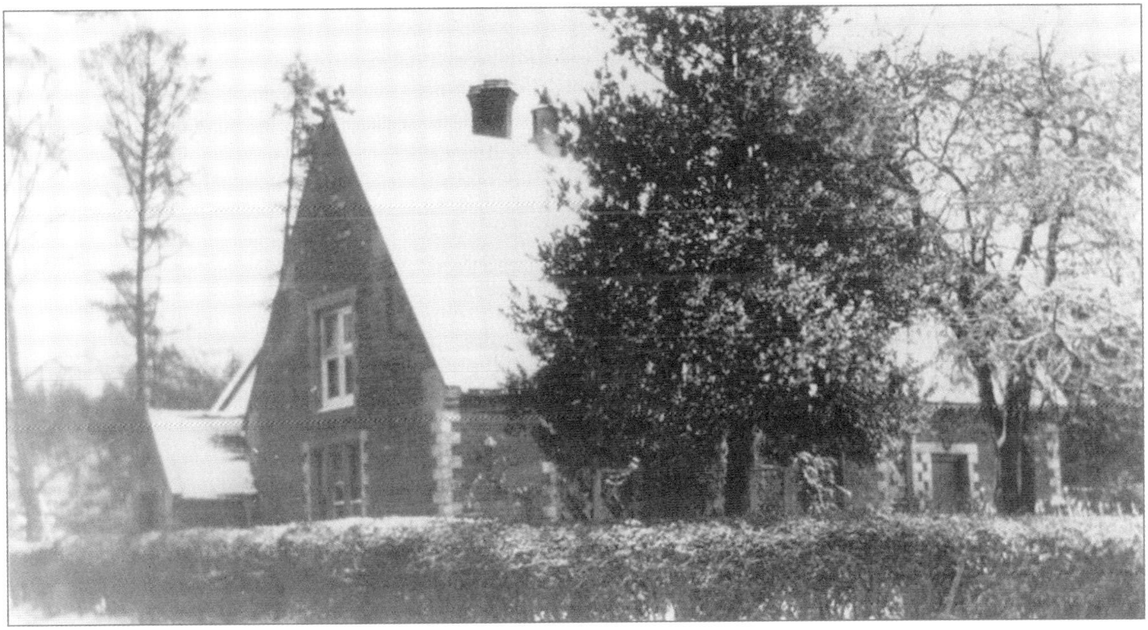

The Curzon C of E School, built in 1850, seen here in the early 1900s. It was badly damaged by gales in 1953 and gradually replaced by the present buildings by 1960. The land all around it was designated in the 1855 Inclosure Award for the use of the 'labouring poor', but was quickly exchanged for the much more suitable common which had been allotted to Earl Howe. (*Alice Timms*)

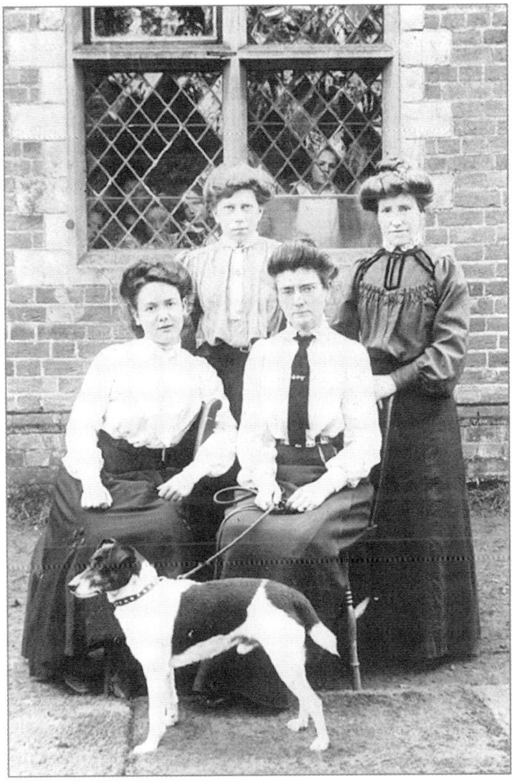

Headmistress and teachers, early 1900s. Back row, left to right: Miss Aston, Miss Lily Winter. Front row: Mrs Wingrove (headmistress) with dog, Ede Wingrove (her niece). Mrs Wingrove was also organist in Penn Street church. Miss Winter retired in 1914 after thirteen years as infant mistress: 'her quiet work and gentle influence will be missed'. (*Alice Timms*)

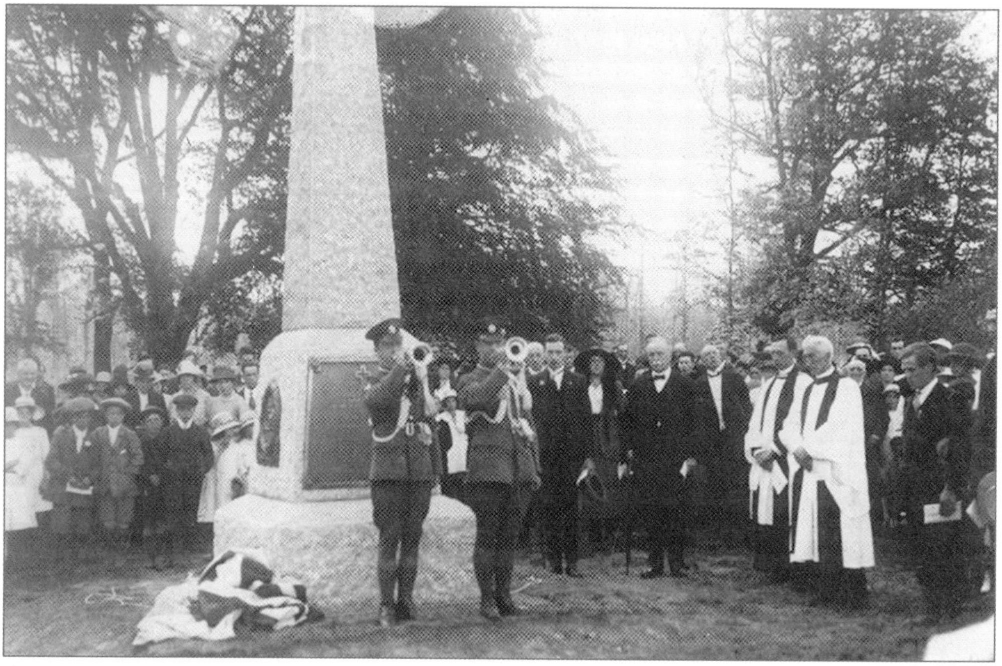

The unveiling and dedication of the war memorial on Trinity Sunday in the presence of nearly 1,000 people, 11 June 1922. The unveiling was carried out by Private Eric Randall and the address was given by the 4th Earl Howe. There were eighteen names, including a Widdowson (see below). The £300 cost was raised by local events and the location decided by a public ballot. (*Alice Timms*)

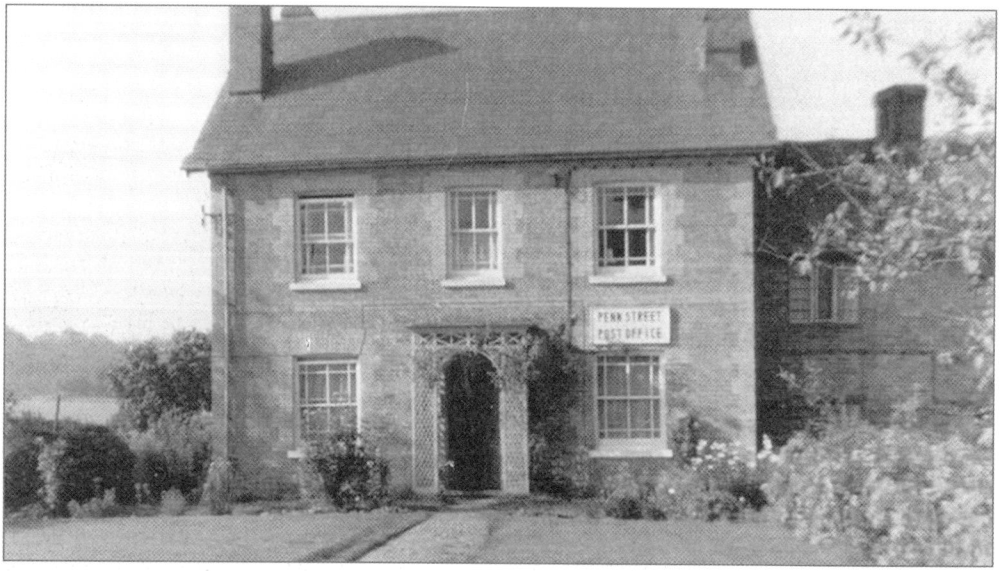

The post office in the Red House, *c.* 1960. It was only here briefly. The post office used to be in a cottage (now Pavilion House) opposite the Hit or Miss, run by the Copestake family from at least 1864. In about 1950 it moved to the Red House where Miss Haynes also had a sweet shop in her sitting room. It closed in the 1960s. Miss Haynes's brother John was butler for thirty years to Earl Howe, starting at Gopsall, which had forty-eight guest rooms, and then moving to Penn House. 'I never thought I would come to live in a doll's house!' he used to say. (*Pamela Leonard*)

The Widdowsons outside the Homestead, *c.* 1879. An article in the *South Bucks Standard*, 12 August 1910, noted that the enclosure of Wycombe Heath, which included Penn Wood, in 1855 'raised the peasantry of the district to a condition of resentful fury'. Newly erected fences were torn down and 'poaching seemed to go on wholesale!' Earl Howe needed 'a strong hand' to contain the situation, and in 1858 brought in James Widdowson (1828–1921) as his agent. Widdowson stayed until his death and was succeeded by his son John (1859–1947), standing on his right. Both were chairman of Penn Parish Council, covering almost all of its first fifty years to 1945. (*Angela Bates*)

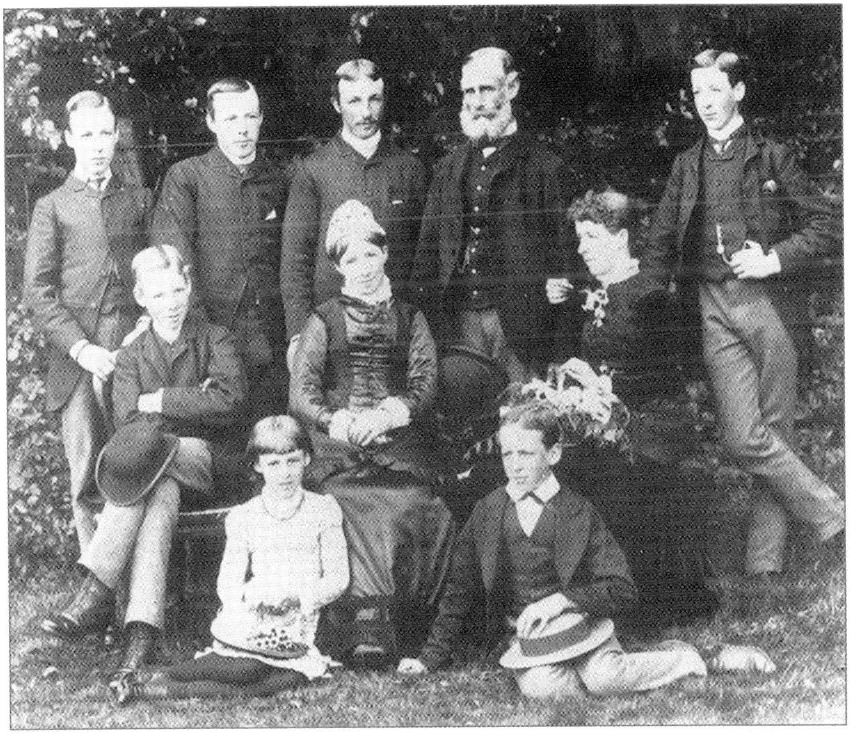

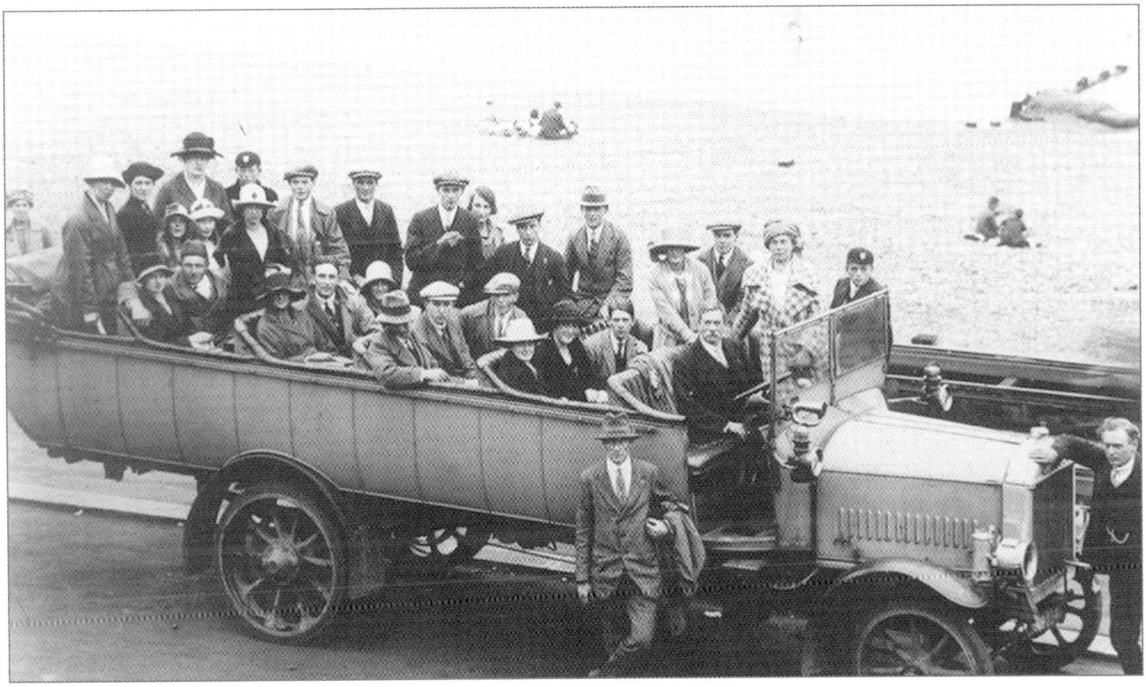

Village outing to Brighton, 1920. A solid-tyred, acetylene-lamped charabanc, thought to be a Thorneycroft, was used. It had a hood and rows of long seats across the bus, with a separate door to each row on the near side. An earlier choir outing to Margate, in 1910, went by 'brake' to Amersham station and thence by reserved carriage on the train. On that occasion few of the children had seen the sea before. (*Alice Timms*)

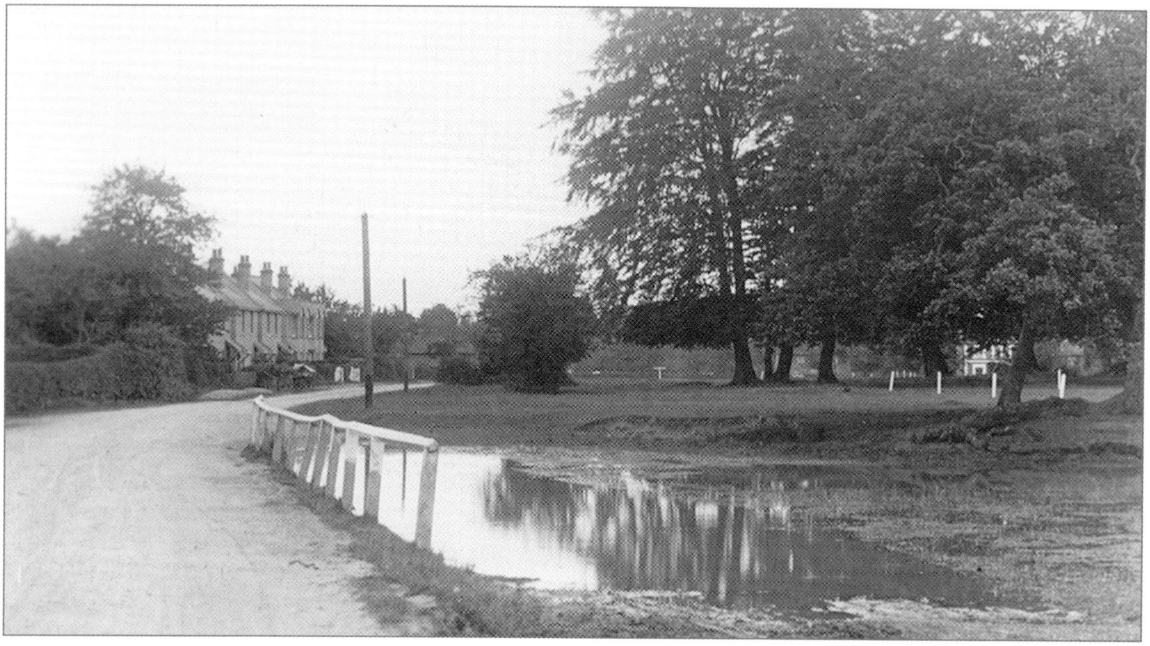

Penn Street Pond, *c.* 1914. The pond went right up to the roadside until 1948. The 1838 Tithe Map shows only one pond, further back and close to what is now the Vicarage hedge. This is remembered as St George's Pond, presumably named after a species of mushroom (agaricus georgii) which still appears there around St George's day (23 April). By 1855 there were two ponds and it is likely that the present pond was dug as an alternative public pond after St George's Pond was initially allotted as private property to Earl Howe by the Inclosure Award. In 1956, both ponds were to be filled in as serving no useful purpose but were reprieved by an eighty-signature petition, although St George's has since been gradually filled in. (*Colin Seabright*)

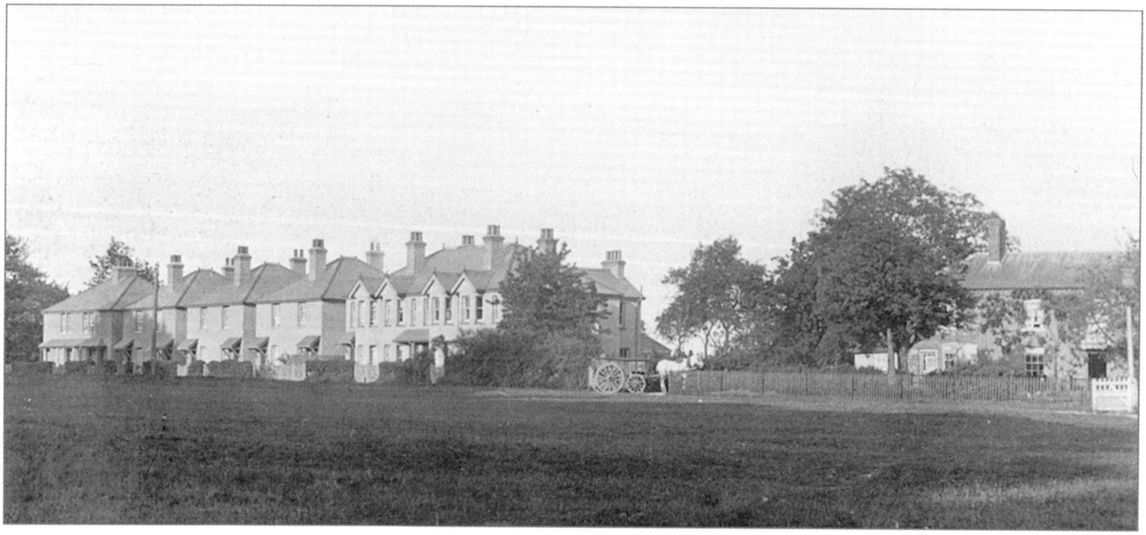

The Squirrel and Penn Wood View, *c.* 1910. The Squirrel was first licensed as a beer house after being rebuilt in brick in 1832 on the site of a much older smallholding (deeds date back to 1689) with an acre of land. The landlord between the wars was very versatile. He baked bread and cakes, sold groceries and made wheelbarrows and coffins. Miles & Co., a five-man chair factory, was in a shed in the yard. Dancer & Hearne built Penn Wood View cottages on the Squirrel's former acre for their family and workers They started to build in 1907, 'shooting' surplus earth into the dell on the common in front of them. (*Colin Seabright*)

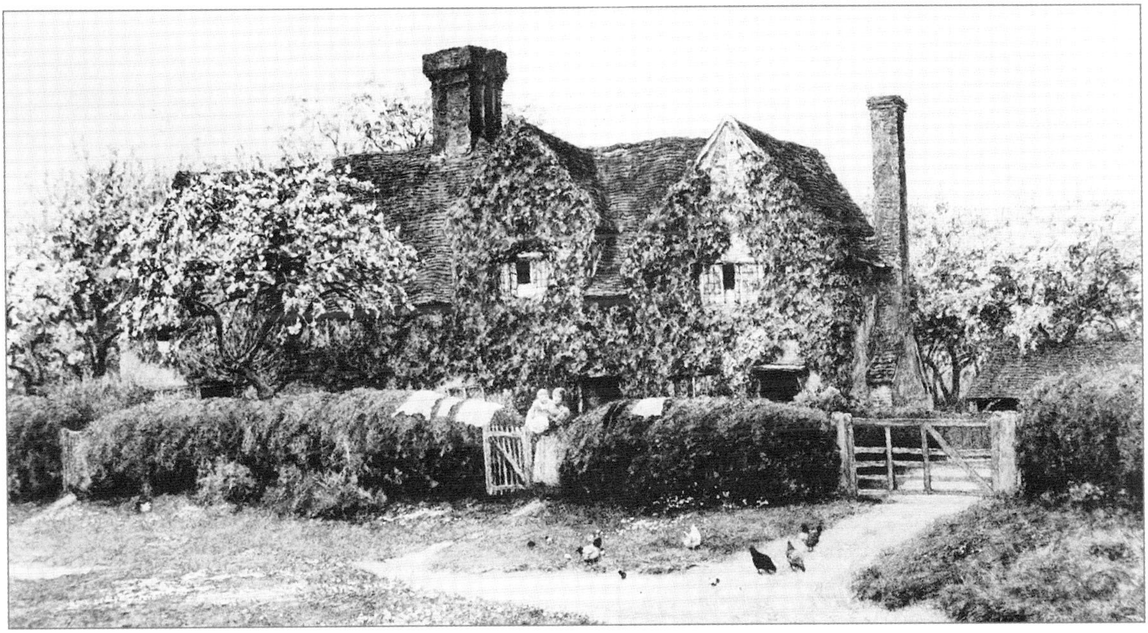

The Forge, in a watercolour, 1891. This is one of the oldest houses, timber-framed and dating from the seventeenth century, with an eighteenth-century wing. It was painted by Helen Allingham, a well-known Victorian painter and conservationist. There were four cottages with the blacksmith's forge on the left, open to the road. George Randall was blacksmith by 1847 and his daughter, remembered as eccentric, had taken over by 1907. Part of the house was later destroyed by fire. The forge closed in the 1930s when cars had finally replaced horses. (*Thomas Wilkie*)

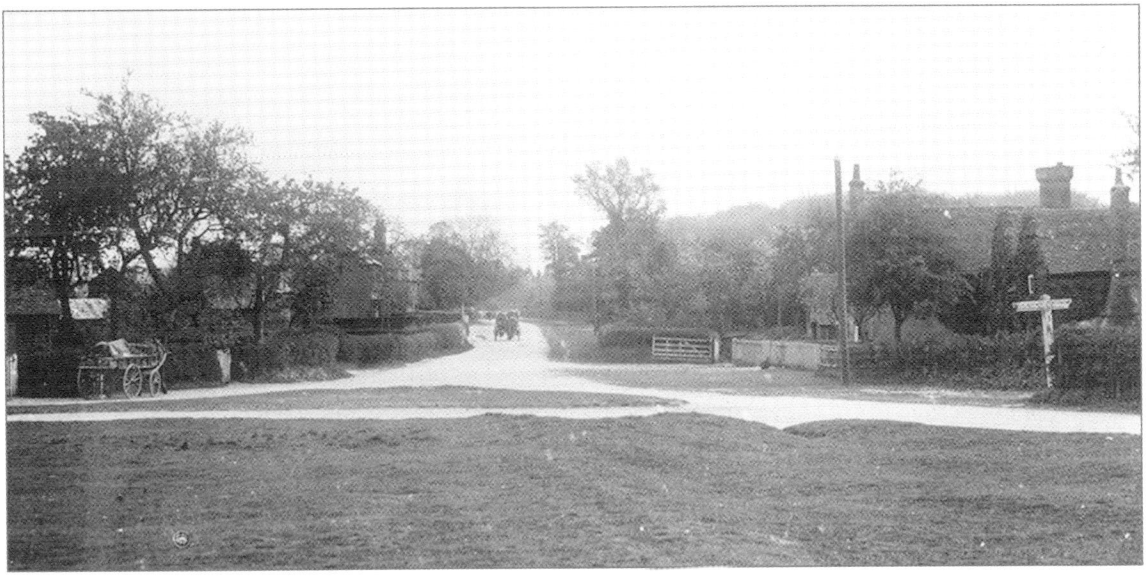

Looking towards Winchmore Hill, *c.* 1914. To the left there were three cottages (now one house called The Cottages, where the last grocer's shop in the village survived until the 1950s and '60s. It was a wine shop until 1999. A rare cruck in the centre cottage indicates a late fifteenth-century date, the oldest known survival in the village. To the right was the still empty site of the Village Hall where, in about 1929, an army hut was put up on land given by Earl Howe, after much fundraising, including a fête at Penn House. It was also intended as a cricket pavilion. During the Second World War it was much used by the army camp on the Common as a canteen and for dances, but was burnt down in about 1952 and replaced by the present hall. (*Colin Seabright*)

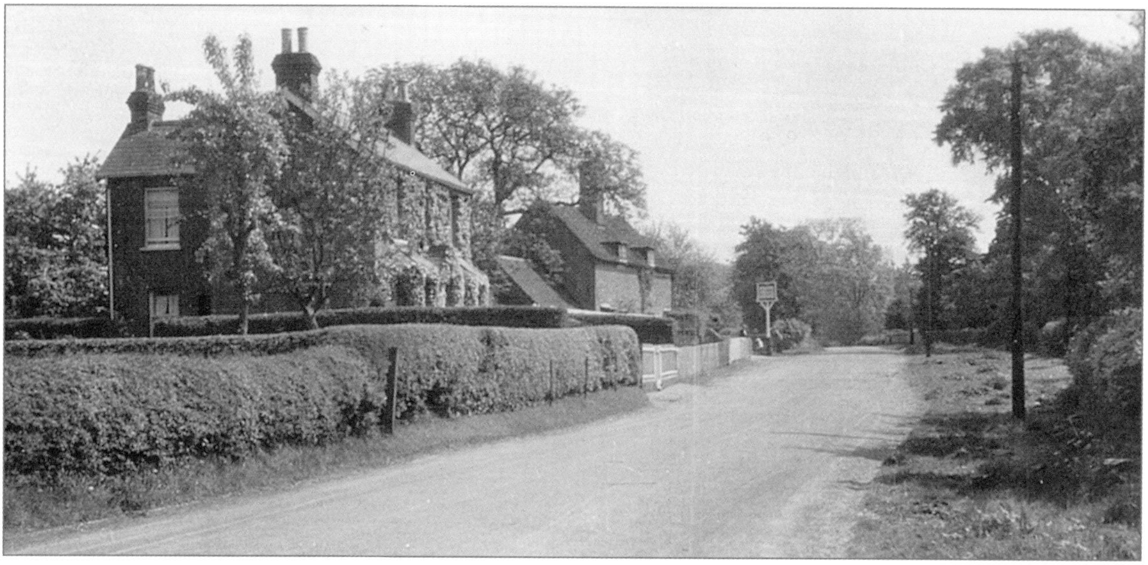

Dancer & Hearne and the Hit or Miss, *c.* 1927. To the left was Myrtle Cottage, a Hearne family house, now unoccupied. In the centre were Factory Cottages, occupied in the early 1900s by a wheelwright/undertaker and a chairmaker/beadle. To the right, and out of sight, is the Hit or Miss, one of the four oldest pubs in Penn parish. It was licensed as the Hit *and* Miss in 1786. It may have been the Green Man in 1756. There was a grocery shop attached to it. (*Colin Seabright*)

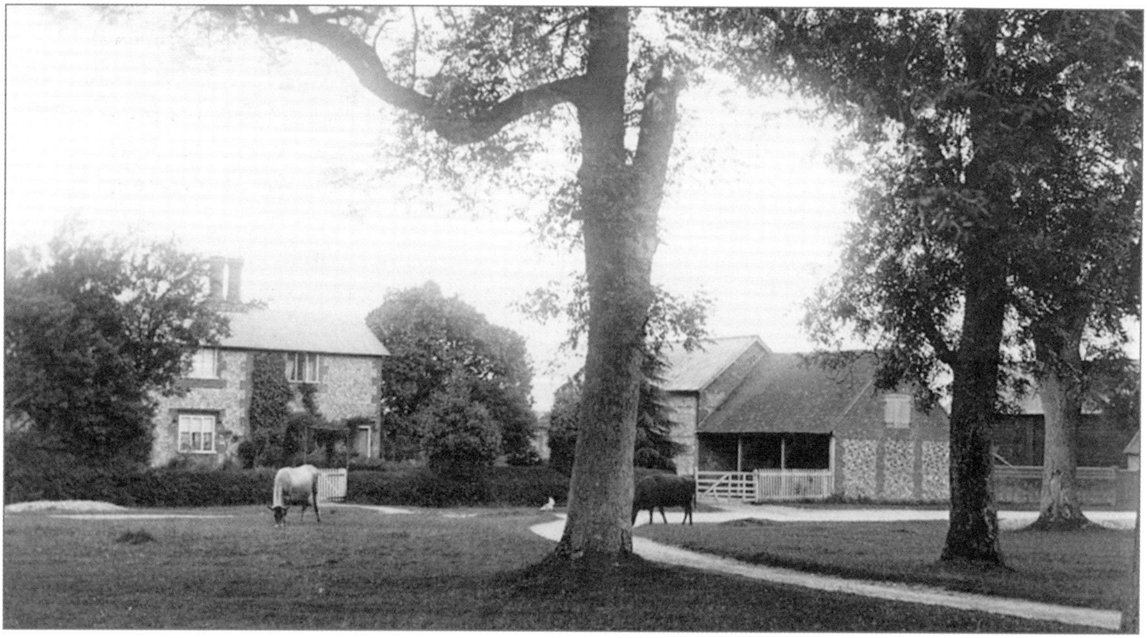

At the entrance to Penn House, *c.* 1914. This is the place referred to in a charter, of probable late thirteenth-century origin, which defines one of the bounds of Wycombe Heath as 'the Gate stakes of Pennbury the Mannor of Sr Roger atte Penn Knight'. The gates of Penn House are exactly the 200 ft from the highway prescribed by a 1285 statute for the removal of dense trees in which highwaymen could lurk. The main common is similarly 200 ft wide all the way down to the Amersham Road. Penn Street Farm was on the edge of the main common until it moved here after the 1855 Inclosure to join the large works which made bricks, tiles and pottery from at least the 1780s to the 1880s, causing the large dell in the wood opposite. (*Colin Seabright*)

CHAPTER SEVEN

THE ROSE FAMILY & RAYNERS

Philip Rose (1816–83) was born in Wycombe where many of his forebears had been mayor. He was articled as a solicitor in Beaconsfield and practised in London. He married at twenty-three and when only twenty-five set up the Brompton Hospital for consumption (tuberculosis) with Queen Victoria as patron. Prince Albert laid the foundation stone, Charles Dickens made a speech and a dozen peers and bishops were on his committee.

He applied the same energy to his profession and profited greatly from the rapid expansion of the railway network. He organised the Wycombe to Maidenhead branch line which brought the railway close to Rayners. His firm acted in the Tichborne case of 1871/2, and he rightly judged the claimant to be an impostor.

Rose was a close friend of Benjamin Disraeli, having helped him in his local electioneering in 1834, and became the national agent for the Conservative party. He looked after Disraeli's legal and financial affairs and was eventually his executor. Disraeli recommended his baronetcy in 1874.

He was equally energetic in his private life. In 1845 he bought Rayners and Colehatch farms, and for the rest of his life took the utmost pleasure in extending and improving his estate, including designing and building a road to get to the station at Loudwater. He owned 1,200 acres.

In 1854 he built St Margaret's Church, and organised the creation of an ecclesiastical parish largely covering his estate but also taking in a part of Penn parish. Earl Howe gave the land for the church as well as several properties to provide an income for the vicar.

The second Sir Philip continued his father's role as the squire of Tylers Green until his death in 1919. His son and heir had been killed in the First World War and the estate was inherited by his young grandson who became the third Sir Philip. 543 acres, two farms, two pubs and many houses and cottages were sold in 1920.

(The originals of the photographs and paintings in this section are owned by the third Philip Rose's daughter, Mrs Petica Waley)

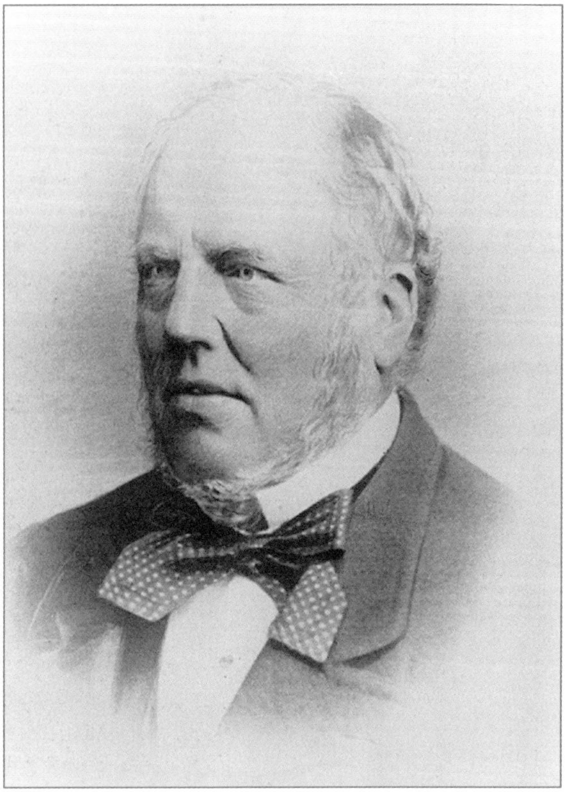

Sir Philip Rose (1816–83), seen here *c.* 1874. He was a solicitor, a man of formidable energy, drive and achievement, with little time for leisure. Novels were taboo, cards the devil's playthings, theatres and balls were sinful vanities; twice every Sunday to church, and woe betide any servant who did not make an appearance or a child who did not remember the text of the long sermon.

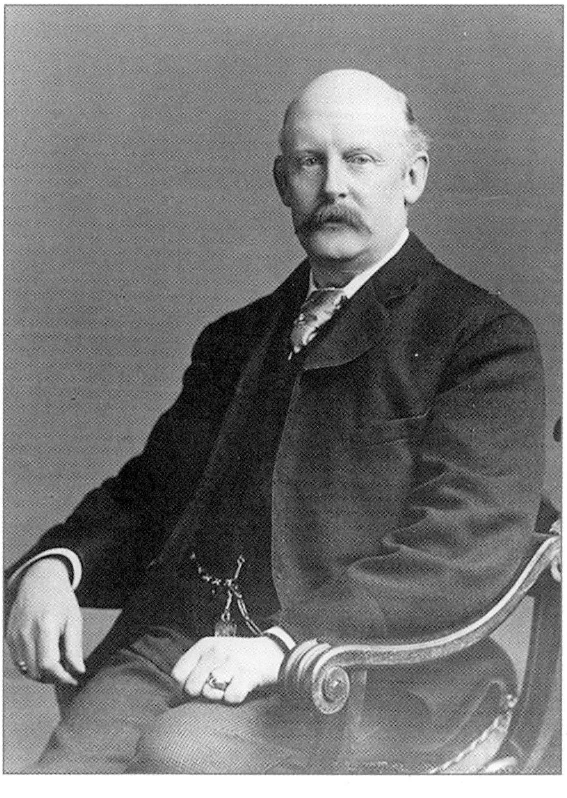

The second Sir Philip Rose (1843–1919), pictured *c.* 1890. He was also a solicitor, a meticulous, hard-working man, very proud of his father's achievements and the fond father of a large family. He continued his father's role as squire of Tylers Green and, like his father, he was High Sheriff, a magistrate and chairman of the South Bucks Conservative Association. He became a Roman Catholic and set up a private chapel at Rayners.

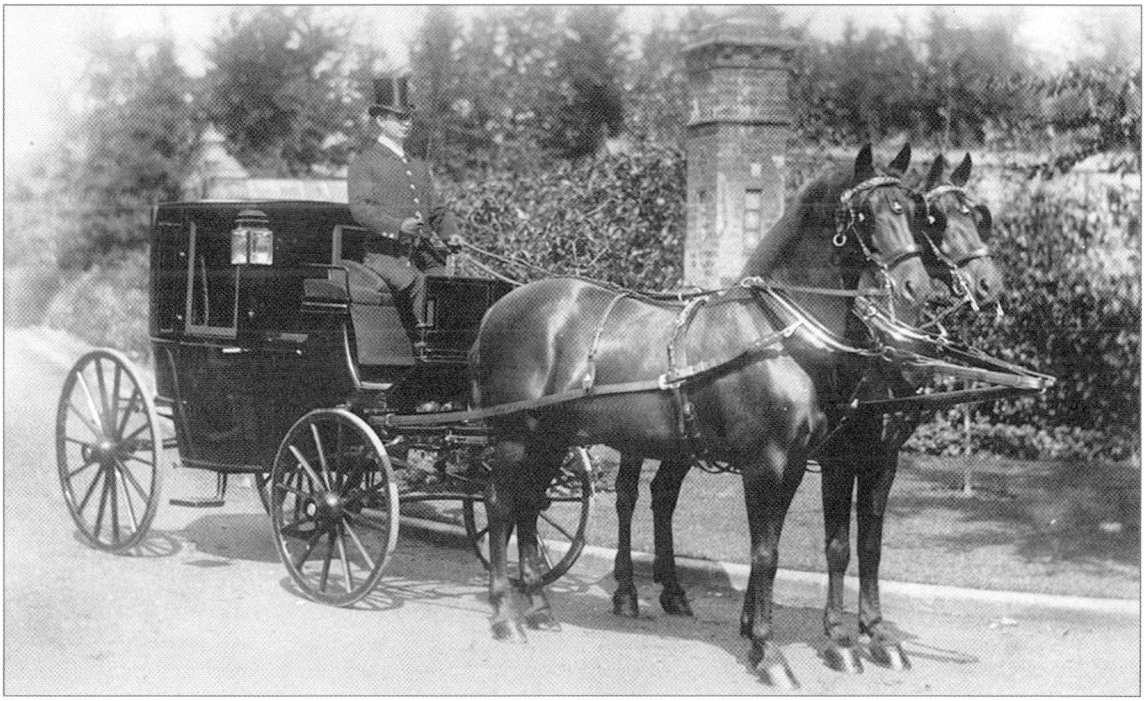

Carriage and pair at Rayners, *c.* 1880. The men wore cockades in their silk hats. Lady Rose is remembered as driving out daily. She never reproved a maid by word of mouth. At the spot where reproof was needed the erring servant would find a note stating the nature of her guilt.

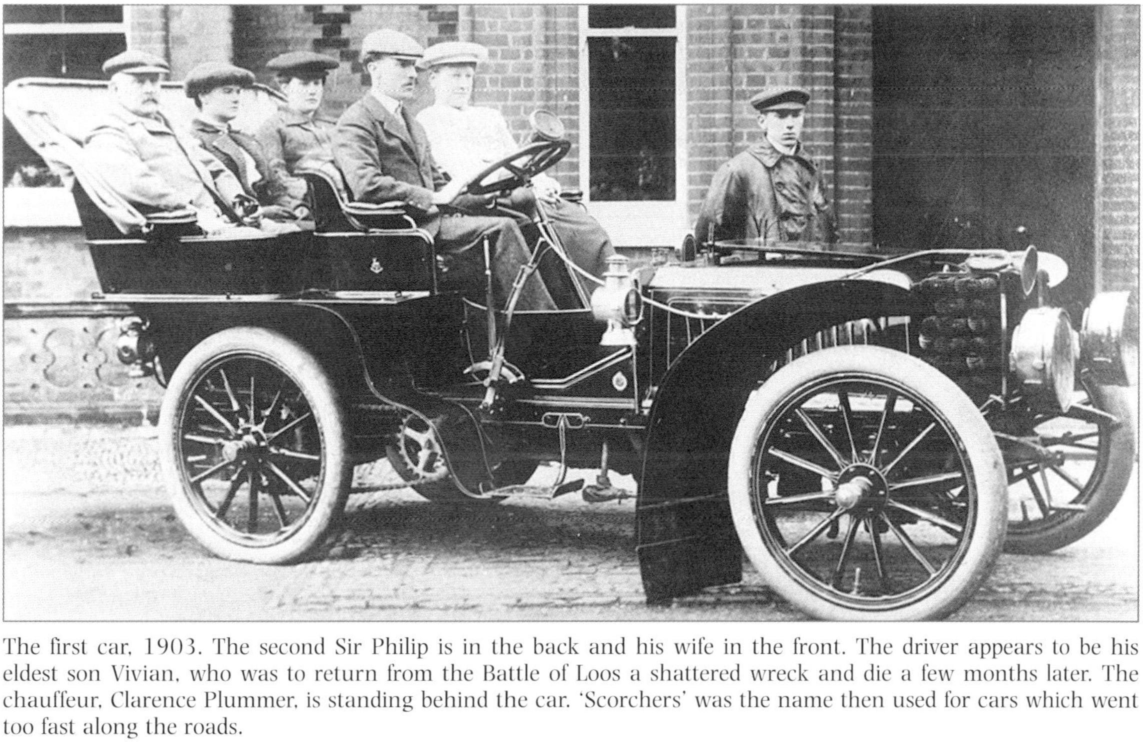

The first car, 1903. The second Sir Philip is in the back and his wife in the front. The driver appears to be his eldest son Vivian, who was to return from the Battle of Loos a shattered wreck and die a few months later. The chauffeur, Clarence Plummer, is standing behind the car. 'Scorchers' was the name then used for cars which went too fast along the roads.

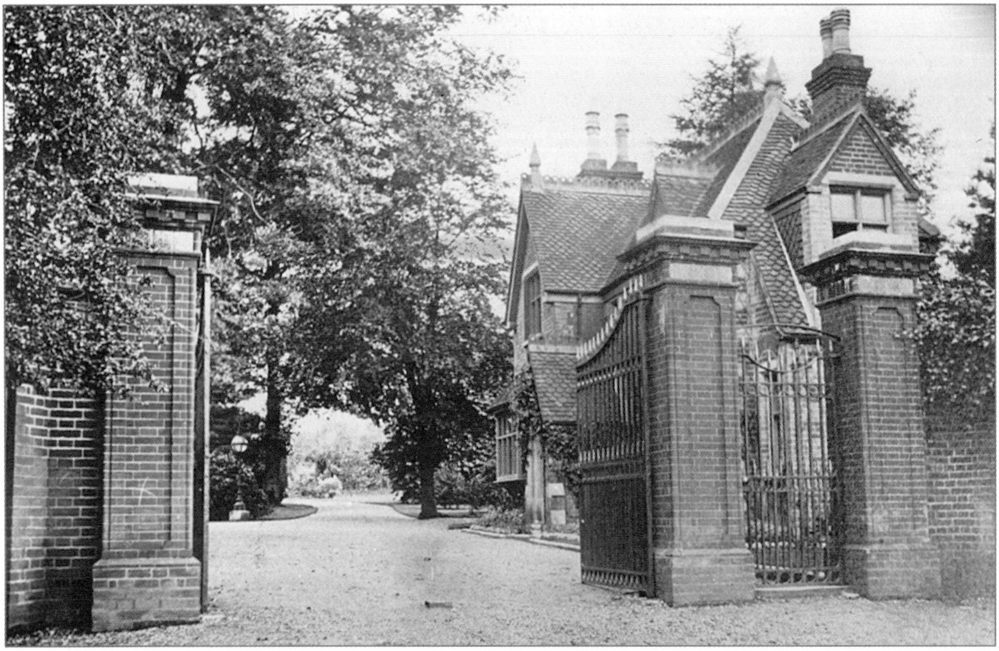

Rayners gates and lodge, early 1900s. The iron gates were taken down in the Second World War to be used for the war effort. A round hole in the wall just out of the picture to the left was for the end of a pole to make a road barrier against invading Germans. There is an obelisk, just beyond the Lodge, commemorating Queen Victoria's journey from Windsor, via Rayners to Hughenden, when Disraeli died in 1881.

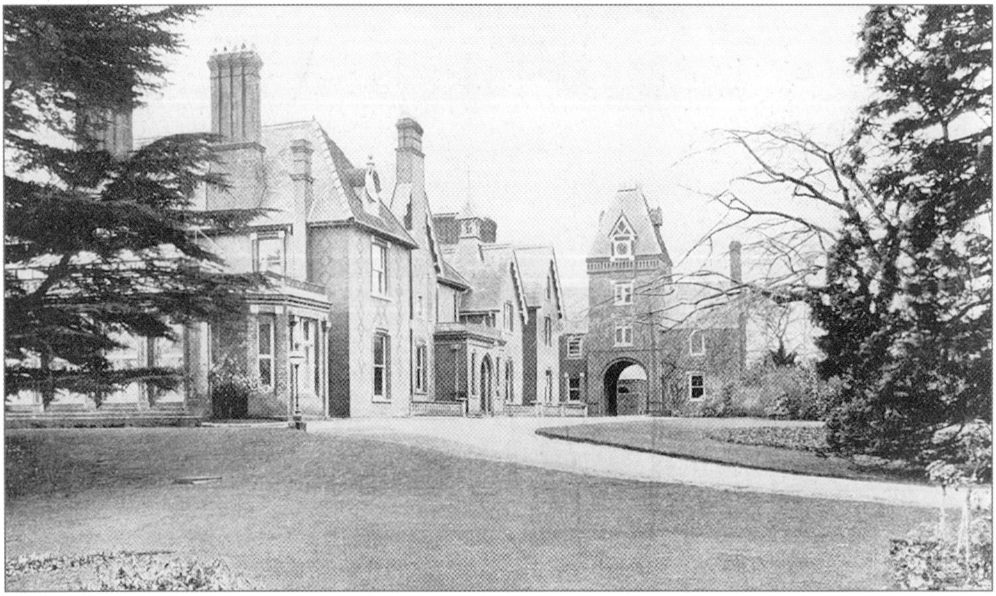

Rayners, early 1900s. The house replaced a farm of the same name and the earliest part was completed in 1847 with bricks made on the spot from the clay dug from the farm pond, which is now a much larger pond in front of the house. The pond was completely concealed by shrubs and trees after Disraeli observed that he did not consider it an ornament. The house was substantially enlarged in the 1850s and 1867.

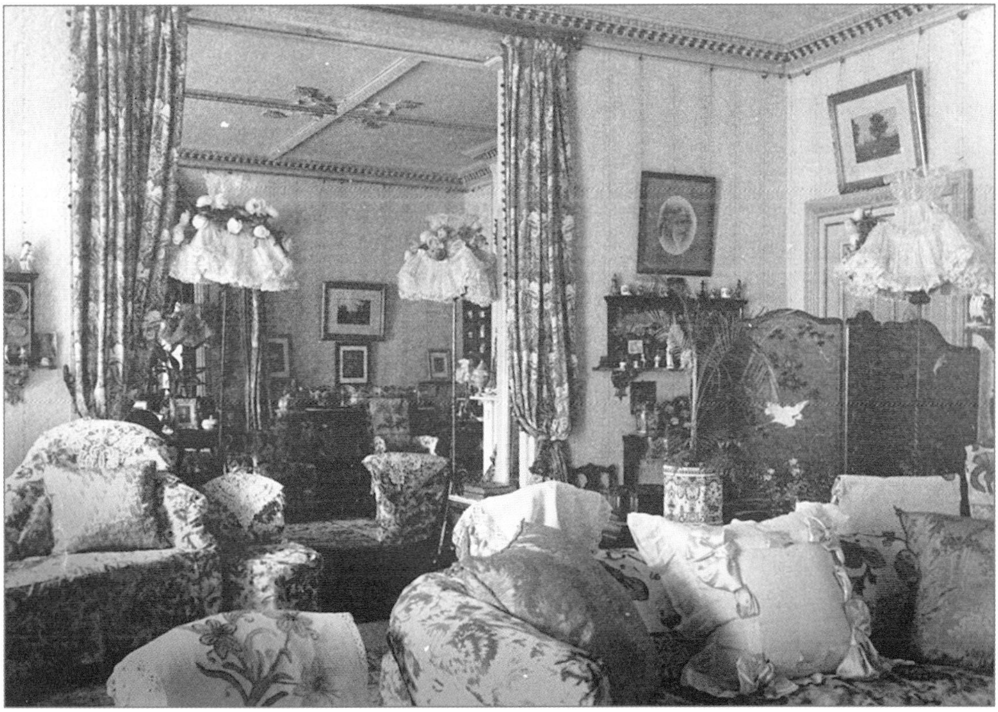

Drawing room in Rayners, 1906. The photograph is one of many taken by Cecil Rose, a younger son of the second Sir Philip.

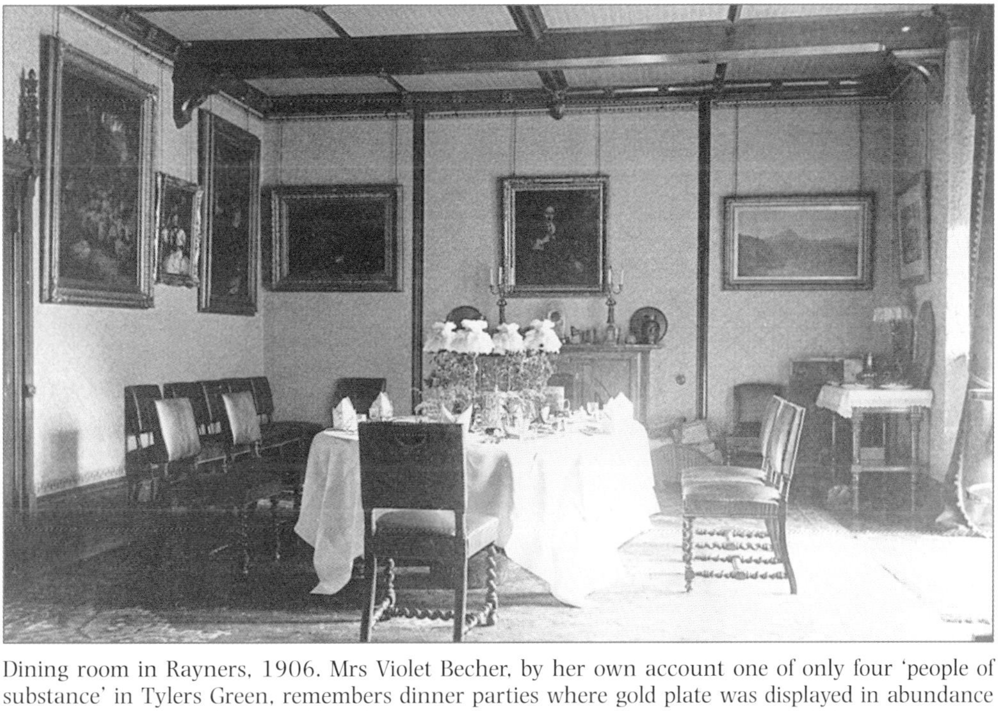

Dining room in Rayners, 1906. Mrs Violet Becher, by her own account one of only four 'people of substance' in Tylers Green, remembers dinner parties where gold plate was displayed in abundance and an occasional whisper told of the price of ingredients making up a special dish. There were always nine courses, which Sir Philip would invariably finish off with two boiled eggs.

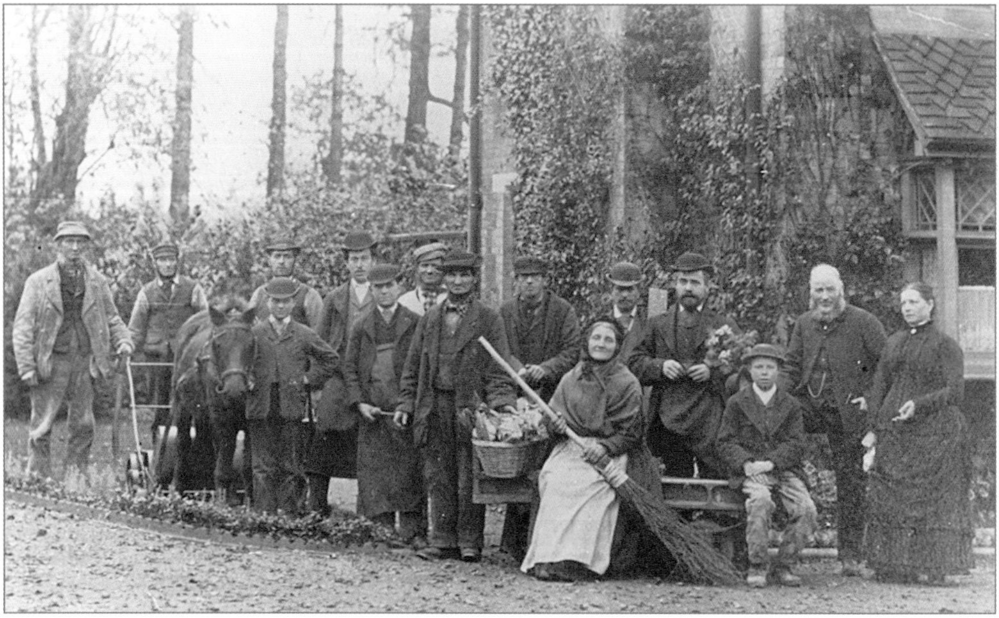

Rayners 'estate men', 1880. In 1889 there were seventy men and boys working on the estate, on the farm and in the gardens. Some 200 tenants and estate workers and their wives sat down for a celebration in 1891, representing nearly two-thirds of the adult population of Tylers Green.

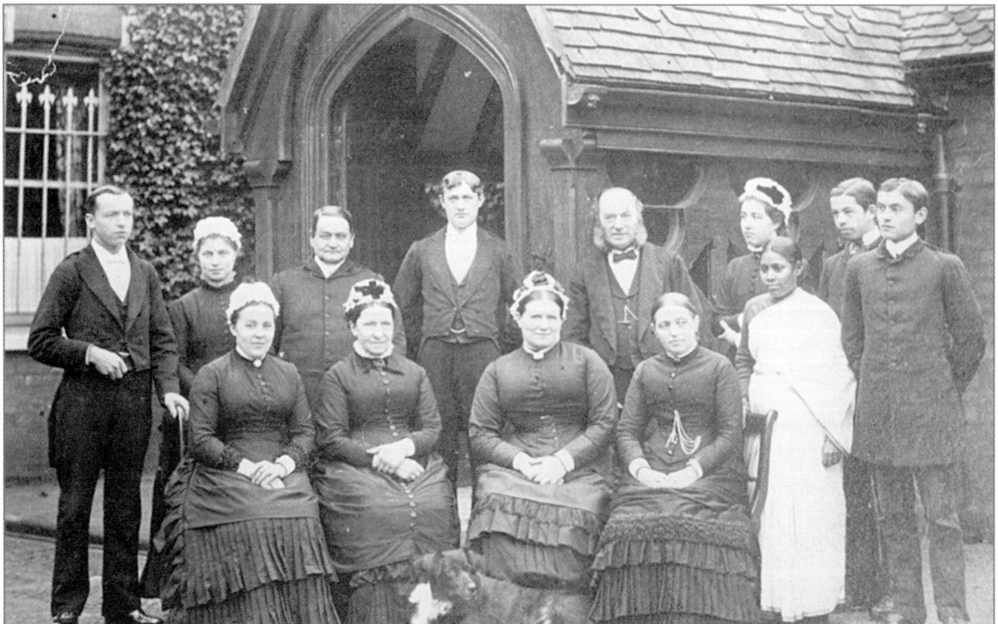

Rayners 'home workers', 1880. There was a large household staff: a butler, coachman, footman and hallboy, cook/housekeeper, scullery maid, kitchen maid and daily woman, first, second and third housemaids. No special occasion (national, local or family) was left unmarked by a large gathering, usually at Rayners, for a meal and often games and fireworks. The last such celebration was 'In Celebration of Victory and Peace', in 1919.

CHAPTER EIGHT

PENN VILLAGE & TYLERS GREEN

What we now think of as Penn Village takes in three originally separate developments along the length of the road between Penn church and Rushmoor Corner (see Map, p. 4). The earliest was the area around the church which was the main focus for the six separate hamlets of the parish and was generally known as Penn Village as far as Beacon Hill. Tyler End Green was a separate hamlet of Penn which ran from the gate near the entrance to Rayners down to Potters Cross. The third development was along the road between Potters Cross and Hazlemere after the 1855 Inclosure of Wycombe Heath had allotted plots of the former heathland to private owners. The population of Penn Village in 1900 was about 600 and is now about 900.

Tyler End Green was a name shared by both the Penn and Wycombe sides of the parish boundary. It was also a tiny hamlet of the 'forrens' of Wycombe, one of the 'ends' of the 4,000-acre Wycombe Heath which stretched up as far as Great Kingshill, and was the source of clay for the highly successful fourteenth-century, Penn tilers.. The Wycombe side expanded in response to the rapid growth of Wycombe's chair industry at the very end of the eighteenth century.

In 1840 the population on the Wycombe side was about 400 with fewer than 100 cottages, but was growing fast as a result of illegal enclosures on the common. In 1854 Sir Philip Rose wrote: 'Within living memory Tylers Green was an open common without any house or building upon it . . . but gradually, within 40 or 50 years, a population has grown up upon the Waste of several hundred souls.' He built St Margaret's Church at that time and soon afterwards created the ecclesiastical parish of Tylers Green.

By 1900 the population of Tylers Green had risen steadily to about 900. In 1906 St John's Wood, which had been enclosed from the Heath in 1868, was sold off in small lots in response to demand created by the new railway, but development was slow and it was still a very small community. In 1916 there were just over 1,000 inhabitants; a newly arrived war widow noted that 'excluding the vicarage, there are but four people of substance living here'.

In 1919 there was a further sale of St John's Wood and between the wars there was steady development along Hazlemere Road, New Road and St John's Road. It was not until 1957 that serious building started with the first houses of the Deer Park Estate. The population today is about 4,500, of whom 85 per cent live on what used to be a part of Wycombe Heath. Mains services arrived in Tylers Green: water (1921), gas (1926), electricity (1928) and sewerage (1957/61).

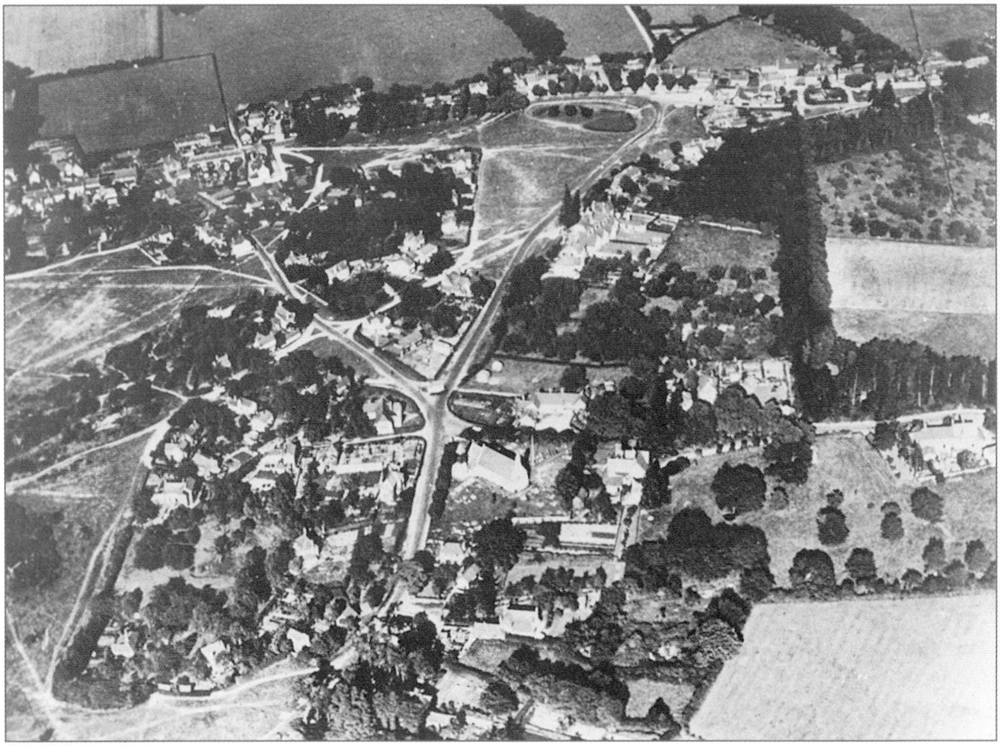

Aerial view of Tylers Green, *c.* 1920. This may have been taken for the sale of the Rayners Estate in 1920. Note the orchards and fields where the Village Hall now stands, along School Road and where part of Wheeler Avenue now runs. (*P. Barnes*)

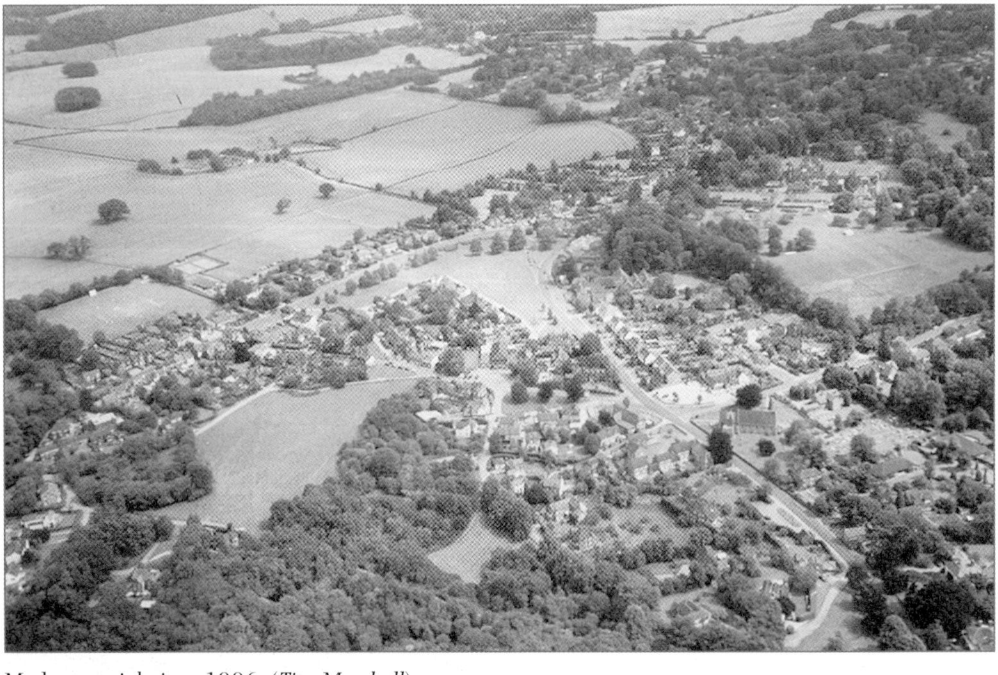

Modern aerial view, 1996. (*Tim Marshall*)

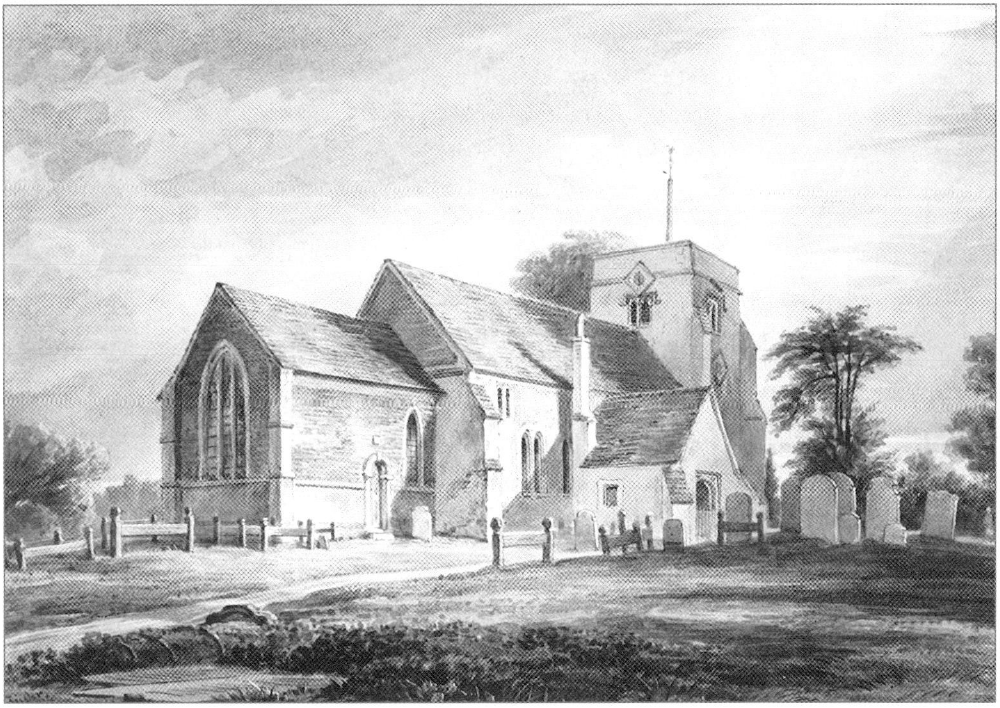

Penn Church, *c.* 1850: a watercolour by H.B. Ziegler (1798–1874), drawing master to Queen Adelaide. His drawing is very precise and he has captured the church before the Victorian 'improvements' replaced the brick east wall and window with knapped flints and a new window. (*Earl Howe*)

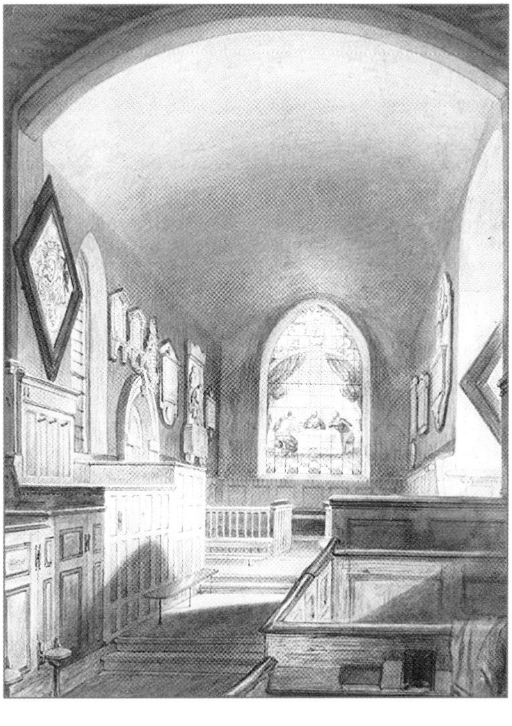

The chancel of Penn Church by H.B. Ziegler, *c.* 1850. It shows the earlier east window of Christ and his disciples at Emmaus, put up in 1737, and a modest 'three-decker' pulpit which allowed the priest to preach from the top and conduct the service from the middle, while the parish clerk below read out each line of a psalm to his largely illiterate congregation before it was sung. (*Earl Howe*)

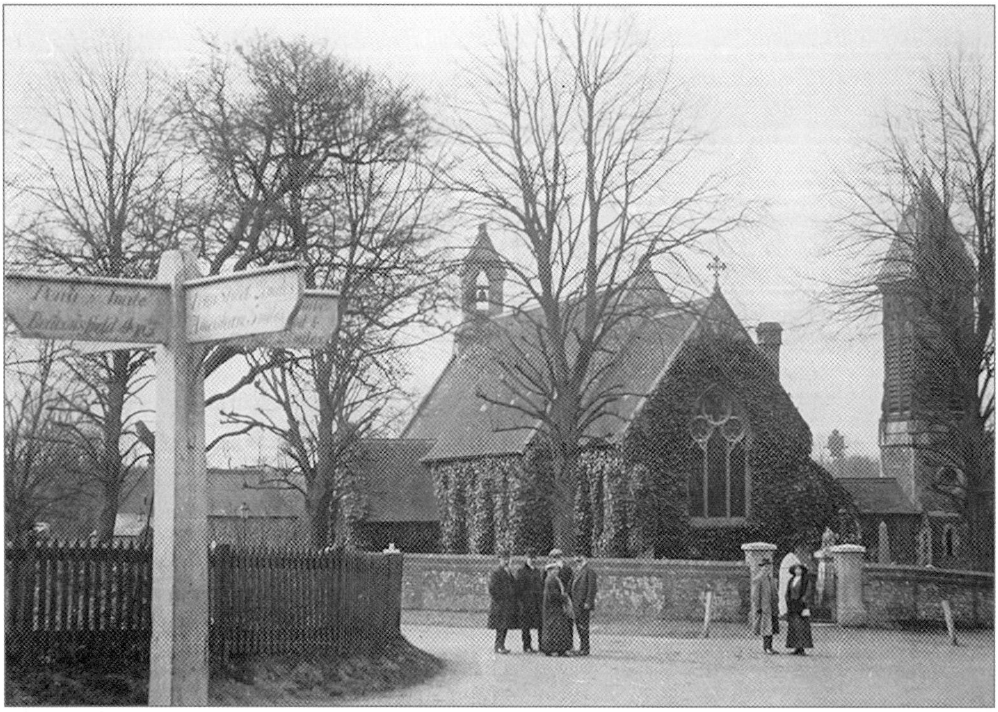

St Margaret's Church, 1905. The church was built in 1854 at a cost of over £2,000, of which more than half was met by the first Sir Philip Rose. It was designed by David Brandon, a young Jewish architect who went on to be Vice-President of the RIBA. The bell tower contains a peal of eight tubular bells and was built by Zachary Wheeler in 1889, for the second Sir Philip in memory of his mother. The brick and flint boundary wall and three gates were built for only £90. (*CWPC*)

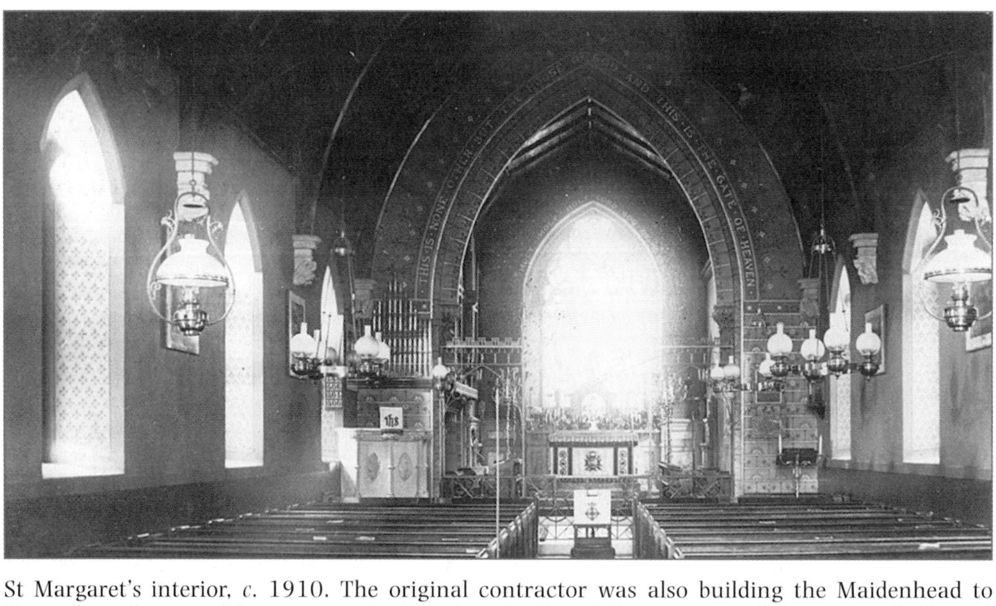

St Margaret's interior, *c.* 1910. The original contractor was also building the Maidenhead to Wycombe railway and his contract for the church allowed him to use railway materials, but he went bankrupt. Zachariah Wheeler, a local builder, did most of the work. Labourers were paid 3*s* 6*d* per day and bricklayers 4*s* 6*d*. 1,700 bricks cost £3. (*CWPC*)

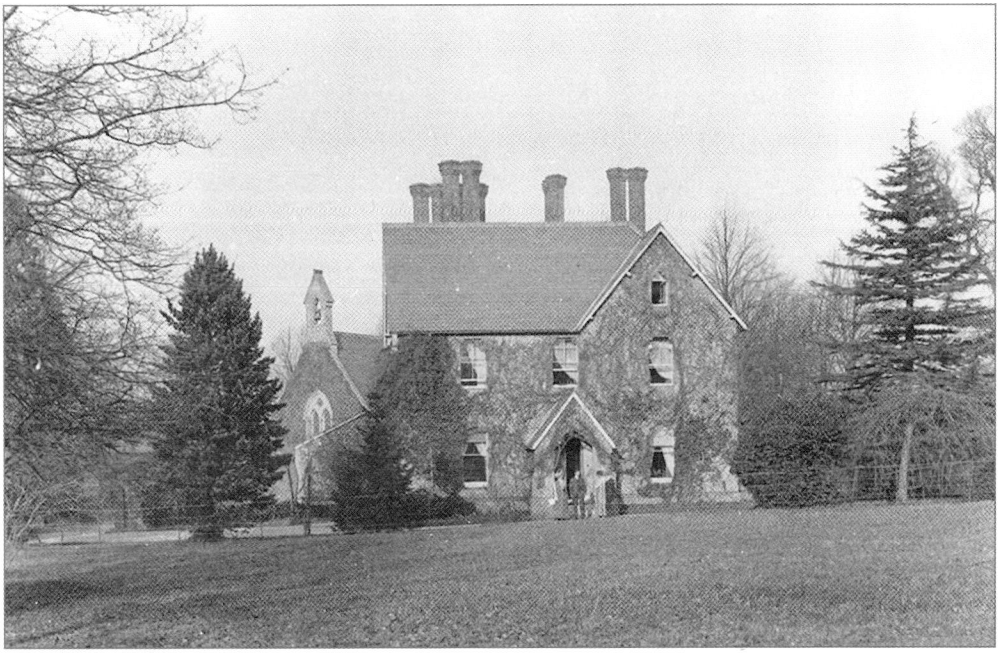

St Margaret's Vicarage, photographed by C.G. Rose, 1906. David Brandon was again the architect and the house was completed, in 1865, after great difficulty in raising the £1,233 required. It had the seven bedrooms and three reception rooms considered appropriate for a vicar at that time. By 1900 it was too big, and successive vicars lived in various smaller local houses: Ivy Cottage (now Tyler End), The Firs (now the Old Rectory), Brown Tiles (now Vicarage Cottage) and Westbury House. The new vicarage replaced the old in 1960. (*Petica Waley*)

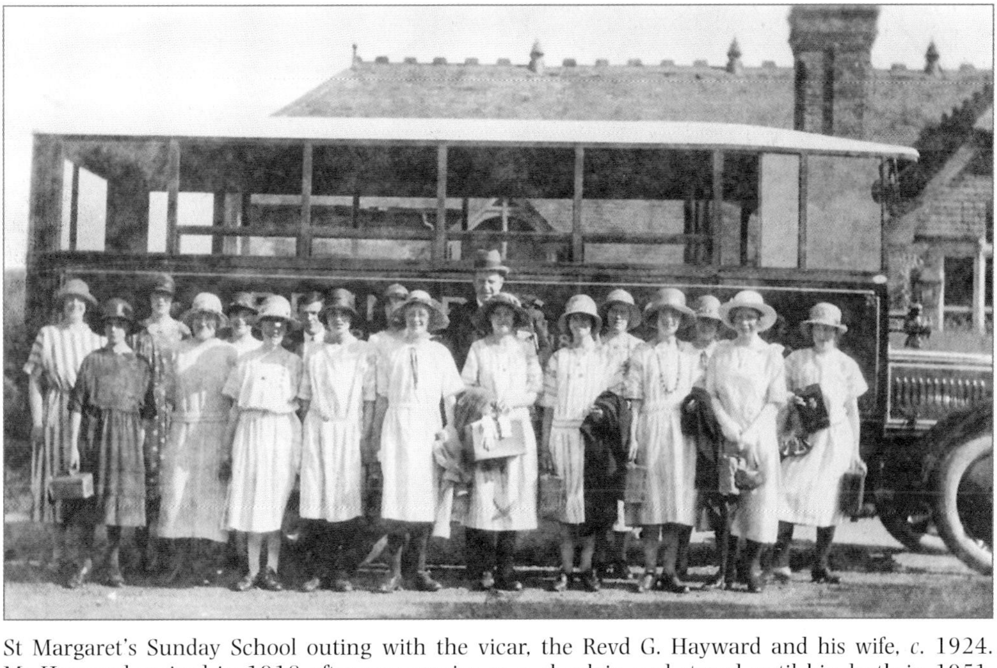

St Margaret's Sunday School outing with the vicar, the Revd G. Hayward and his wife, *c.* 1924. Mr Hayward arrived in 1918 after war service as a chaplain and stayed until his death in 1951. (*Cissie Ginn*)

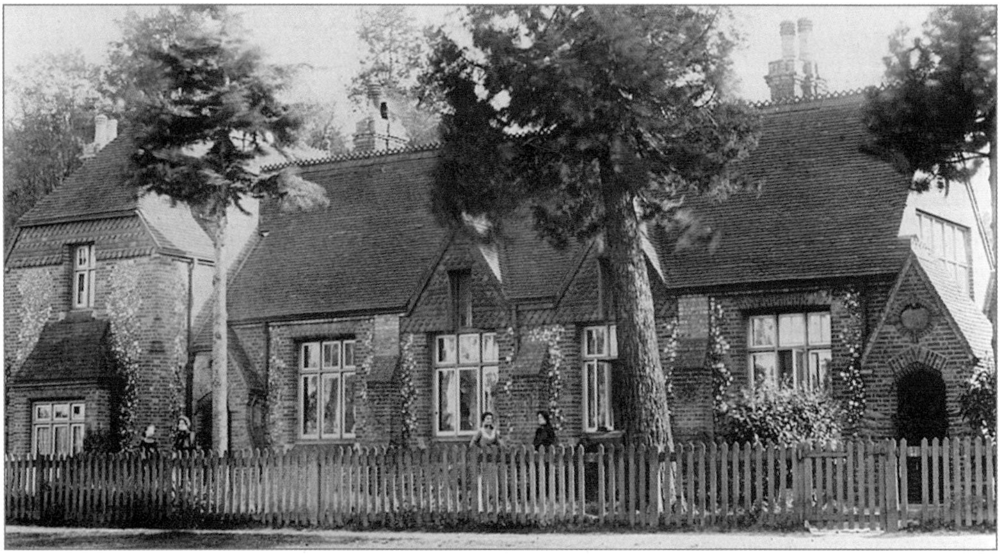

Tylers Green Board School before the major extension of 1910. Sir Philip Rose laid the foundation stone on 15 October 1875. Arthur Vernon of Wycombe designed the building for 150 pupils at a cost of £1,870. There were separate entrances for boys (right) and girls (left).The three young Wellingtonia trees were planted in 1876. One survived until 1980 and still provides a seat on the common in front of the school. (*Eric Hearne*)

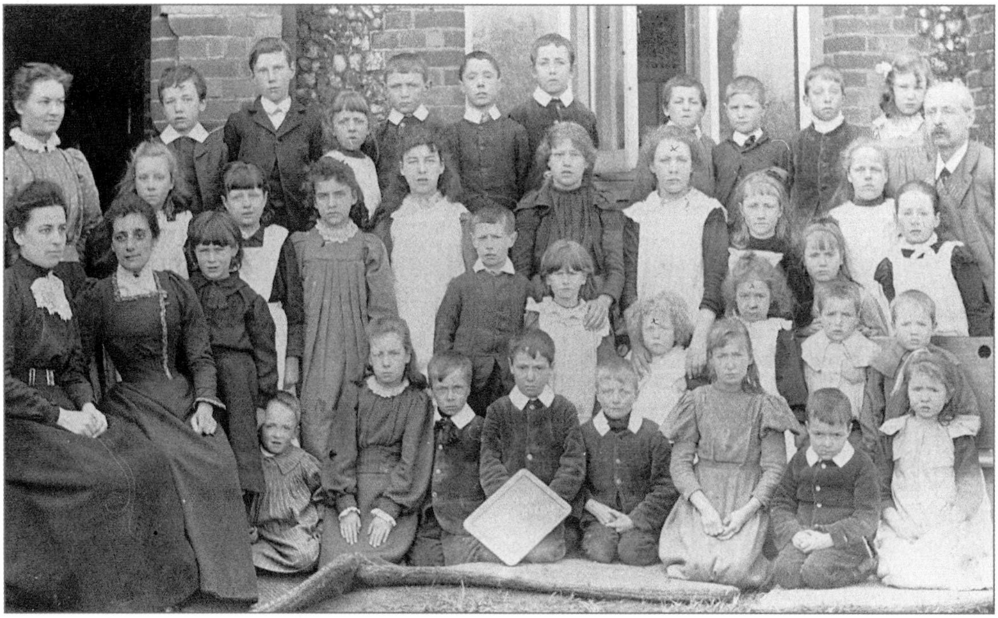

Family groups at Tylers Green School, 1901. Mr Rees, the Headmaster, is on the right. On the left are the teachers, Miss Emma Sutton (standing), Miss Alice Evans (sitting left) and Miss Castle. The two girls standing centre left are Maud and Miriam (Minnie, in white smock) Evans, sisters of Alice Evans and all daughters of Walter Evans the blacksmith (p. 97). The three girls, centre right, marked with a small cross are the Ball sisters. The youngest, Lilian (1897–1985), was a postwoman in the First World War, married Charlie Clarke, the butcher (p. 97), and is the forebear of the Bowyer family. A video was made of her reminiscences shortly before she died. The names of almost all the children have been noted. (*Lilian Clarke*)

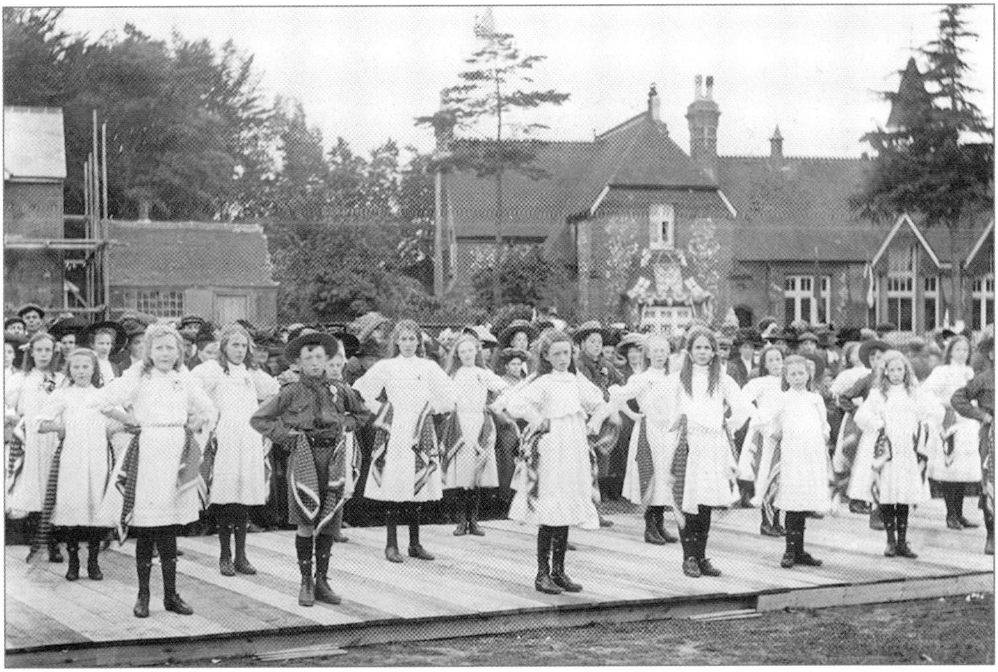

Celebration of King George V's coronation, 1911. By 1909 there were 239 children and still only two classrooms, and so the infants were moved to the Parish Room. In the First World War 'air raid' children arrived. Mr Rees was remembered as a good teacher but 'a cruel man', frequently using his cane on the pupils' hands. To the left a new house is being built. The hut at the side was used by a cobbler who came on Friday charging a penny for re-stitching reins, satchels, etc. The house burned down only a few years later. (*Eileen Brown*)

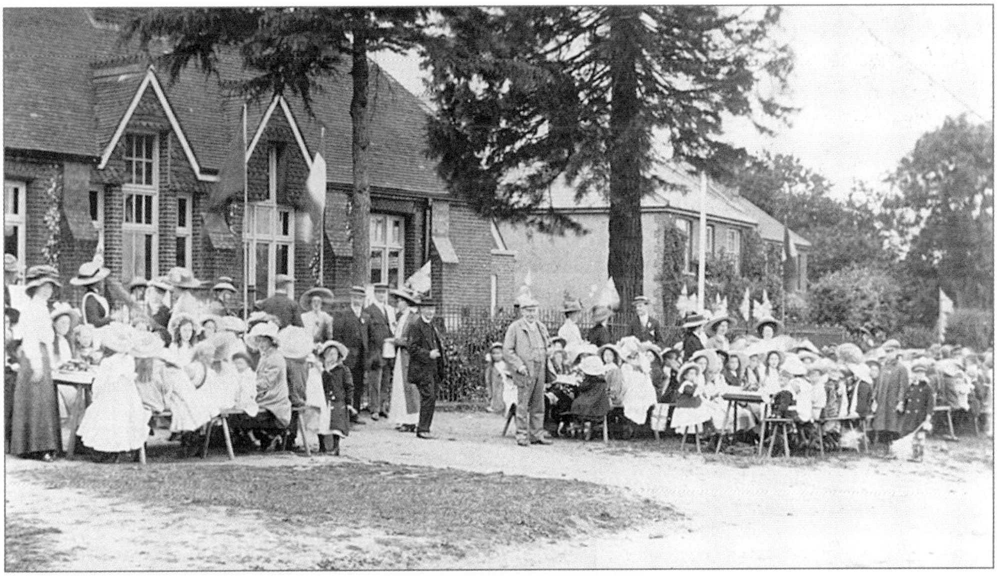

Tea party to celebrate George V's coronation, 1911. Harold Wheeler remembers receiving a coronation mug, carrying the Union Jack and going to Rayners for a celebration which ended with 'God Save the King' in fireworks. Twenty-nine years later, the children lined School Road to welcome Queen Elizabeth (now the Queen Mother) when she visited the Parish Room. (*CWPC*)

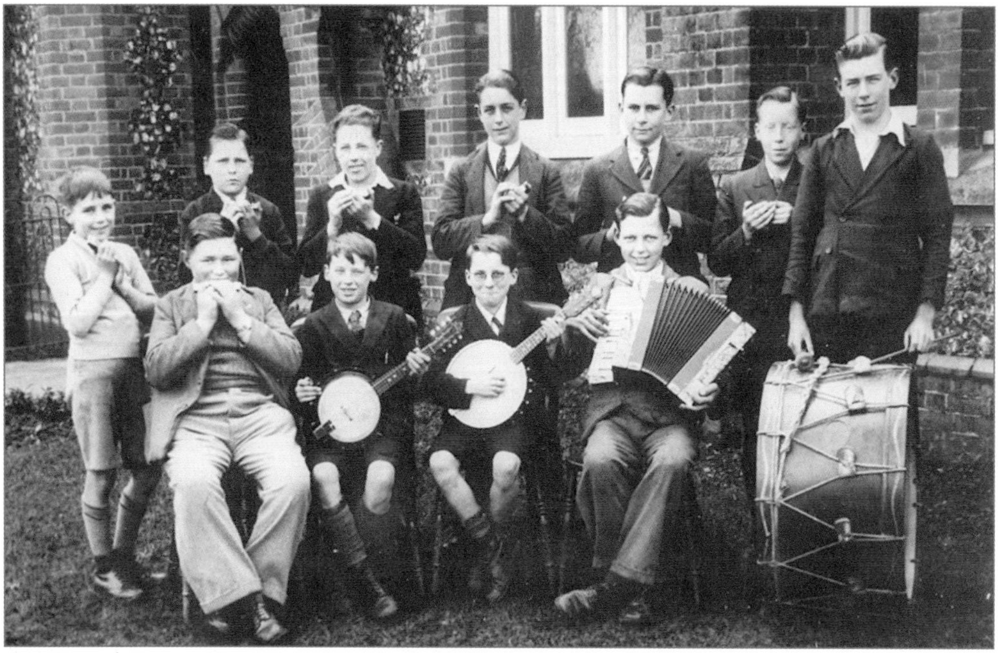

The school band, 1937. They were heirs to a long tradition which started in 1881 when Sir Philip Rose gave the school a big drum and twenty small drums and fifes, and engaged a Drum Major to instruct the boys. 'God Save the Queen' was the first tune they were to learn. (*CWPC*)

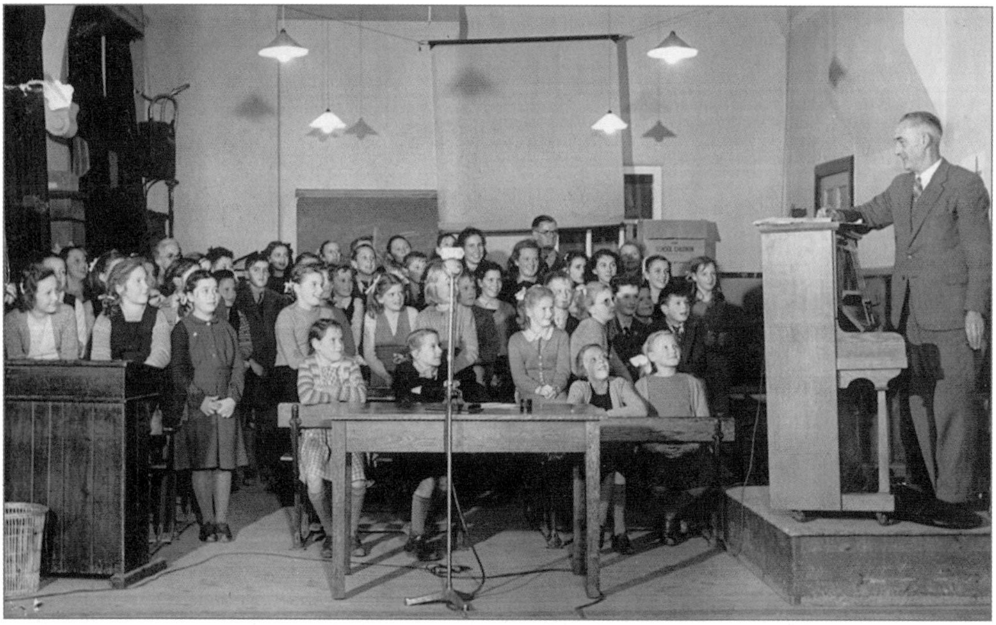

Mr M.K. Filby (headmaster 1931–61) leading the school through their recording of Christmas carols and hymns for a BBC radio programme, 9 December 1949. It was called 'A Country Christmas' and was relayed to the North American service. It was recorded in the school log that in 1932 Mr Filby had arranged for the installation of a 'wireless receiving set'. He was only the third headmaster since 1877. In 1939 evacuees from London had doubled the number of pupils overnight to 334, and the school had to be run in two shifts. (*CWPC*)

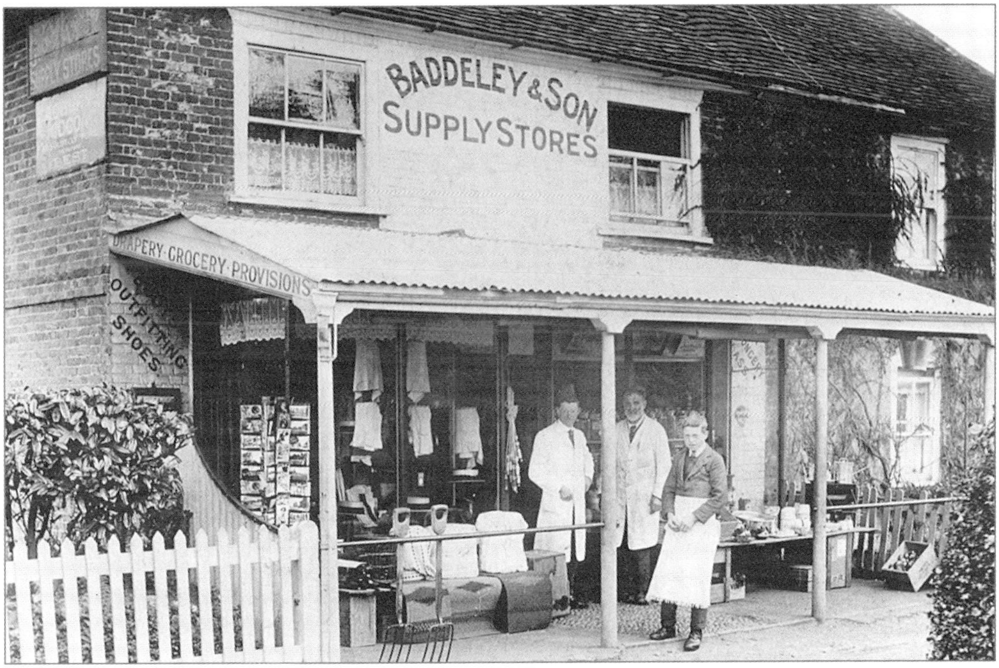

Mr Cyril Baddeley (centre), Jimmy Palmer (left) and Harold Wheeler, *c.* 1920. The shop sold a huge variety of things – groceries, cottons, materials, linos, rugs, medicines, candles, paraffin, gunpowder and shot, clothing, shoes and so on. It was a grocer/draper in the 1870s. Signs reading 'Close and open carriages let on hire' and 'Brougham for hire' have been painted over on the outside of the shop. It closed in the 1960s and was an antiques shop until 1993; it now stands empty. (*F. Baddeley*)

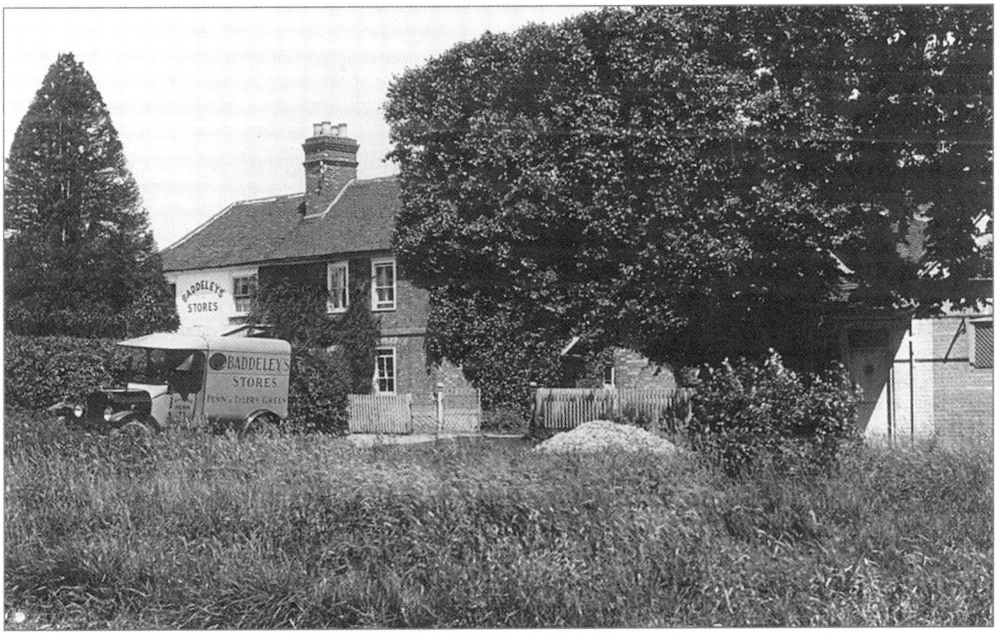

Baddeley's first delivery van, early 1920s. It replaced a horse and cart, and was a left-hand-drive Ford. Note the low telephone number on the door of the van. The elm which was said to 'part the village' conceals W.G. King, the butcher. (*F. Baddeley*)

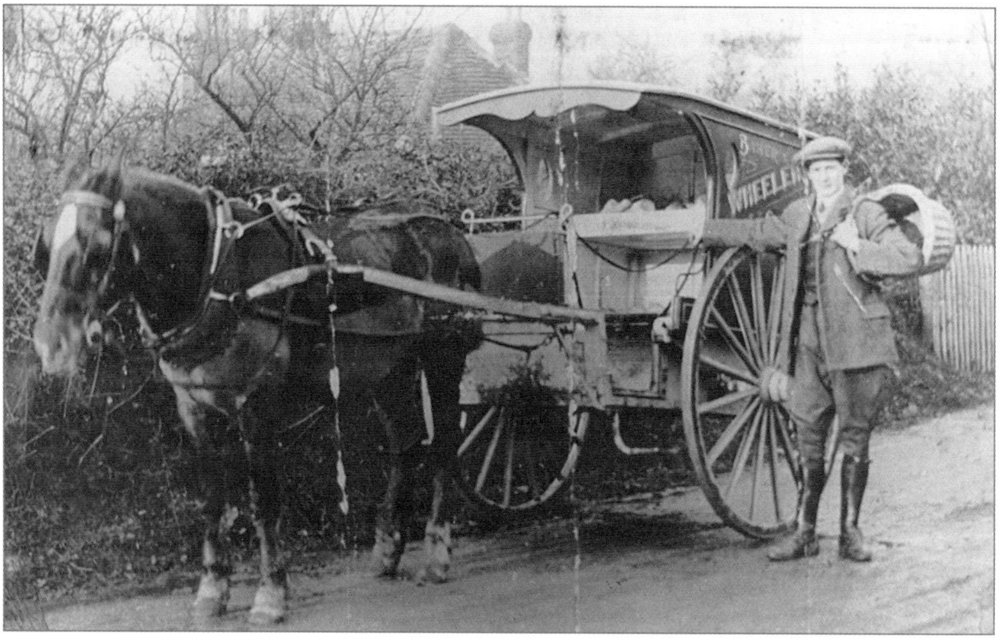

Arthur Wheeler (b. 1884) with delivery van, 1913. His father, 'Brusher' Wheeler, had the grocer/baker/post office opposite Baddeley's which he sold to his employee Billy Woodbridge in 1915, moving to Wayside, Church Road, where he kept the post office until 1919. (*Brian Randall*)

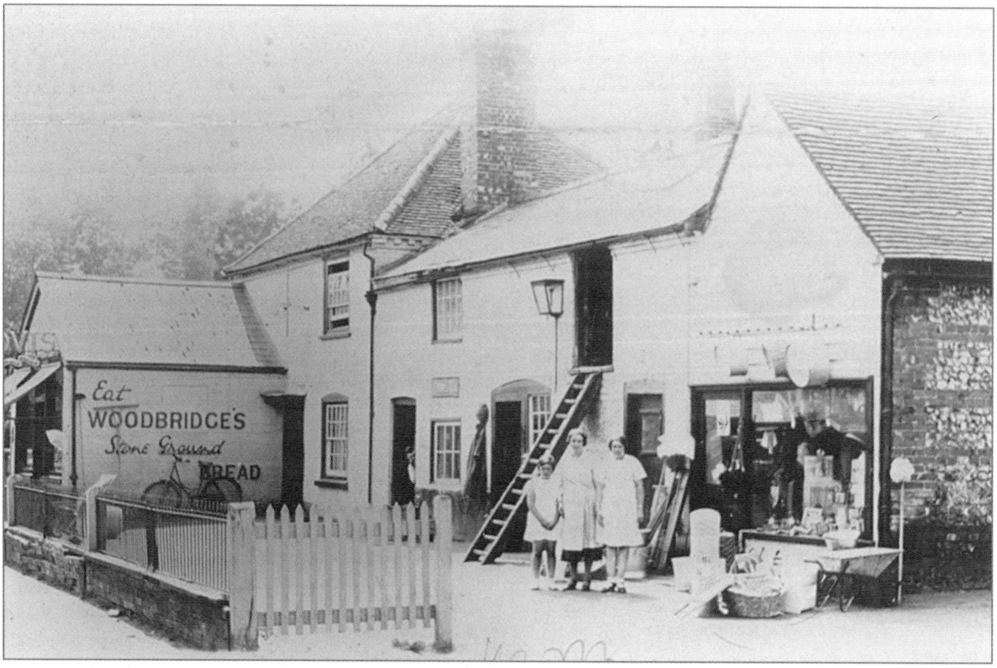

Woodbridge's in the 1930s. It was described in 1920 as 'grocer, baker, corndealer and Jobmaster. Phone 19 Penn'. The grocer's shop was on the left, the bakery (oven built in 1846) in the centre, and out of the picture to the right were the stables and barn where the jobmaster, Mr Reid, kept his horses and carriages for the horse bus service to Beaconsfield. Bread was baked until 1964 and the shop closed, amidst champagne and lamentations, in 1986. (*Brian Randall*)

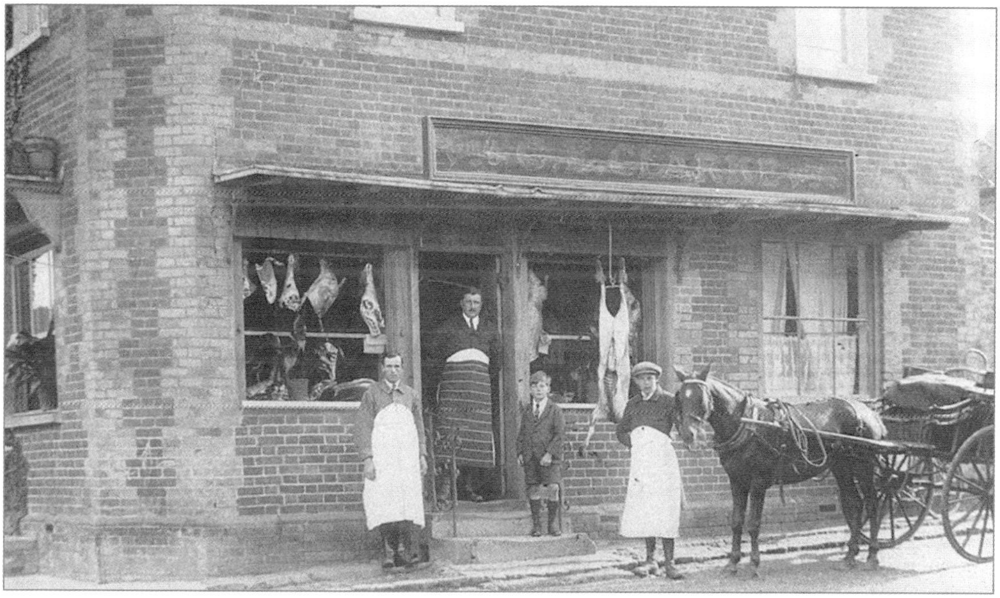

Charlie Clarke the butcher is in the doorway, and Bert Hawes on the left, *c.* 1926. There was a slaughter house in the yard with some of the animals coming from Puttenham Farm. Mr Clarke died in 1934 but his wife carried on the business. It remained a butcher's shop (Streeters) until 1 April 1988. It is now a ladies' beauty salon. (*Lilian Clarke*)

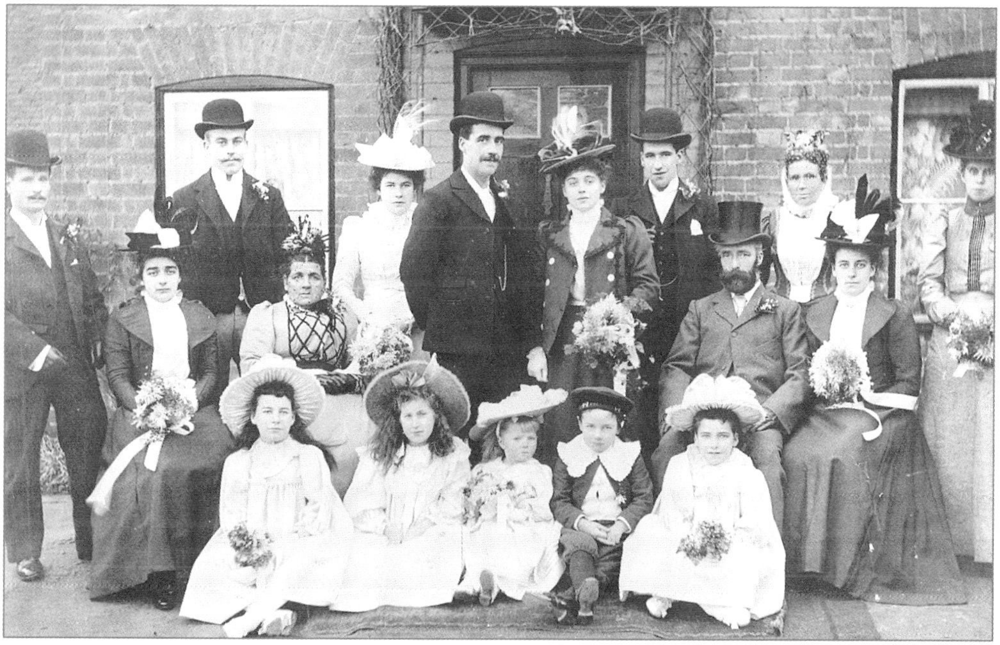

The marriage of Charles Evans (centre, bowler hat) to Maggie Stretton, *c.* 1898. He was the son of Walter Evans (in top hat) who owned the blacksmith at Beacon Hill where the photograph was taken, and later also Beaconsfield Motors and Farnham Motors. Mrs Evans (with a veil) is seated to the left. Sitting in front of her mother is Minnie Evans (b. 1888), mother of Geoffrey Perfect and later infant mistress at Tylers Green School. Next to her is Kathleen Finch, who as Mrs Saunders inherited the post office and shop from her mother, Ellen Finch. (*Geoffrey Perfect*)

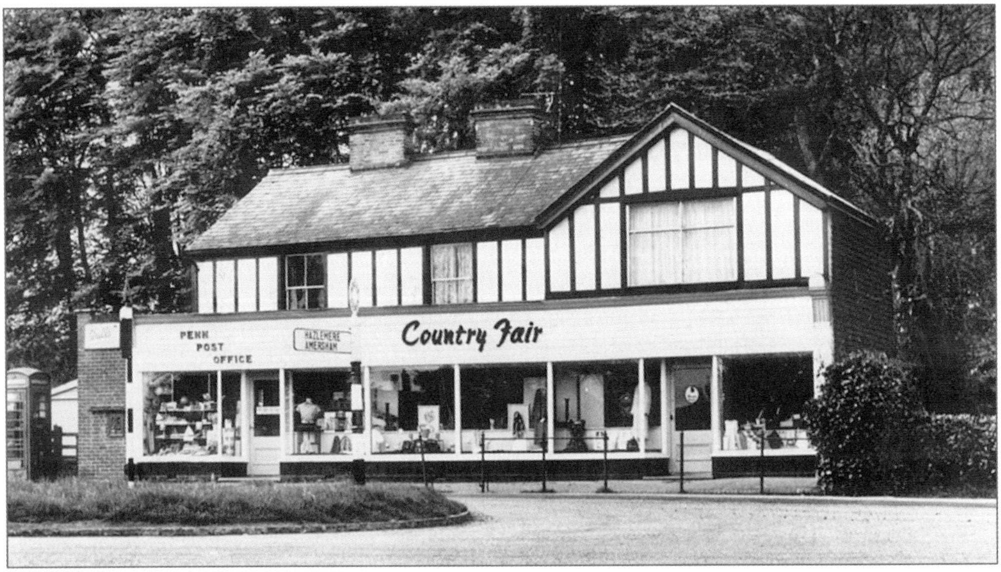

Country Fair, 1960. In 1919 Penn post office and sorting office moved from Wayside in Church Road, Penn, to join Mrs Ellen Finch's drapery in School Road. The telephone exchange (in Wheeler's by 1915) was also moved there at that time and, in 1927, relayed the first ever transatlantic call to Lord Dawson of Penn. Mail came from Wycombe (it used to be from Amersham until 1903), at first on foot and then in a pony and cart. Local mail was sorted on the spot and delivered the same day. Postmen and women got 12*s* 2*d* per week plus 2*s* 6*d* for running their own bikes. In 1988 the sorting office moved to Hazlemere and the post office to Church Road, Tylers Green. (*Eric Britnell*)

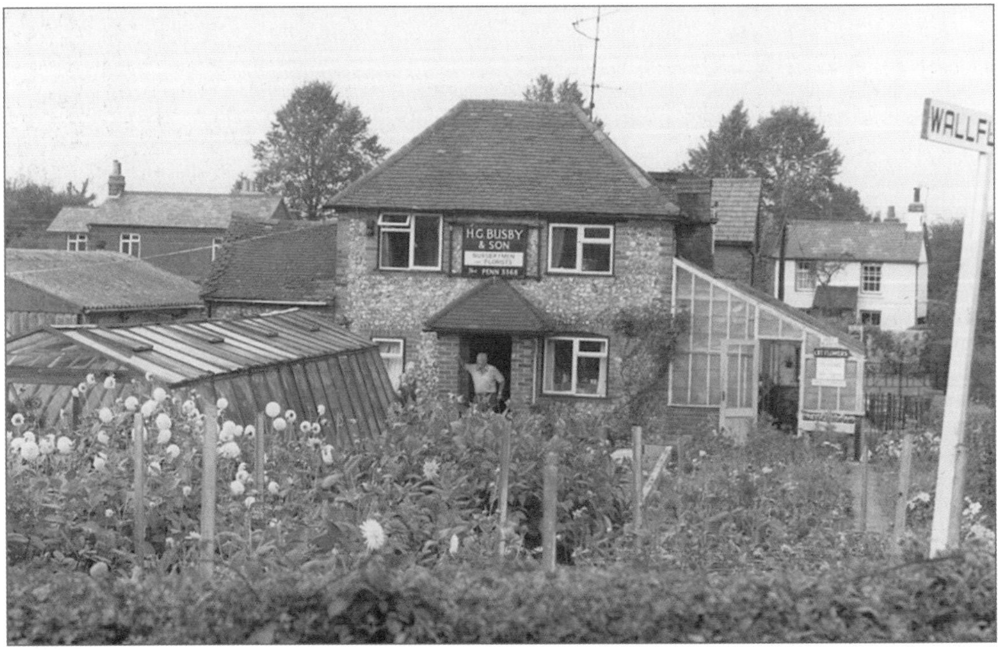

Henry Busby at the door of the Nursery shortly before it was replaced by Nursery Close, 1985. The cottages were built in about 1827 by a tea dealer and became a nursery in 1872 when purchased by Henry Beale, Harry Busby's grandfather. Nursery Lane used to be known as Wizzle Street until the 1950s, and the footpath which forks off it as Tickle Belly Alley. (*Miles Green*)

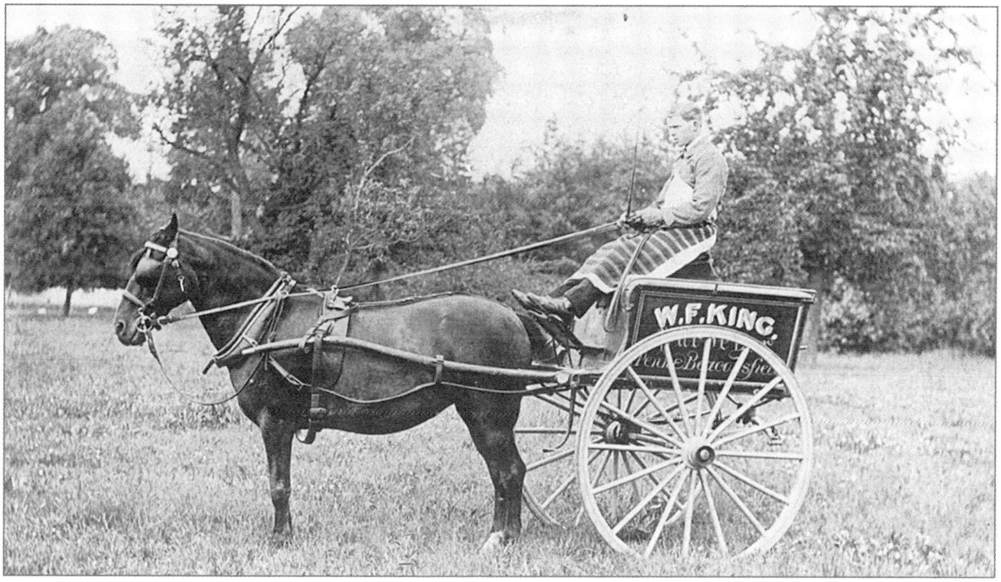

Charlie Wheeler, brother of Harold Wheeler, is remembered making daily deliveries for King the butcher, early 1920s. 'TCW 1797', inscribed on the side wall of Kings, probably stands for Thomas and Charlotte Weller. He was a Penn butcher in 1780 and her father held Puttenham Farm. The former shopfront claims 'Established 1782', and it was closed in 1982 after exactly two centuries. Penn post office was here in 1871. (*Harold Wheeler*)

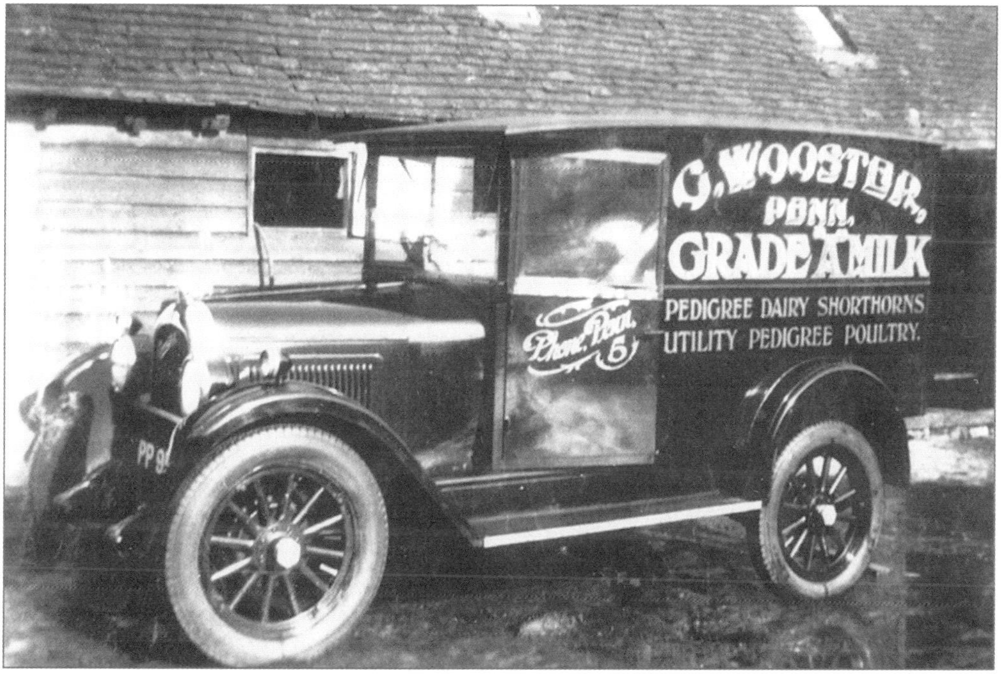

Wooster's first milk delivery van from Penbury Farm was an Overland Whippet which took the place of a horse and cart; it is seen here in 1928. George Wooster farmed Penbury from 1889 to 1938 and bred dairy shorthorn cattle and shire horses, winning prizes for both. From 1942 to the 1960s milk was delivered around Penn and Tylers Green by Joyce Windsor from the Broadway Dairy, Beaconsfield, using an electric hand cart. (*David Wooster*)

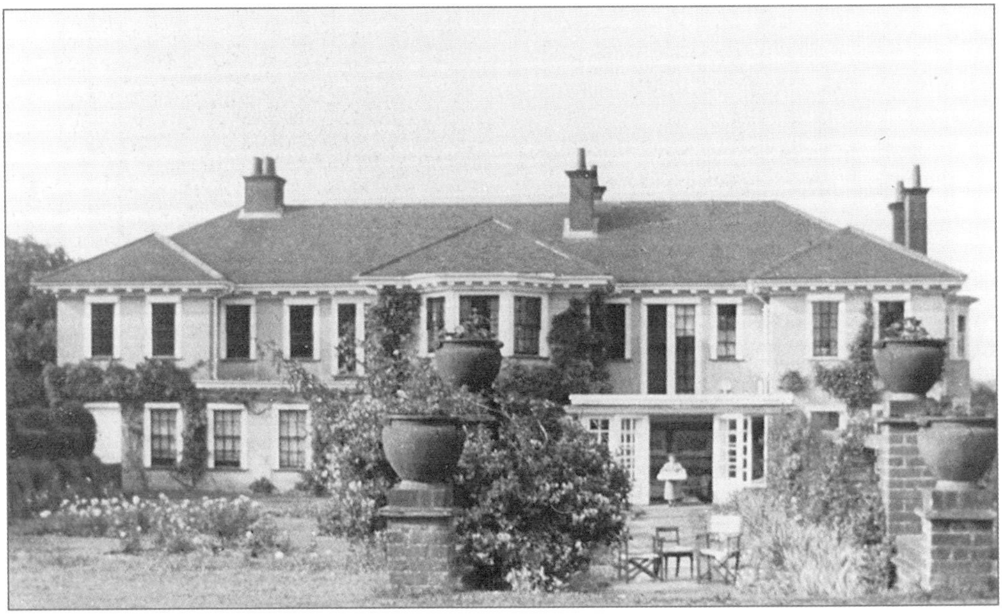

The Wight House, 1930s. It was called The Retreat when built by James Wight, a builder, in 1875. Bateman Lancaster Rose, brother of the second Sir Philip, bought it in 1903 for £950. It was extended in about 1920. The butler and chauffeur lived in the adjoining cottages and the gardener in the one behind. Mrs Lancaster Rose was still there in the mid-1950s and her grandson, the present baronet, Sir David Rose, was brought up there. Veronica Walley (née Papworth), the journalist, bought the property in about 1955, divided the house into three and apparently renamed it the White House. (*CWPC*)

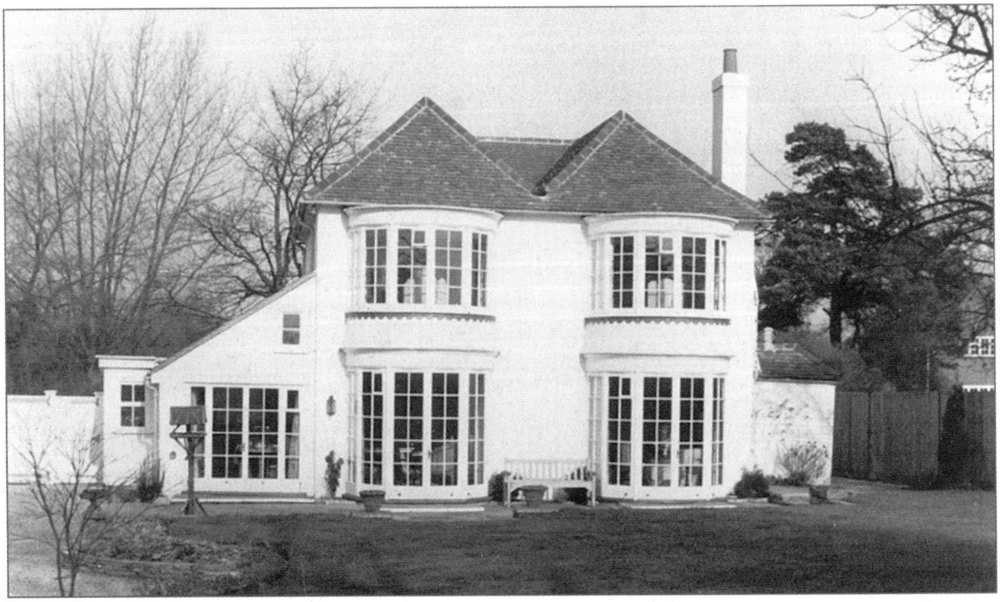

The Manor House, Church Road, Penn, was the centre of the medieval Manor of Segraves where the bailiff lived. It was never the residence of the lord of the manor. As late as 1804 the Manor Court was still being publicly proclaimed the required three times outside the house before the officials moved on to 'the usual Court House', the Red Lion. The house has an eighteenth-century exterior, though much altered. (*CWPC*)

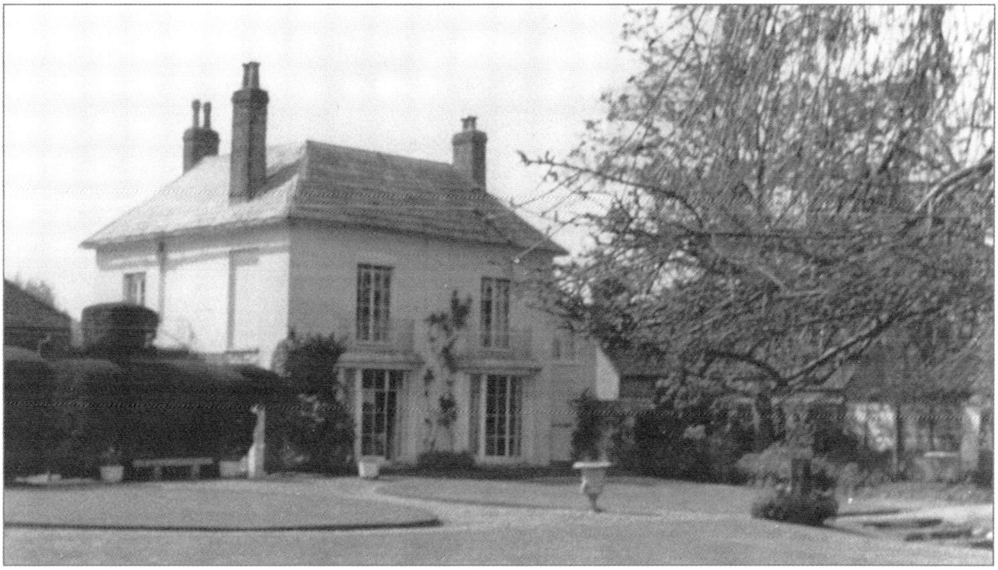

Watercroft. An early nineteenth-century listed building, built by John Grove (1777–1868) who left Penn for London with only a horse and a guinea and made his fortune as a fishmonger. Charles Dickens recorded buying fish from his shop. His nephew, Sir George Grove (1820–1900), originator of the famous *Dictionary of Music and Musicians*, later owned the house and Arthur Sullivan, a close friend, is supposed to have composed *The Lost Chord* and *Onward Christian Soldiers* in the summerhouse. (*CWPC*)

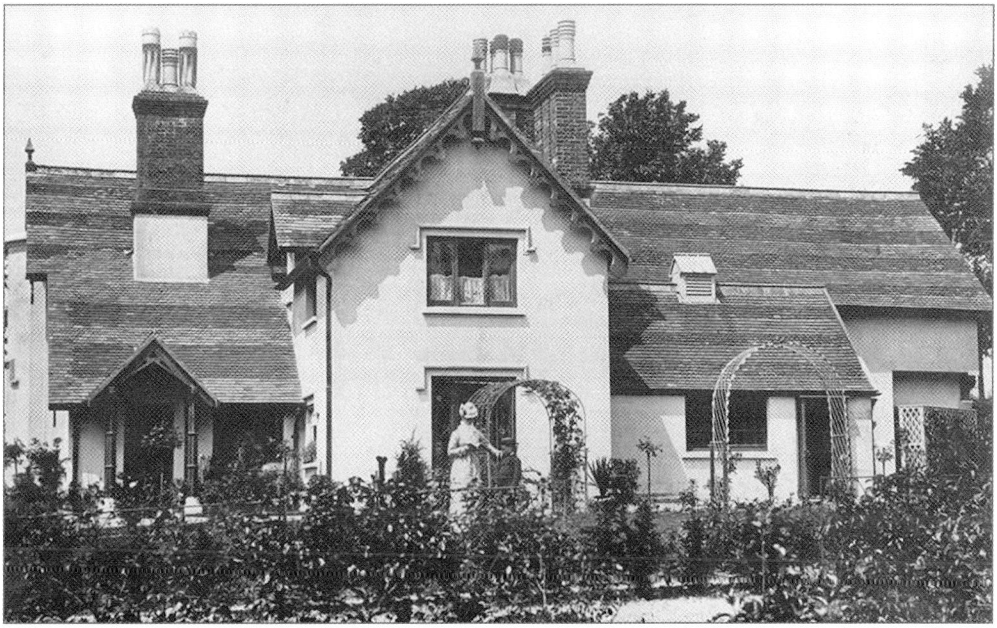

Colehatch House, Hammersley Lane, *c.* 1880. The first Sir Philip Rose bought Colehatch Farm in 1845 and converted the farmhouse into a 'villa residence' where his grandson, Vivian Rose, lived before the First World War. Two elderly daughters of the deposed emperor of the Sikhs, Duleep Singh, who gave the famous Koh-i-Noor diamond to Queen Victoria, lived there from 1938 to 1948. They were addressed as 'Your Highness'. Their name for the house, Hilden Hall, comes from Germany: one of their grandfathers was German. (*Penn School, Rayners*)

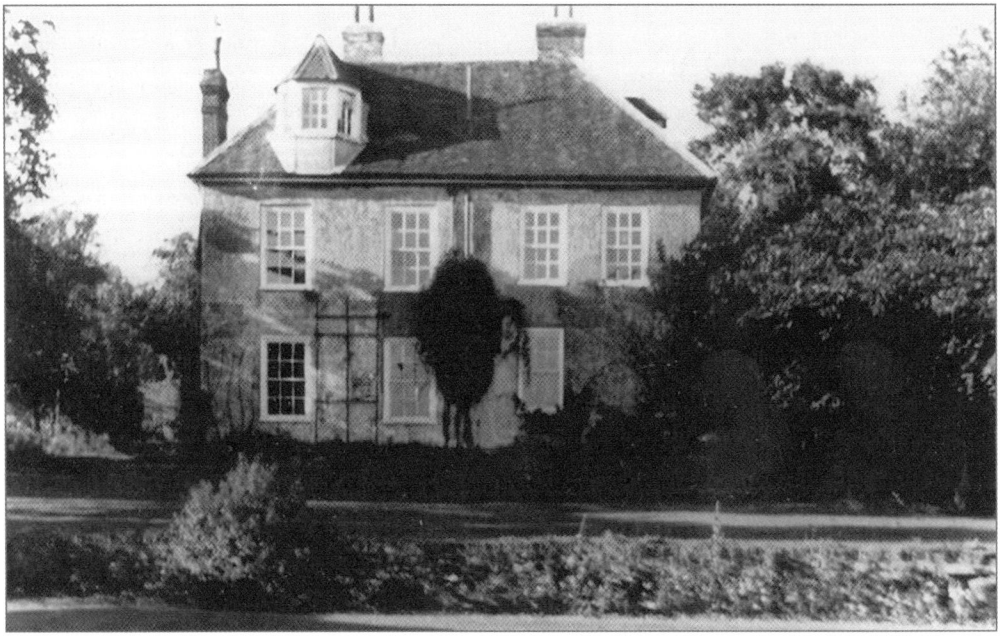

The Knoll, Paul's Hill, 1940. In about 1671 Sir John Curzon built 'a pretty house at Penn' for his son Nathaniel who had married Sarah Penn, heiress to the Penn estate. The house remained with the Curzons, and Countess Mary Howe, divorced wife of the 5th Earl, lived there after the Second World War, followed by her son, Viscount Curzon, and his young family. It is a listed building. (*Lady Charlotte Dinan*)

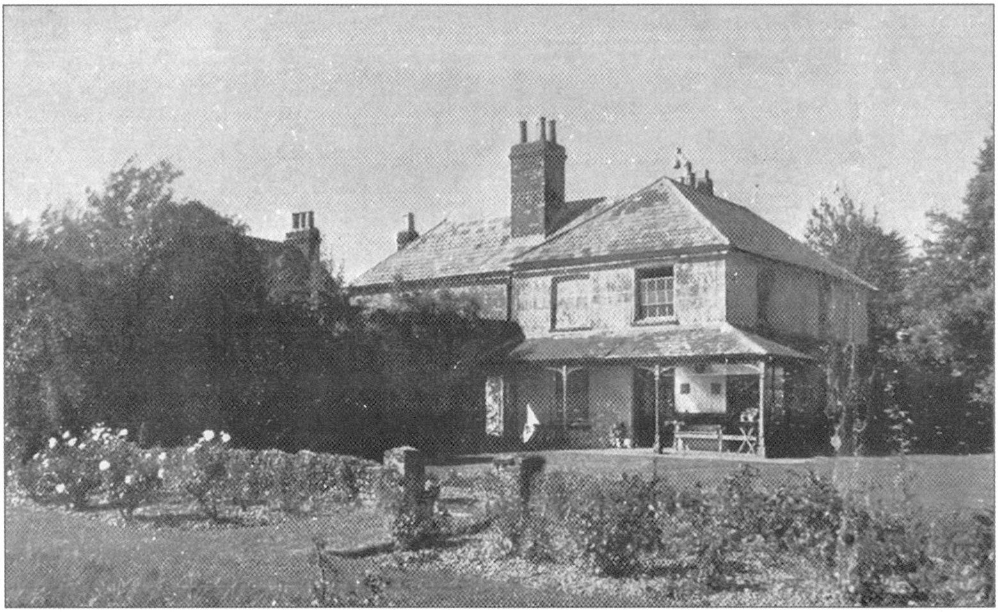

Stonehouse, Church Road, Penn. An early nineteenth-century refacing conceals an earlier house which for over six centuries, until 1953, was owned by the Grove family. In 1868 John Grove owned 540 acres, half of which was in Penn. 'Yeoman' Edmund Grove (1729–1823) was reputed to be friendly with George III who, it is said, visited the house and claimed to be able to see his host from Windsor through his telescope, eating cherries on the lawn. It is a listed building. (*CWPC*)

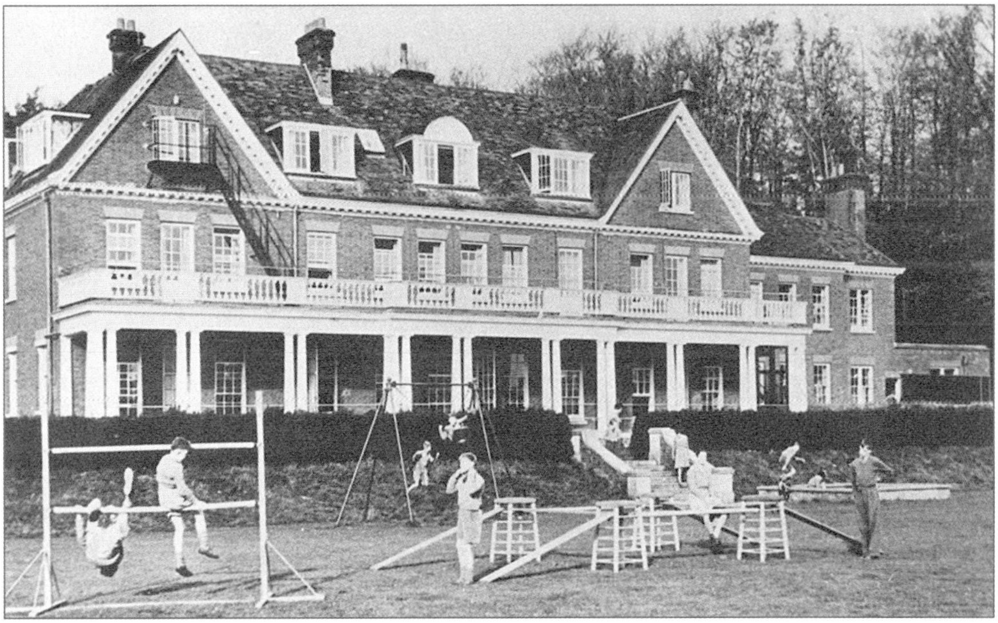

Penbury Grove, *c.* 1960. In about 1907 the Penn Estate sold 53 acres of Penbury Farm to Dr Horace Parshall, a gifted American electrical engineer who became chairman of what is now the Metropolitan Line. The house is modelled on William Penn the Quaker's late seventeenth-century house in Morrisville, Pennsylvania, which he had called Pennsbury supposing his ancestors had lived at Penbury Farm. There were fifteen bedrooms and five bathrooms, with no expense spared on imported Italian marble, and exotic trees and shrubs in the garden. It was the first local house to have electricity, using a paraffin generator. Huge blocks of Derbyshire stone were imported to create a large rockery. (*Fred Payne*)

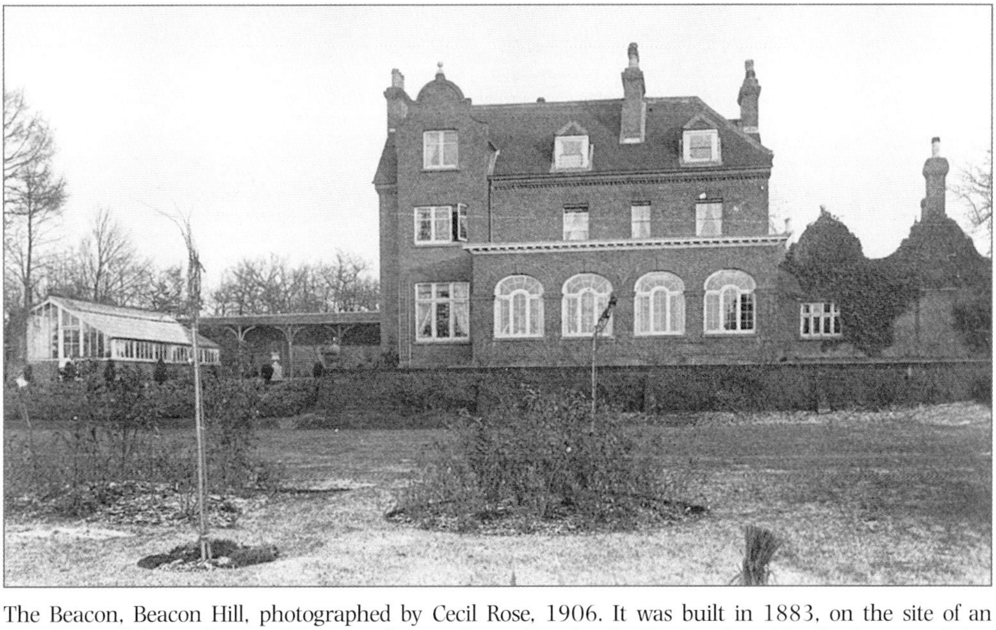

The Beacon, Beacon Hill, photographed by Cecil Rose, 1906. It was built in 1883, on the site of an existing small house, by Sir Philip Rose for members of his family. His daughter, Mrs Bartlett, was living there in 1899. It was sold with the Rayners Estate in 1920. Sir Robert Evans, an educational expert, lived there from 1926 to 1948. The parish boundary line runs through the middle of the house. (*Petica Waley*)

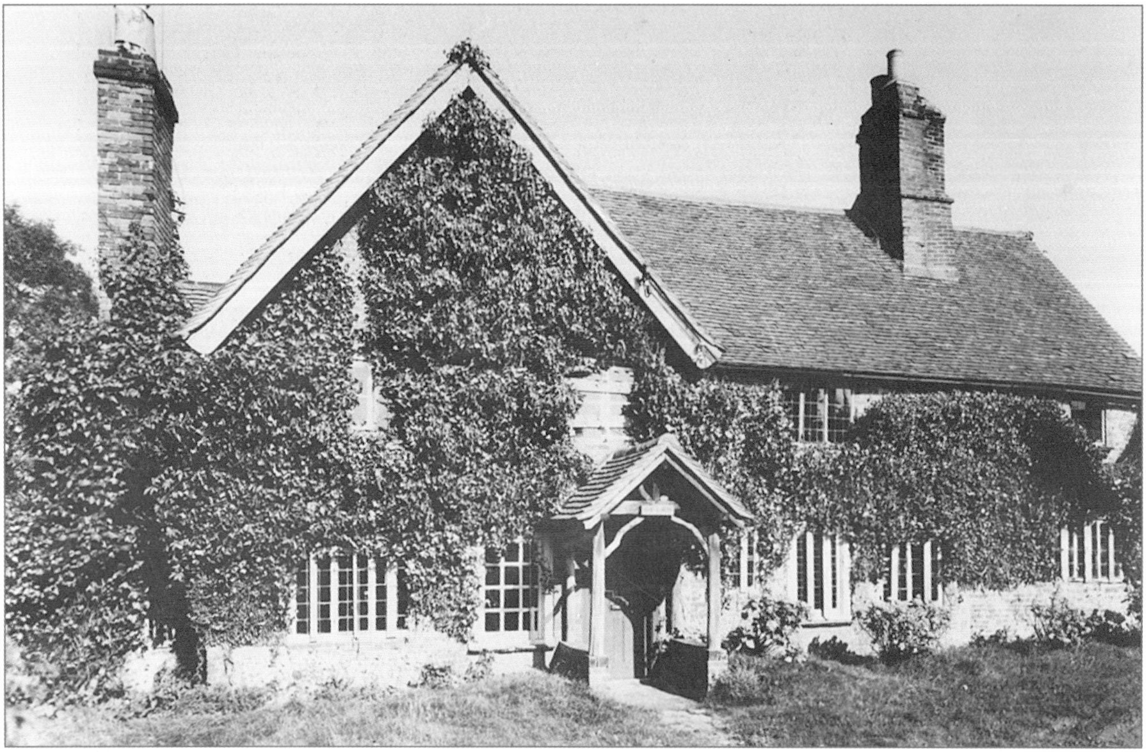

French Meadow Cottage, Elm Road, *c.* 1961. This is a listed seventeenth-century timber-framed house, clad in eighteenth-century brick, which is likely to have been a farmhouse for Puttenham Place. It had no direct connection with the French School, its near neighbour on the Green, and takes its comparatively recent name from a field name relating to the school. It was called The Gables and occupied by Thomas Griffen who built the Parish Room in 1887 and by his son who built the new Penn Vicarage in 1925. There were also a blacksmith, wheelwright and carpenter working in the yard. (*Monica Bazell*)

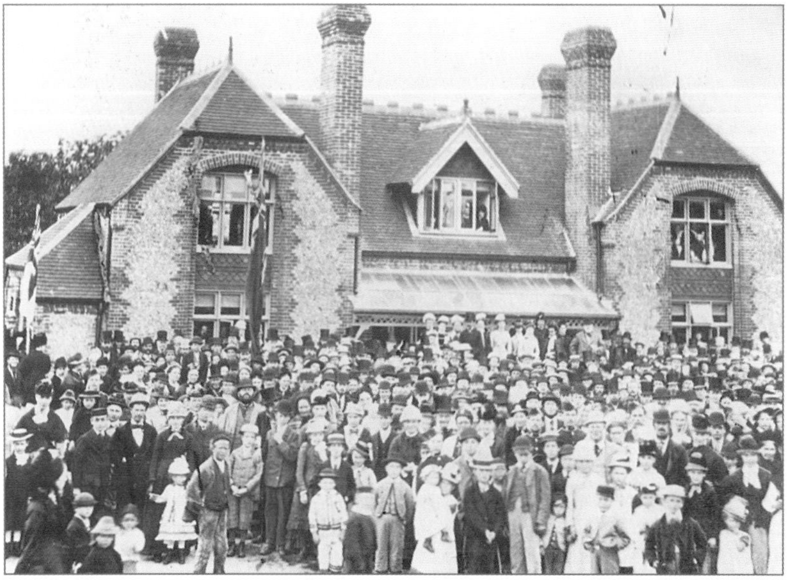

Opening of St Margaret's Club (now Tylers Green House) by Lady Carrington, 1878. Sir Philip Rose, following the example of Earl Howe's Penn Institute, set up a working men's club with the aim of keeping the men out of public houses. Arthur Vernon, architect of the nearby school, designed the building to be converted into two cottages if the scheme failed. It cost £1,000, and started with 123 members. Sir Philip proudly recorded, a year later, that there had not been a single case of drunkenness from Tylers Green before the Wycombe magistrates. By 1895 initial enthusiasm had waned, there were only twelve members and the Club was closed. (*CWPC*)

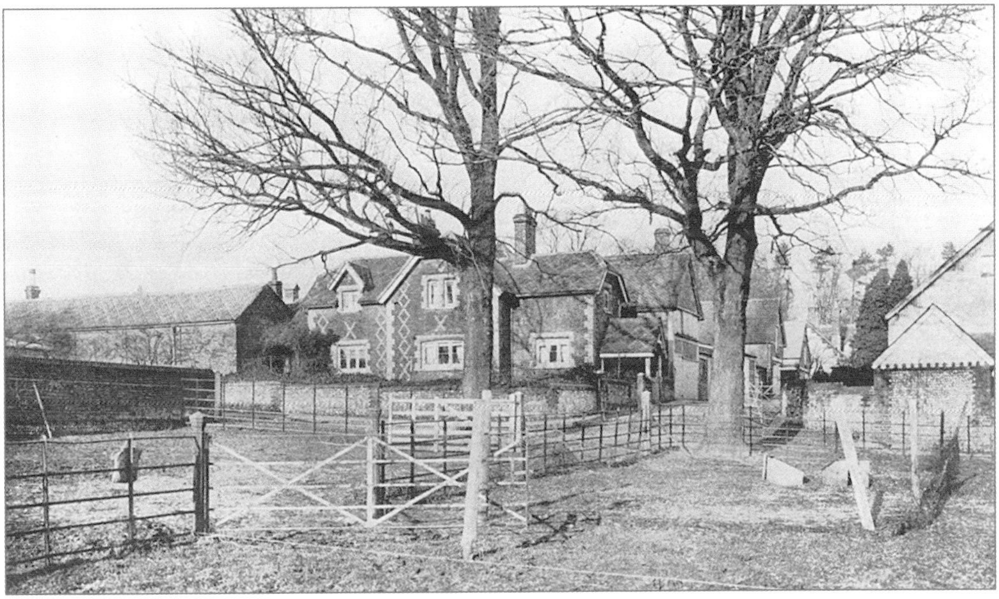

Colehatch Farm (now Pastures Farm), Hammersley Lane, 1920. Sir Philip Rose bought Colehatch Farm in 1845 and converted the farmhouse into a residence. He therefore built a new house for his bailiff and converted and added to the farm buildings to make a model farm in which he took a close interest. Prizes of all kinds were won in local agricultural shows. (*CWPC*)

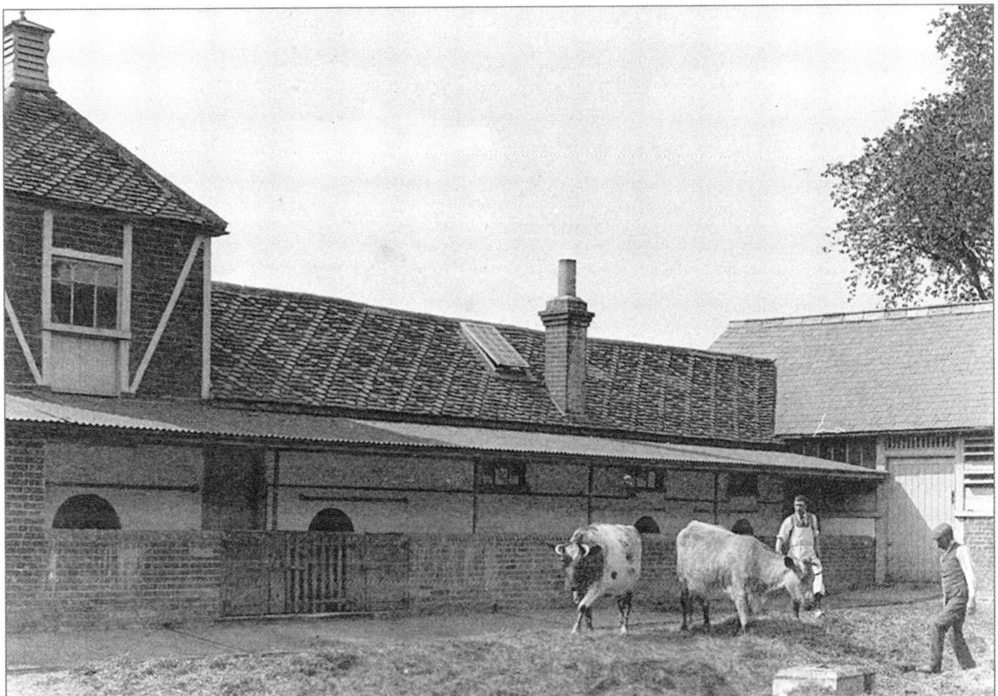

Farmyard of Colehatch Farm (now Hammersley Hatch), with Mr Crispin Winter and his son, early 1900s. Mr Winter came as farm bailiff to Sir Philip Rose in 1905, after twenty years with Earl Howe at Penn Bottom Farm. (*Evelyn Clark, née Winter*)

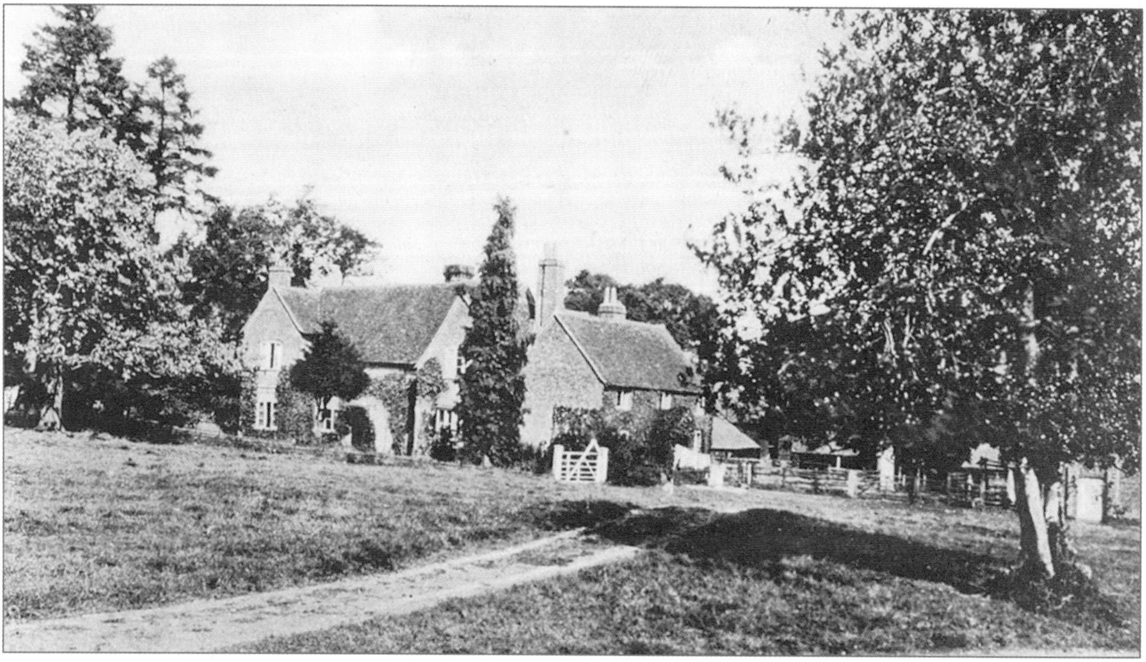

Puttenham Place Farm. This is a listed medieval hall house dating back to the fifteenth century. It takes its name from the Puttenham family, descendants of the Turvilles who were overlords of the Pennes. In 1199 the house was called Withiheg (hedge of withies) to which Witheridge Lane led from Beaconsfield via Penbury and Church Knowl. It has recently been restored. (*CWPC*)

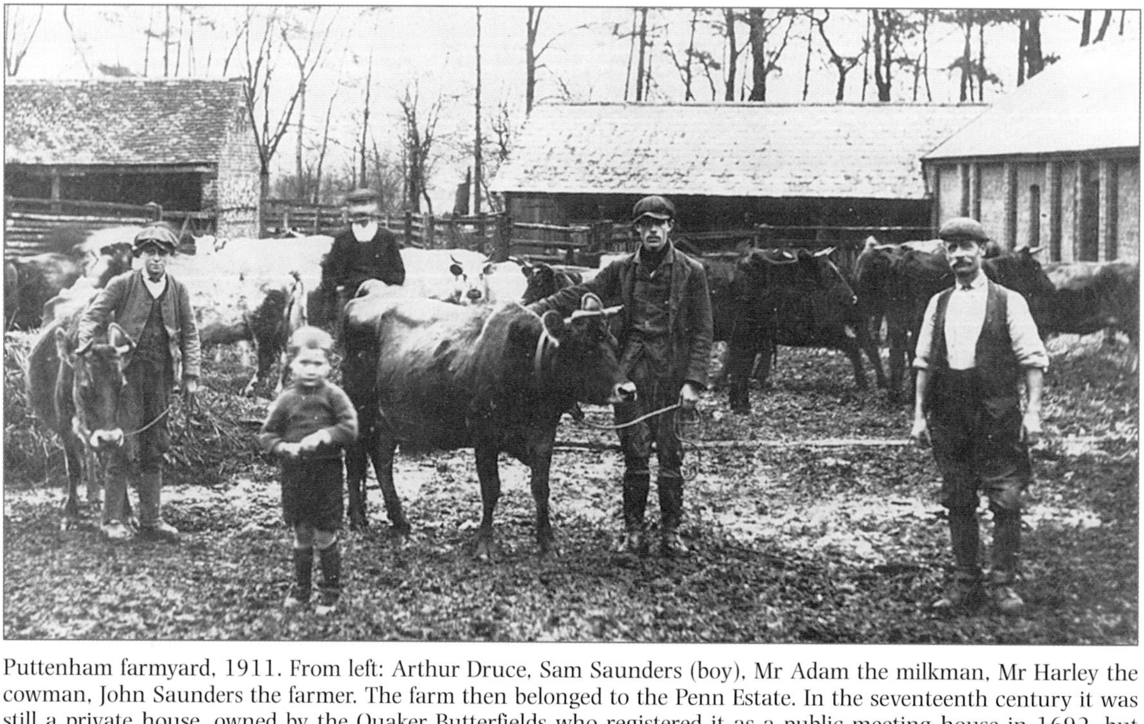

Puttenham farmyard, 1911. From left: Arthur Druce, Sam Saunders (boy), Mr Adam the milkman, Mr Harley the cowman, John Saunders the farmer. The farm then belonged to the Penn Estate. In the seventeenth century it was still a private house, owned by the Quaker Butterfields who registered it as a public meeting house in 1692, but from about 1725 it became a farm and remained one until a few years ago. (*Edith White, née Saunders*)

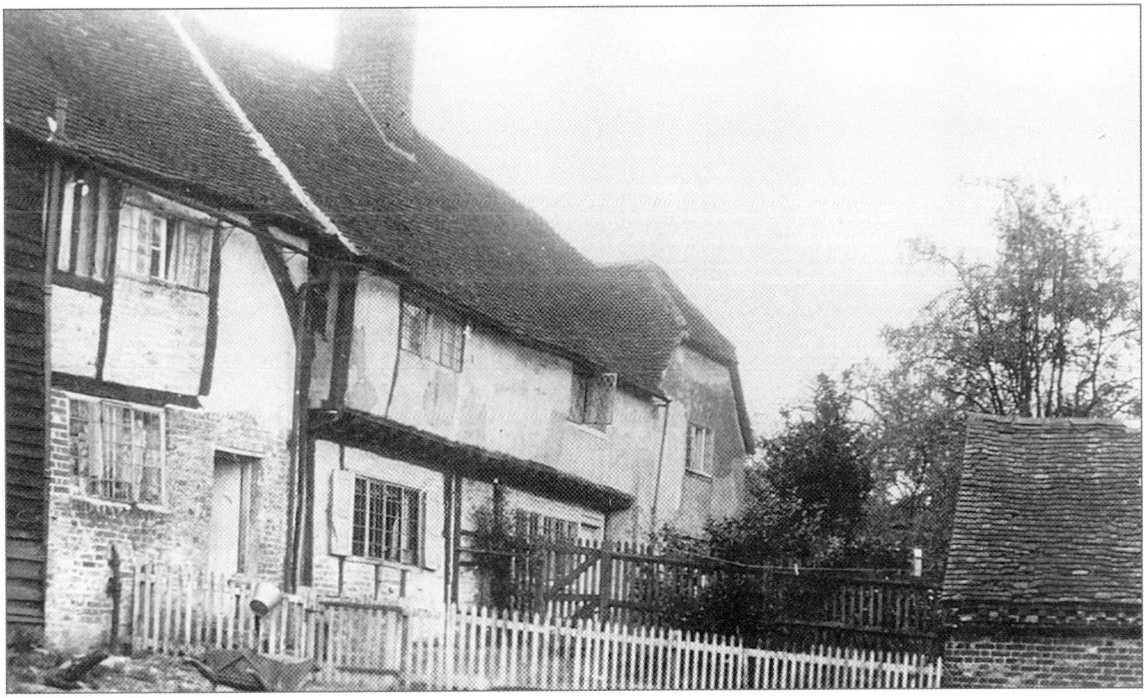

Town Farm, Beacon Hill, 1925. A listed early to mid-sixteenth-century farmhouse, timber-framed with 3-inch wattle and daub, this is the oldest building in Tylers Green. It was recorded in 1185, called Remes or Rhemes, and was owned by the Hospital of St John in Wycombe. In 1531 it was given, with about 200 acres (now the golf course), to the Borough of Chepping Wycombe and hence its name, Town Farm, although the earlier name was still in use in 1691. It was the main source of income for the Borough's charities. (*CWPC*)

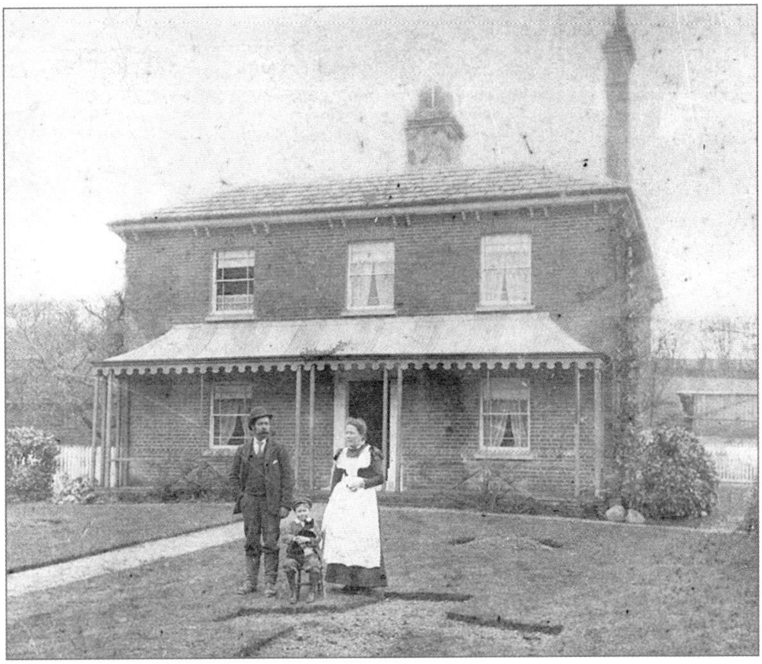

Penn House Farm, with Mr and Mrs Crispin Winter and son Herbert, late 1890s. Mr Winter was Earl Howe's farm bailiff from 1885 to 1905. The listed farmhouse was built following the 1852 enclosure of common land and took over the former Church Knowl Farm buildings. Royal shooting parties lunched here and the house may have been built with that additional use in mind. The 4th and 5th Earls lived here for a time. (*Evelyn Clark, née Winter*)

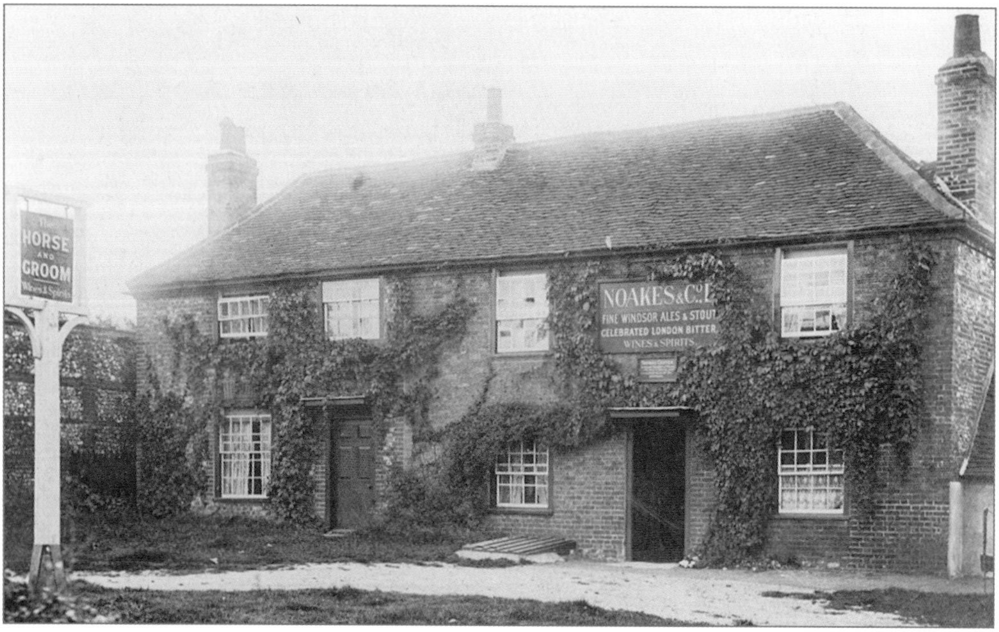

The Horse & Groom, seen here in the early 1900s, was a public house rather than a beer house and was licensed before 1832. The pub is in Tylers Green and the forecourt in Penn. The first Sir Philip Rose roundly condemned the 1830 Beer Act, which first allowed any premises to sell beer without a magistrate's licence. It had encouraged 24,000 new beer houses in three months; this was reflected in the district of St Margaret's where there were six beer houses and four pubs for 187 households, a root cause, Sir Philip maintained, of the prevailing poverty. (*Eric Britnell*)

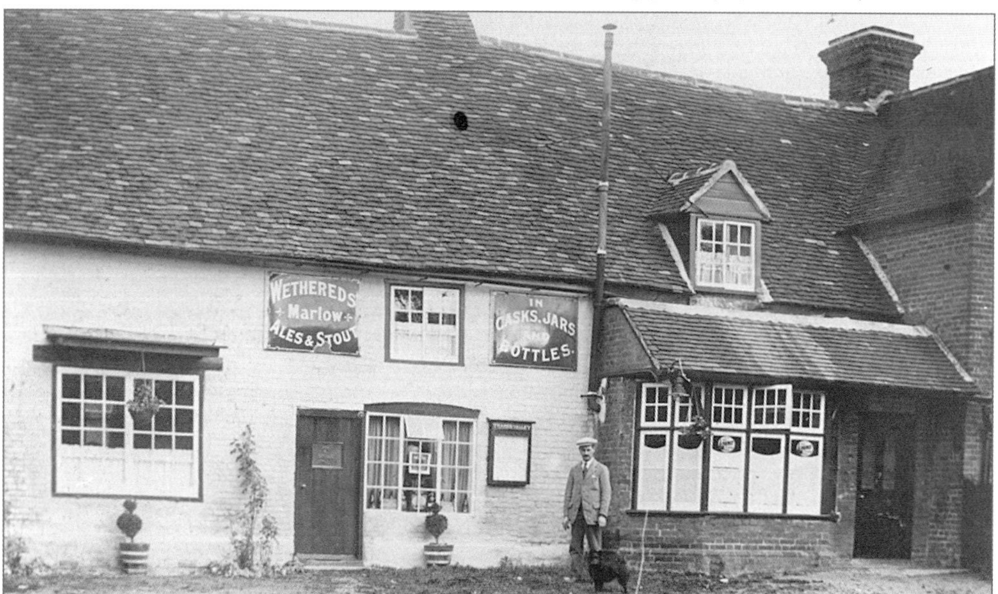

The Queen's Head and Mr Alphabet Ayres, the landlord, 1920s. It is a listed seventeenth-century building and barn, owned in 1666 by a Mayor of Wycombe and physician to Charles II. It first became a pub in 1799 when bought by Wethered's. It had 4 acres of land, once part of Rayners Farm, which has gradually been sold for development, starting with a plot in 1875 for the village school. (*CWPC*)

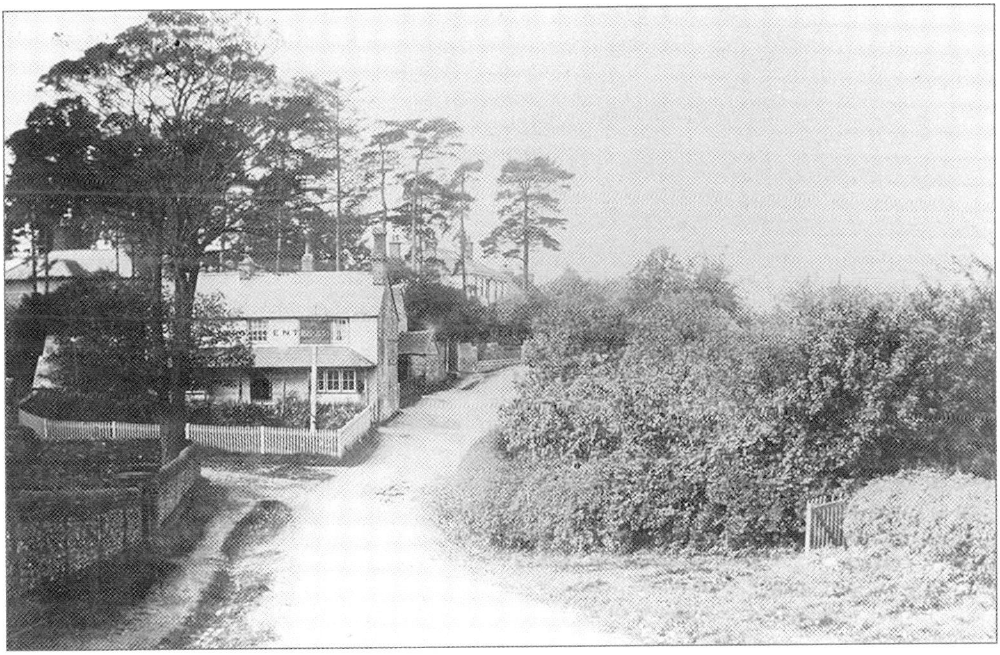

Horse & Jockey, early 1900s. The deeds start with a mortgage in 1837 and a sale in 1842 to Messrs Weller, brewers of Amersham. It was first licensed as a beer house in 1844 as the Horse & Groom. A 1930 conveyance from Weller to Benskin describes it as 'the Horse & Jockey sometimes called the Horse & Groom'. There was already an established Horse & Groom in the village (p. 108). (*CWPC*)

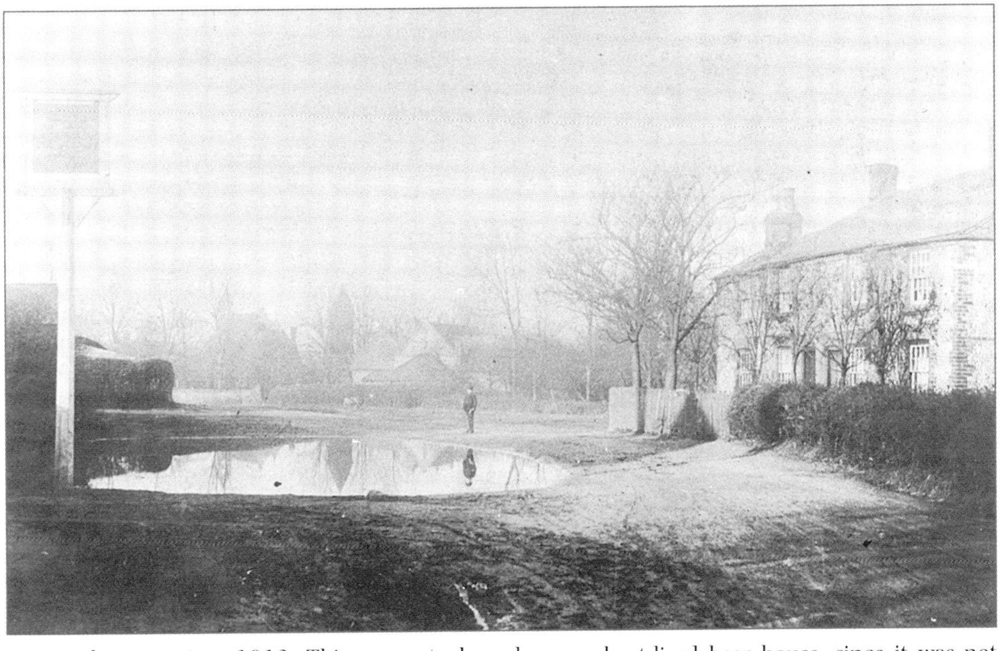

Fox & Pheasant sign, 1913. This seems to have been a short-lived beer house, since it was not licensed in 1872 but was by 1879. The landlord, George Slade, was away for the First World War; when he returned he did not re-open but became a coal merchant and his wife sold sweets. The house was pulled down, in 1936, to make way for the new Village Hall and the pond was filled in at the same time. The footpath behind was known as Slade's Alley. (*Eric Britnell*)

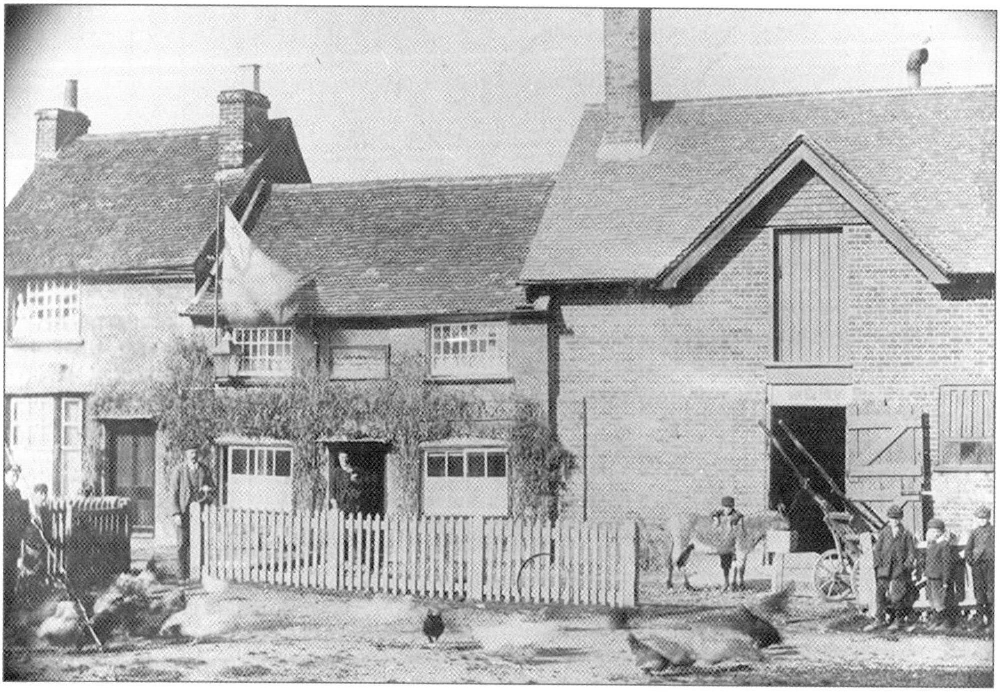

The Old Bell House, early 1900s. The centre cottage was built in 1769 and first licensed as a victualling house that same year. In 1795 it was referred to as 'the name or sign of the Bell'. The left-hand cottage was built in about 1796 and the stable to the right is late Victorian. This is one of the earliest and best documented major encroachments on both Penn and Wycombe commons, in four stages, from 1746 to 1781. It became a private house in 1922. (*CWPC*)

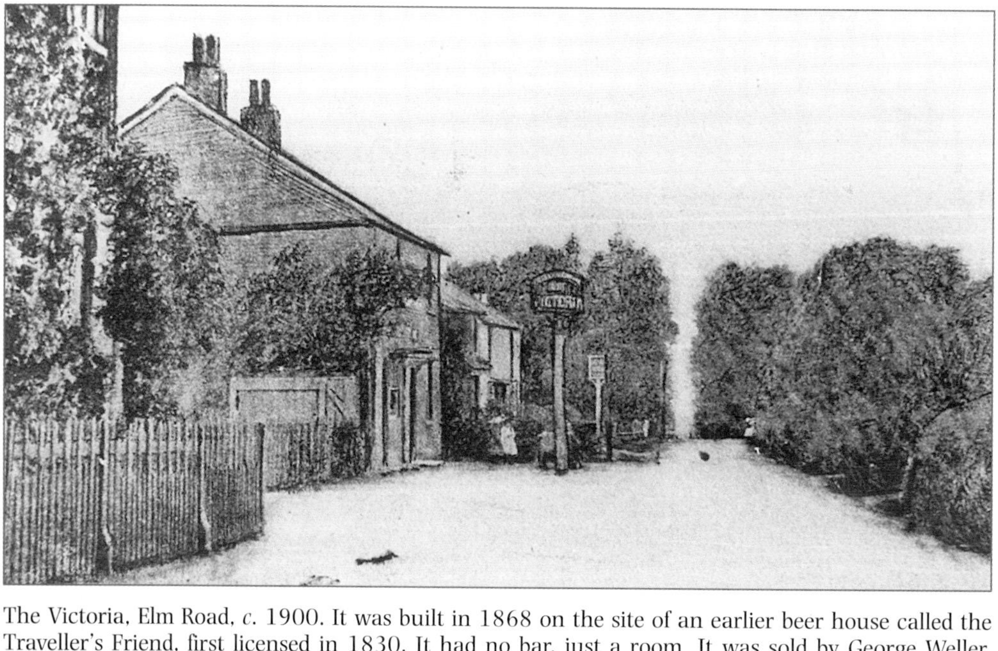

The Victoria, Elm Road, *c.* 1900. It was built in 1868 on the site of an earlier beer house called the Traveller's Friend, first licensed in 1830. It had no bar, just a room. It was sold by George Weller, brewer of Amersham, in 1917, but had ceased to be a beer house some years earlier. It is remembered, briefly, as a grocer's shop from 1906 to 1915. (*CWPC*)

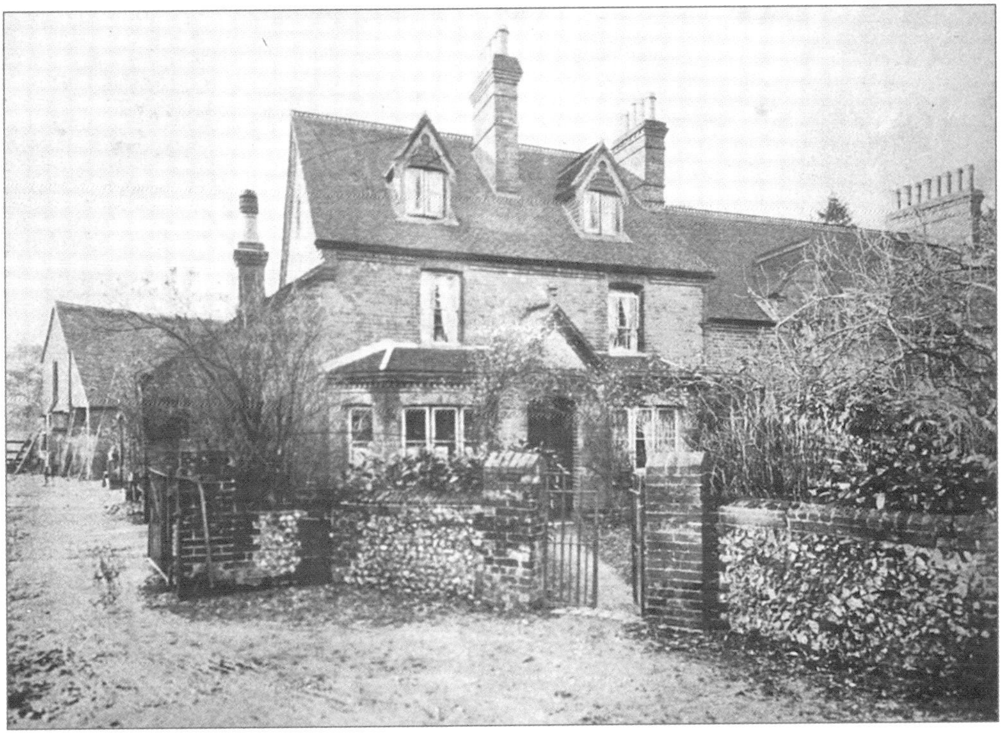

Rosebush, Hammersley Lane, 1920. It was first licensed, in 1830, as a beer house called Rose Cottage. The landlord in 1920 was Mr Thomas Standage, who was also a baker. The pub was sold as part of the Rayners Estate in 1920. It was owned by Wethered's from 1929 to 1958 when it was closed and demolished. Two new houses were built on the site. (*CWPC*)

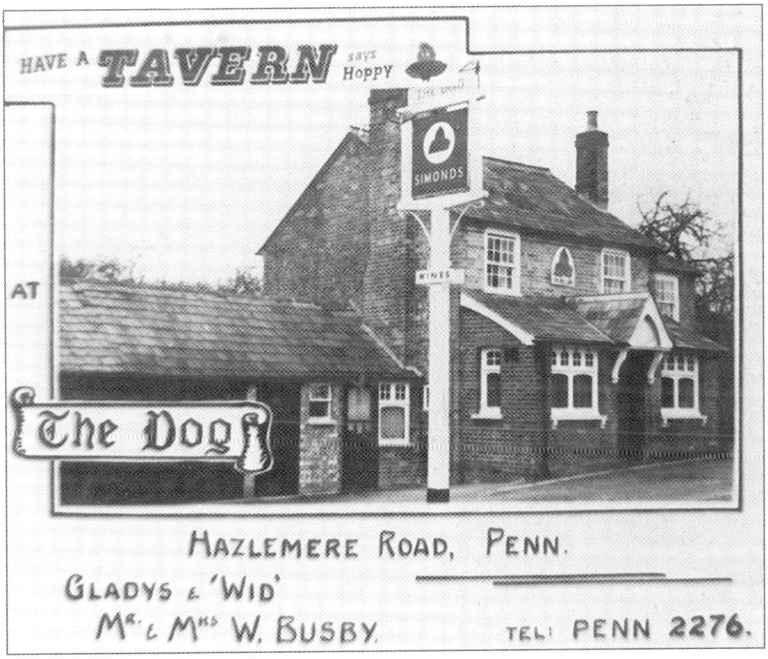

The Dog was a beer house first licensed in 1832, and pulled down in 1965 to make way for Meadow Walk. It gave the name to Dog Hill. In the early 1900s the landlord, Jabez Dennis, made chair legs in the hut at the side. Most landlords had a second occupation of this kind. (*CWPC*)

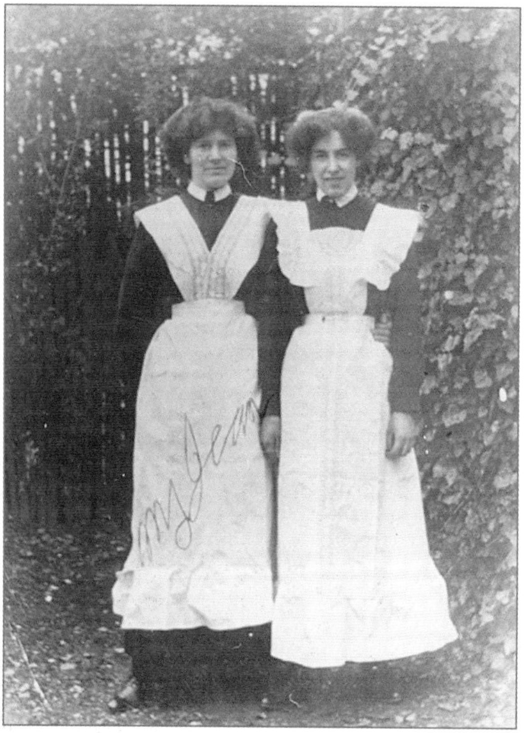

Parlour maid and house maid outside The Knoll, Paul's Hill, *c.* 1912. This was the 'pretty house' built by Sir John Curzon for his son in about 1672. In 1912 it was still owned by Earl Howe but tenanted by Mrs Capel Hanbury. Jean Sims (left) later married William Woodbridge and Edith Bell later married George Woods. Both are buried in St Margaret's churchyard. (*Brian Randall*)

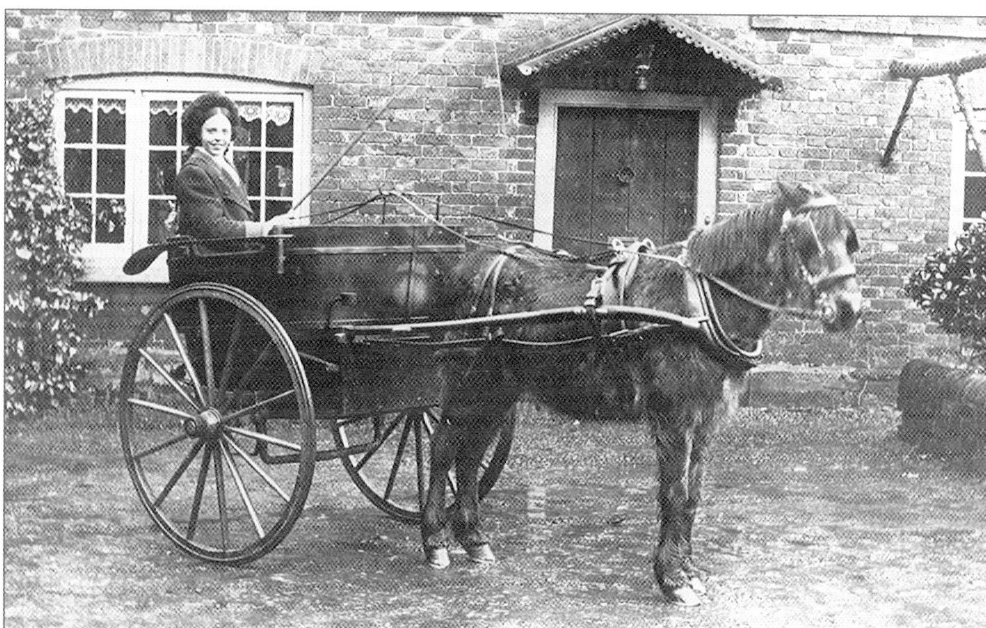

Violet Rayner outside Cotters Barn, Elm Road, in a trap, 1913. She was the niece of Mr Reid, the jobmaster, who ran the horse bus service to Beaconsfield station from the barn near Widmer Pond. He went in the morning and evening, at first in an open wagonette with facing seats. The pony and trap were also on hire with Violet Rayner, who was 'excellent with horses and . . . had a slight stammer'. (*Harold Wheeler*)

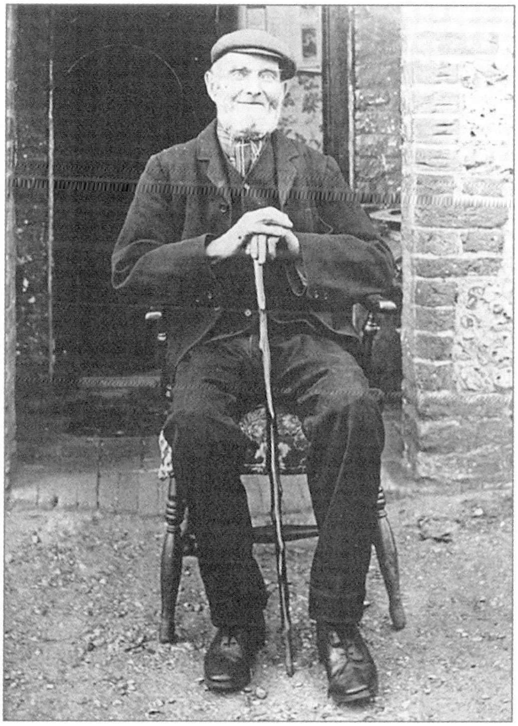

Mr Dover outside his cottage (now Kenilworth) in Elm Road, *c.* 1900. He was born in the 1820s and was keeper/woodman on the Penn Estate. The cottages were built in 1848 and his family moved in soon afterwards. (*Fred Payne*)

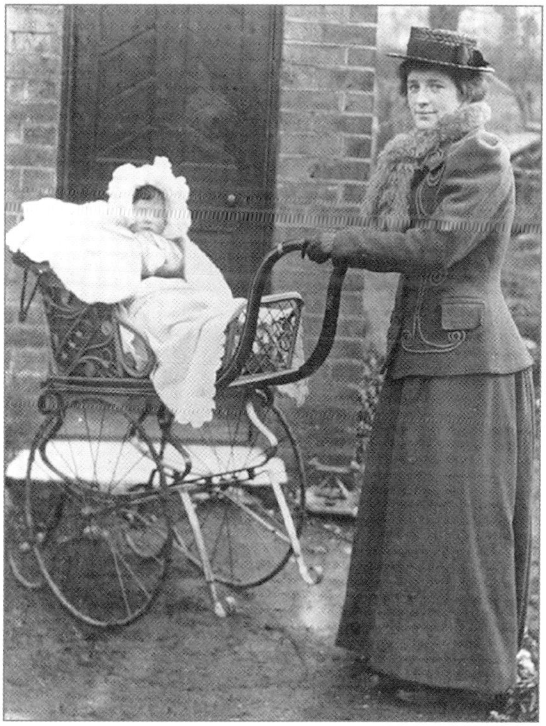

Emily Pusey with her sister Florence outside their home at 5 New Road, known as Muddy Bottom, *c.* 1903. Edith White (née Saunders) lived at no. 11 in the adjoining pair of cottages (rent *2s 6d* per week). She remembers the Potters Cross ponds continually overflowing into the road and the doctor insisting they should come out of that damp, unhealthy bottom. (*CWPC*)

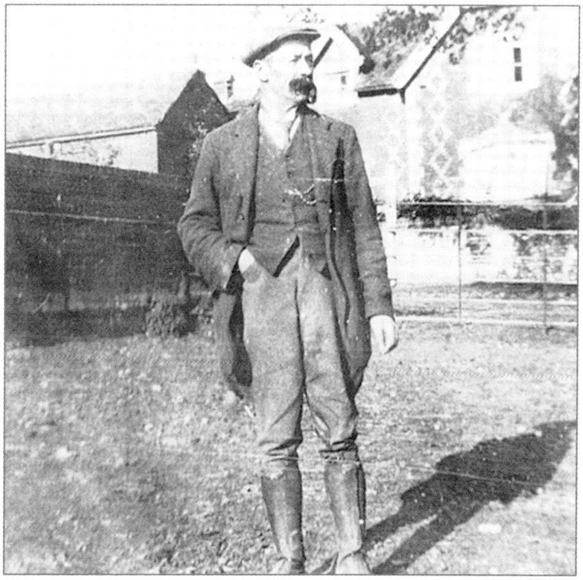

Mr Crispin Winter, early 1900s. He was farm bailiff to Sir Philip Rose at Colehatch Farm, Hammersley Lane (1905–20) and had previously been bailiff to the Penn Estate (1885–1905). The farmhouse in the background was newly built by Sir Philip when he bought the farm in 1845. (*Evelyn Clark*)

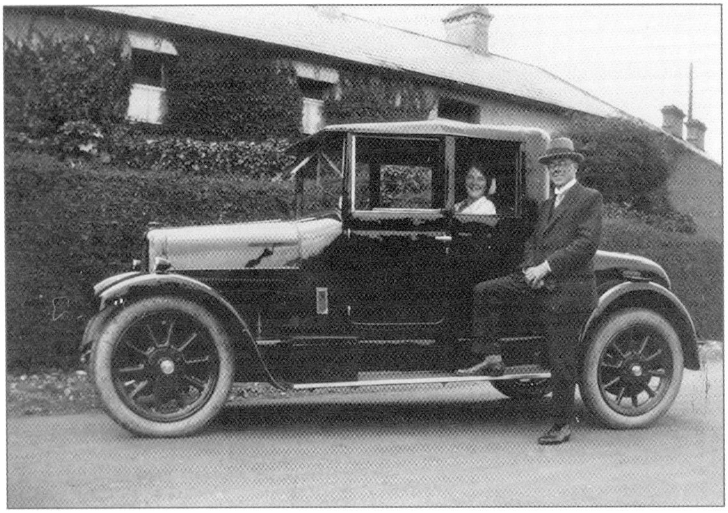

Dr C.S. Wynne, the visiting doctor from Amersham, 1920s. He used to come in a pony and trap, later a motorbike, and then a two-seater car. His surgery was a corrugated-iron hut at the end of School Road near the Parish Rooms. The fee, for those who could afford it, was *7s 6d* a visit. In 1927 he was succeeded by Dr Richard Starkey, also from Amersham. Dr A.J. Milner established a surgery at Tyler Cottage in 1939 and then in his own house, Tylers Green House. In 1951 he was joined by Dr Robin Horn who moved the surgery, first to Madryn (34 School Road) from 1960 to 1969, then to the present Penn Surgery which was opened in 1969, replacing a barber's and a ladies' hairdressers'. (*Pat Cuthbert*)

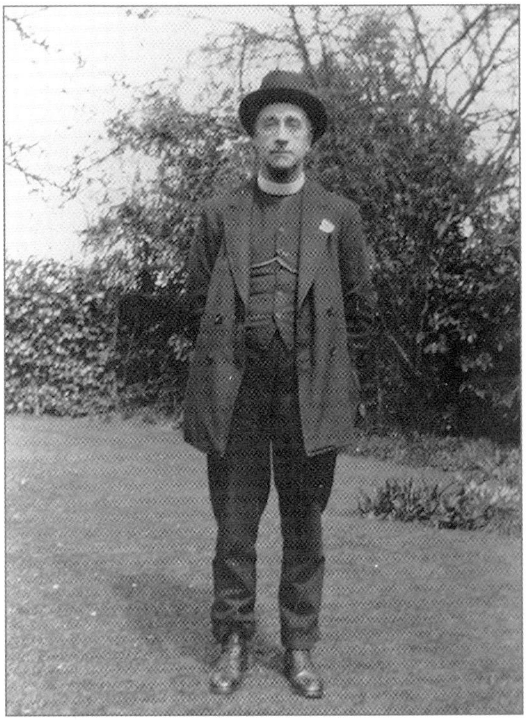

The Revd E A. Smith, Vicar of Penn 1922–37, seen here in the 1920s. He was 'High Church' and added an elaborate surround (a reredos) to the formerly plain altar table. This in turn hid the lower part of the east window and so required a new shorter east window, which was duly installed in 1931. (*Pat Cuthbert*)

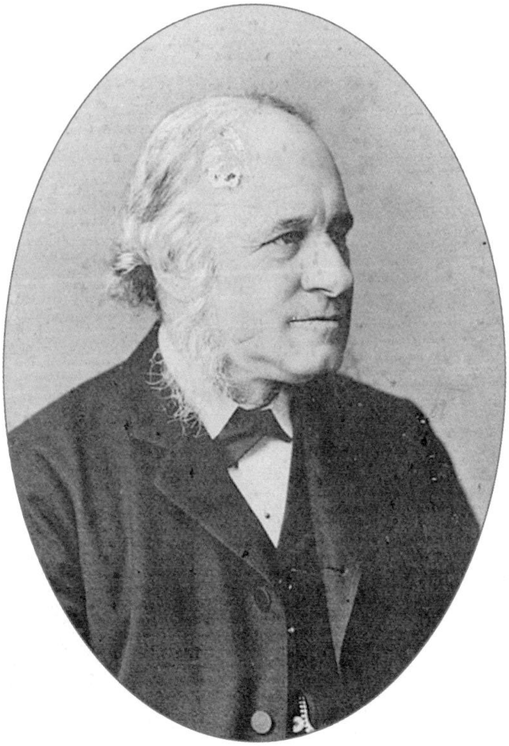

Sir George Grove (1820–1900), was a son of Thomas Grove who, with his brother John, had set up as a London fishmonger and so restored the family fortunes in Penn. George was born and lived in London but visited Penn and eventually inherited the Grove estate in 1897. He was one of the great Victorians: a civil engineer, administrator, archaeologist, musicologist, editor, lexicographer, educator and author. He projected and edited the *Grove Dictionary of Music and Musicians*, which runs to this day. (*Caroline Weeks*)

Tom Burrows, *c.* 1925. His family owned Burrows Nursery in Hazlemere Road. He was blind but wove baskets with great dexterity in his workshop by Pistles Pond in Beacon Hill. He is remembered walking fearlessly and unhesitatingly through the village, expertly tending the oil lamps in St Margaret's Church without spilling a drop, and ringing the tubular bells with great skill. (*CWPC*)

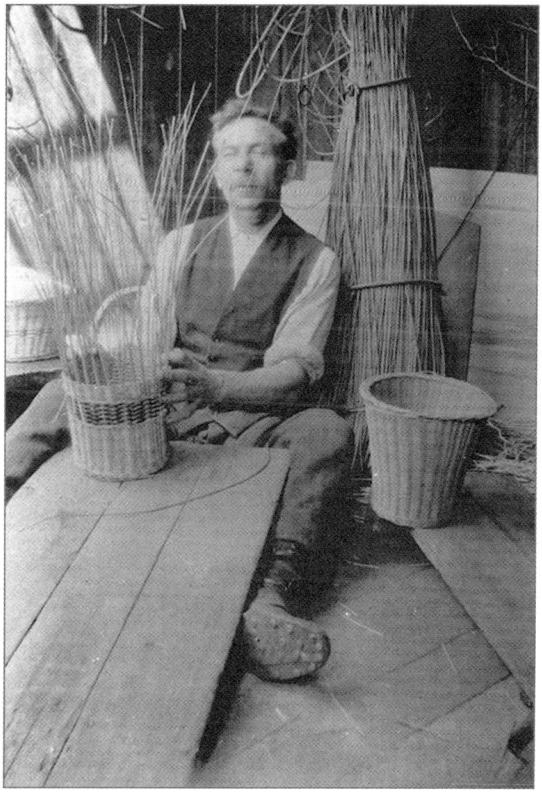

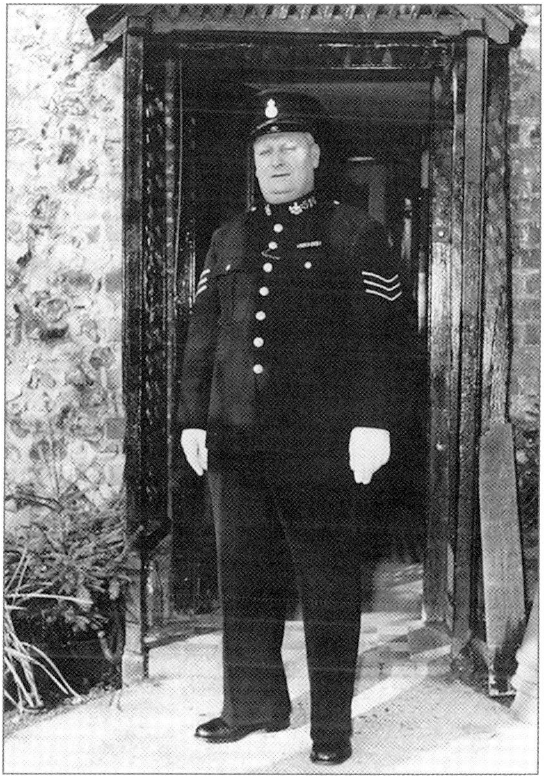

Harry Busby (1907–94) at the door of Nursery Cottage, *c.* 1970. He had inherited the cottage with the nursery in 1953. He went to the Royal Grammar School and was very musical, playing the tenor horn and cornet in the P&TG Brass Band and was in the choir of the Methodist chapel at Hazlemere where he met his wife. He was a Special Constable from 1942 to 1972, reaching the rank of sergeant. (*David Busby*)

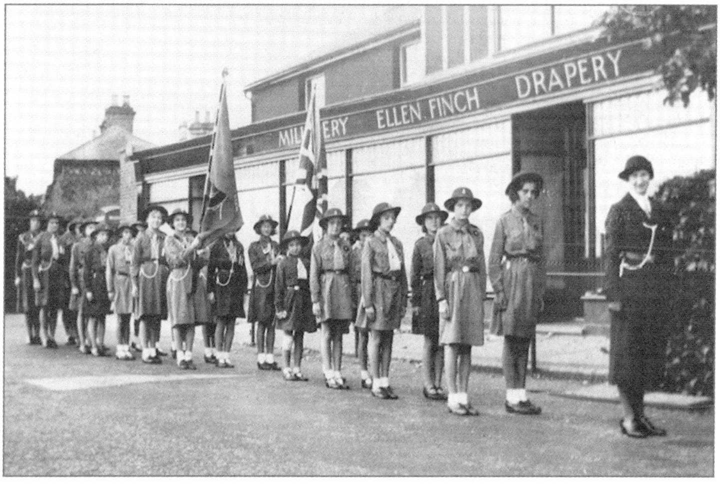

Penn and Tylers Green Guides on a church parade, probably for Armistice Day when they used to march to St Margaret's with ex-Servicemen and the local brass band, *c.* 1940. The guides were started in 1922 by the two Beattie sisters, who lived in New Road, Dorothea (captain) and Norah (lieutenant.) who stayed in charge for thirty years. They met in the Parish Room. (*CWPC*)

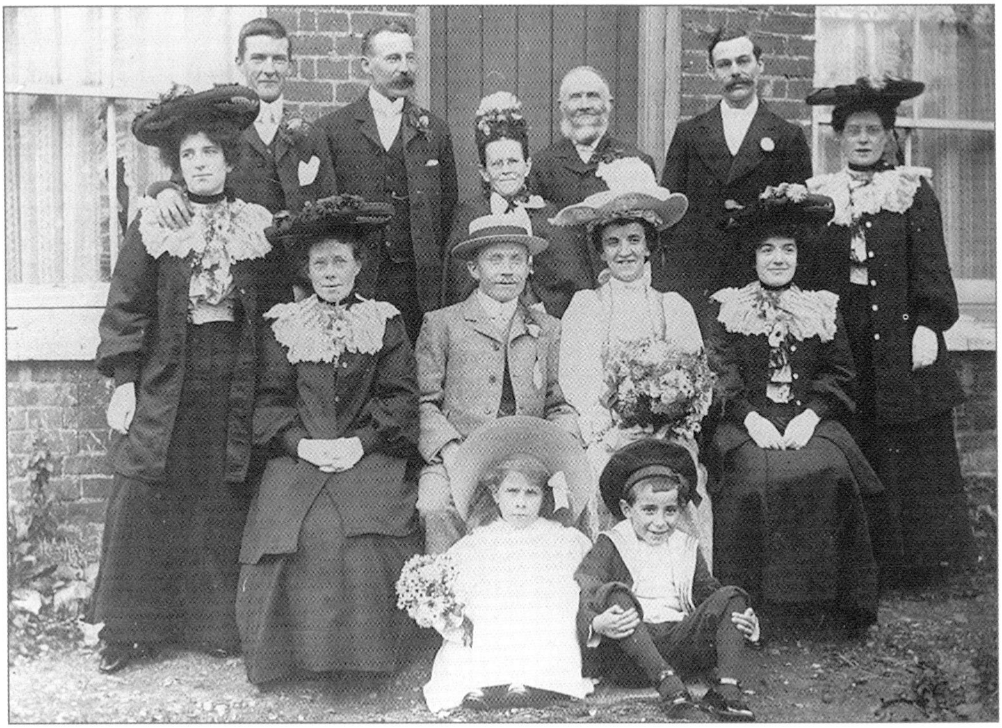

Wedding party for Billy Simmonds and Mrs Ada Barnes, a widow, early 1900s. They lived in Eastleigh on the back common. He was a blacksmith at Walter Evans'/Slade's, Beacon Hill, played the cornet in the brass band and taught Methodist Sunday School. After the First World War Mrs Barnes's son, Len, set up a shoe repair shop in an army surplus hut adjoining Eastleigh. (*CWPC*)

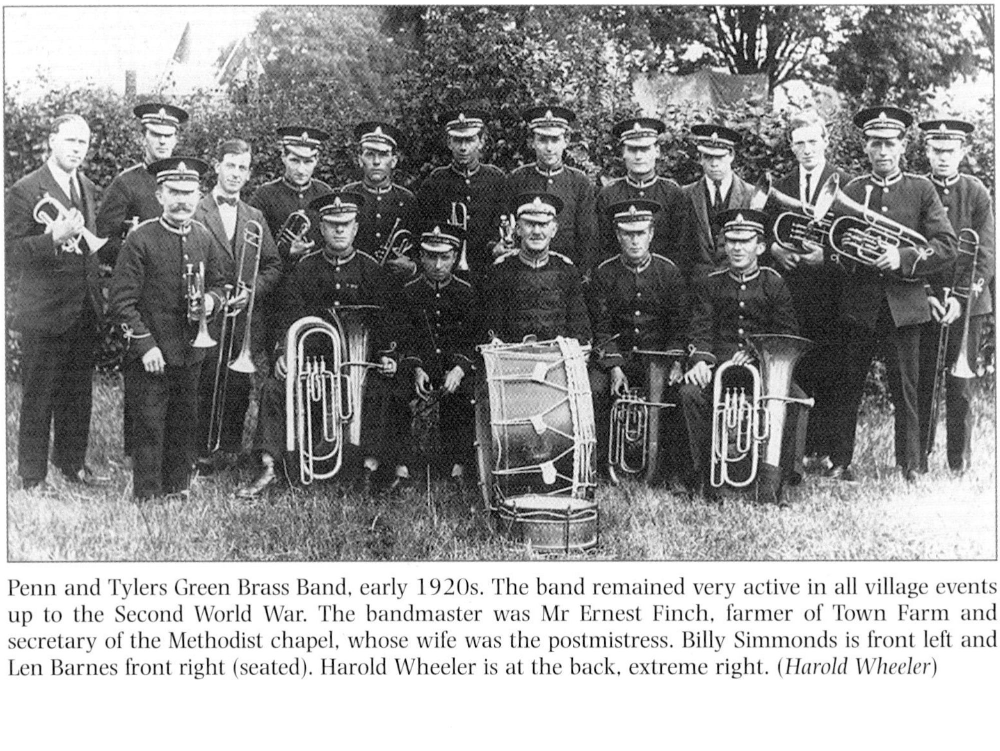

Penn and Tylers Green Brass Band, early 1920s. The band remained very active in all village events up to the Second World War. The bandmaster was Mr Ernest Finch, farmer of Town Farm and secretary of the Methodist chapel, whose wife was the postmistress. Billy Simmonds is front left and Len Barnes front right (seated). Harold Wheeler is at the back, extreme right. (*Harold Wheeler*)

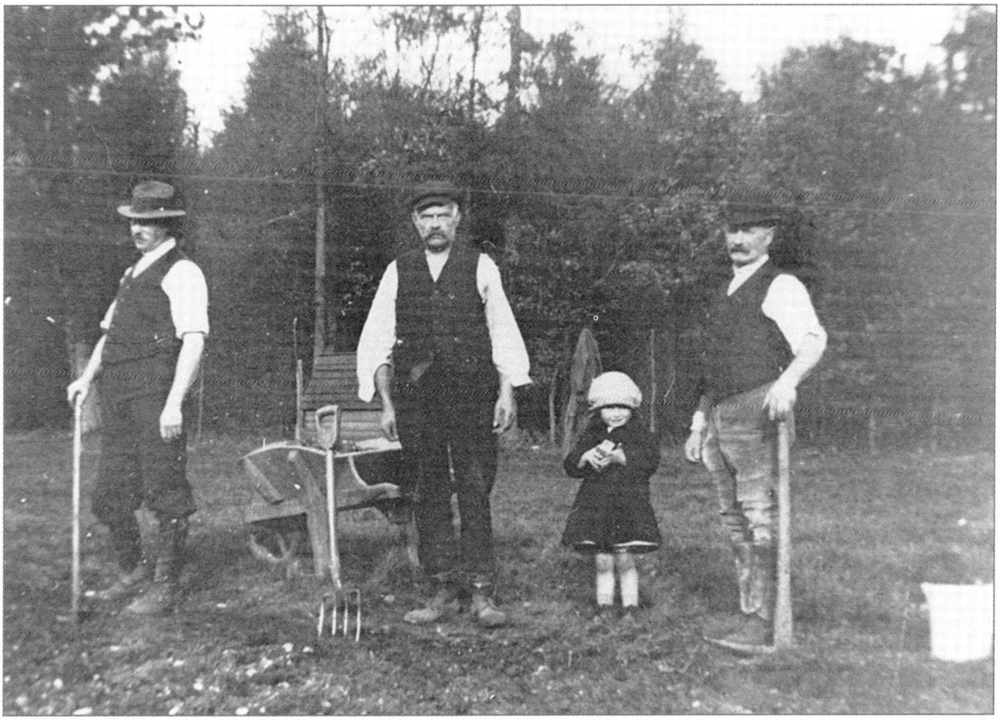

Members of the Weedon family on their plot in Hazlemere Road, opposite their house, Yew Trees, *c.* 1900. The trilby hat helps date the photograph. It was named after the hat worn in the play of the novel *Trilby* by George du Maurier, published in 1894. (*CWPC*)

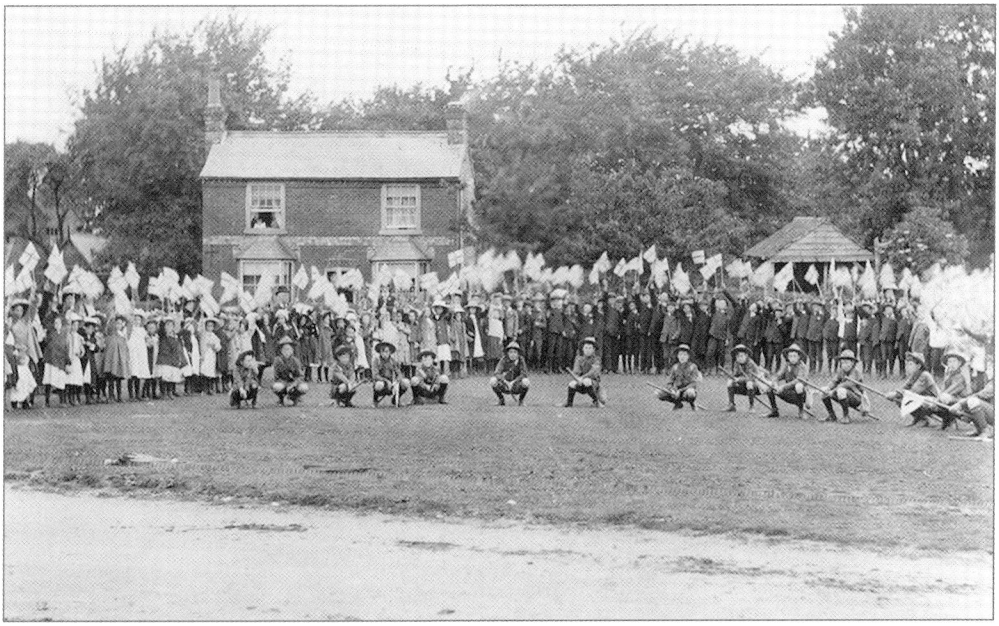

Presumably this is a celebration of the Coronation of George V, 1911. It is on the common directly in front of the school with Hawthorne Cottage behind. The Scout movement was only started by Baden Powell in 1908, so our local Scouts were newly formed. (*CWPC*)

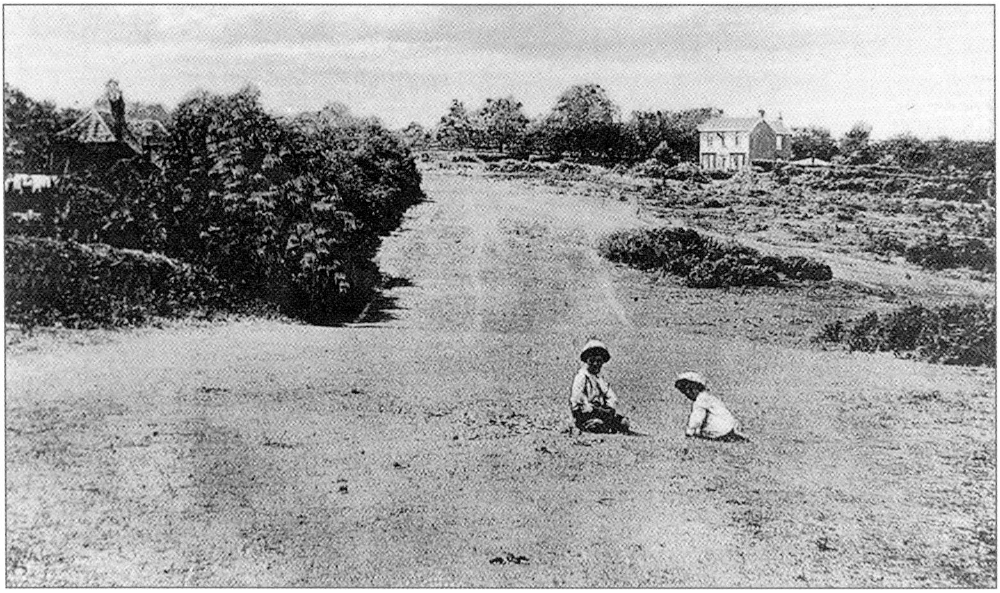

The back common from the track looking south towards the White House (though it is not visible), with Lost Cottage on the left and Mr Silvey's house (no longer there) set back from New Road on the right, *c.* 1915. The common was kept open by grazing, by collecting 'fuzzies' for firewood and by the frequent, unlawful fires lit by boys, often at night. Holidaying London boys were blamed in 1892. There were many fires after the Relief of Mafeking in 1901. (*CWPC*)

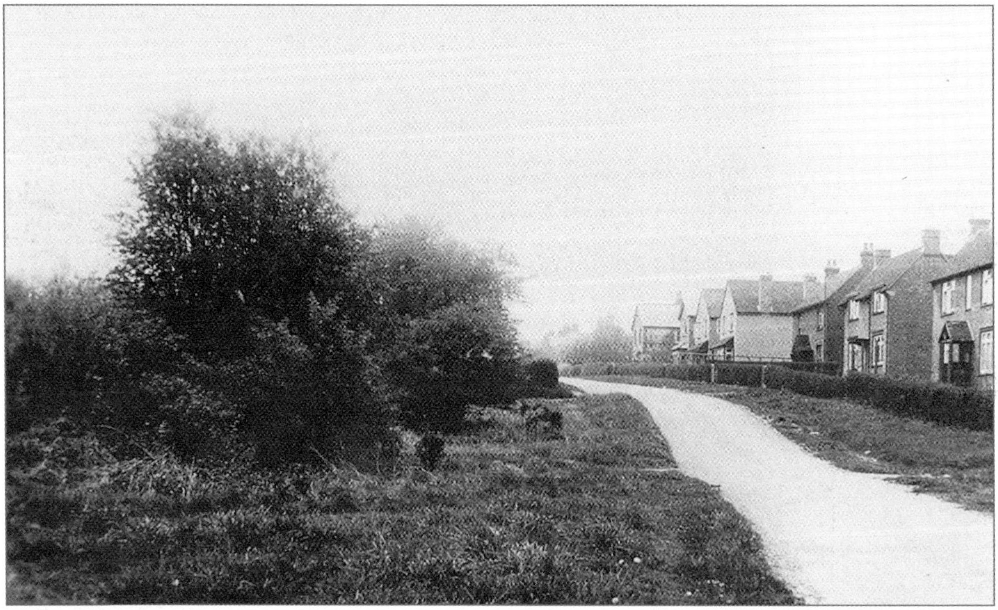

New Road, photographed from opposite where Ashley Drive is now, *c.* 1933. It was called 'New' Road because it was first set out as a '30 foot public carriage road' by the Inclosure Award of St John's Wood, in 1868. St John's Wood, owned by the Crown for two centuries, was part of Wycombe Heath and was divided up into plots allotted to existing landowners instead of their previous rights of common. The houses in the picture were built (1925–30) on roadside 'allotments'. (*Jack Wheeler*)

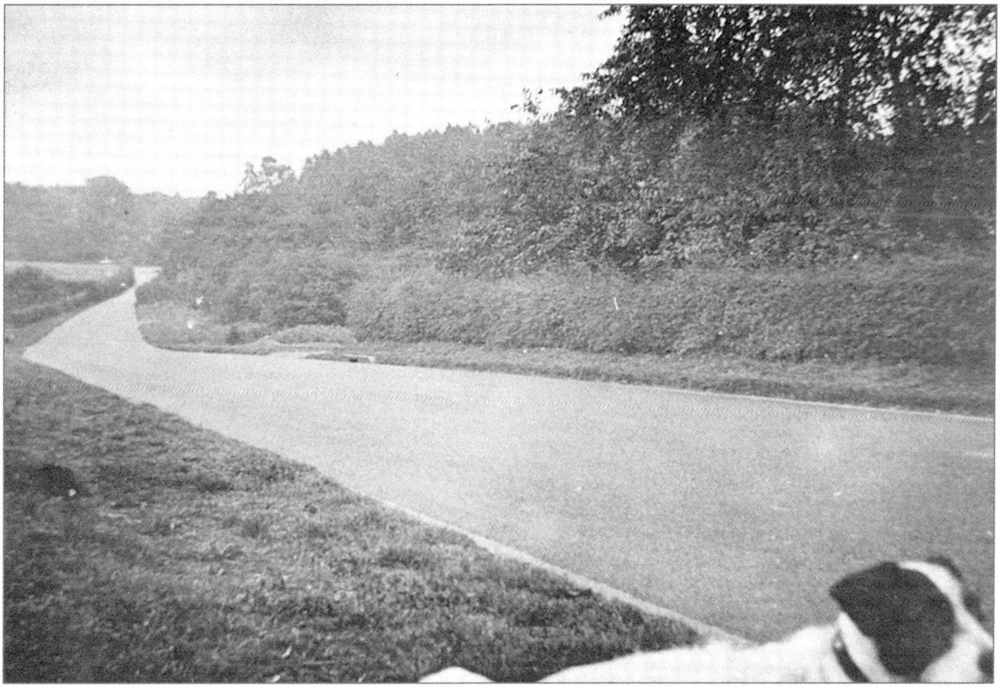

Muddy Bottom or Potters Lane Bottom, *c.* 1930. The photograph was taken from 50 yards above where Ashley Drive was built thirty years later. It was a muddy, swampy cart track across Tylers Green common with only two pairs of late Victorian cottages at the Potters Cross end. In 1927, after a public meeting, Wycombe Rural District Council took over the track, widened it and made it up as a public highway as an extension of New Road, at a cost of £1,510. (*Jack Wheeler*)

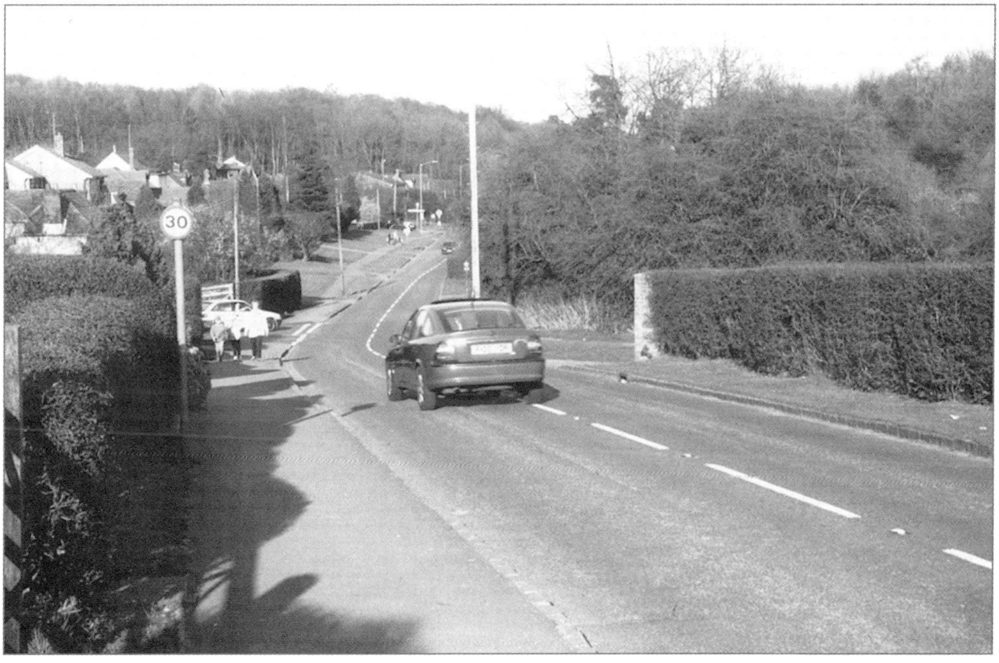

A modern view. (*Eddie Morton*)

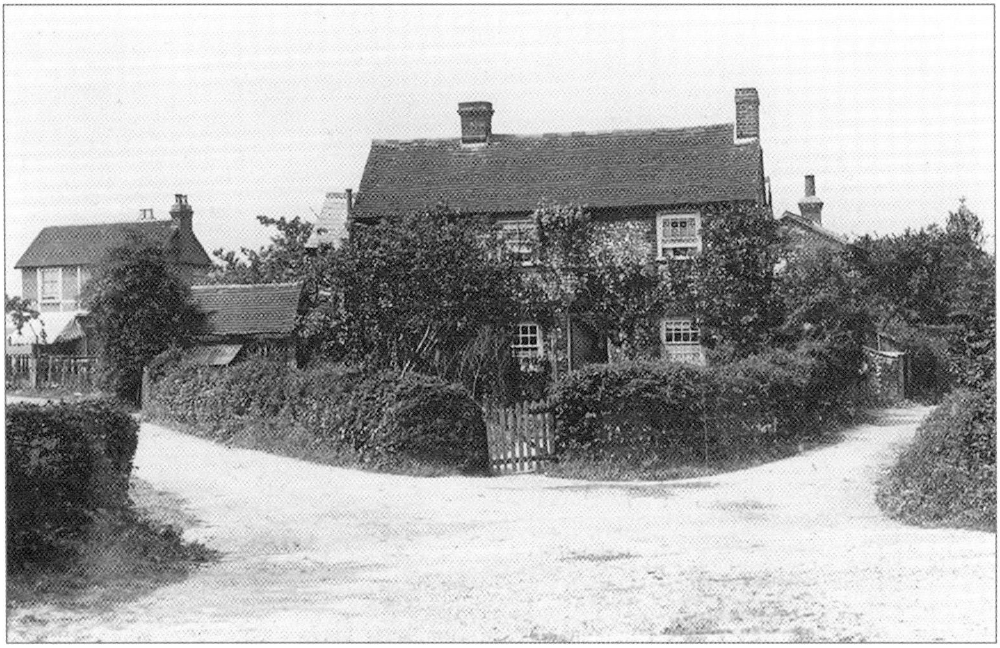

This photograph was taken in the 1930s from the side of the present carpet shop (Byzantium) looking down the track to the left to the present post office, and to the right along the footpath which goes along the side of the Old Bell House garden towards the back common. The cottage was occupied in the 1930s by Mrs Sarah Lacey who sold sweets. It was pulled down in the late 1930s. (*Anthony Ainslie*)

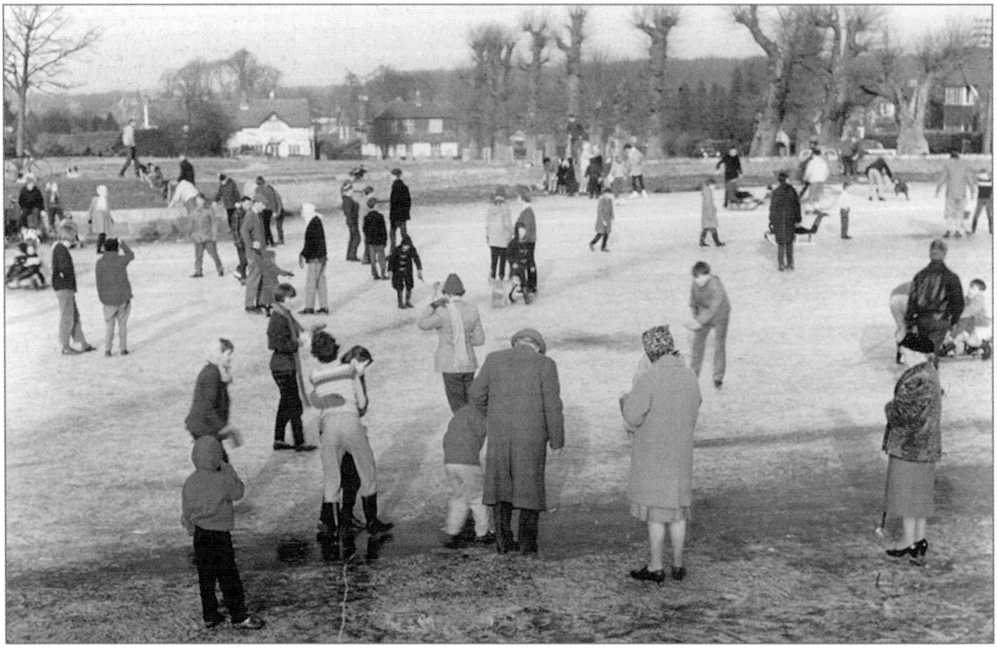

Skating on Widmer Pond, 1963. It was a particularly cold winter when rivers and ponds remained frozen solid for weeks on end. (*Geoffrey Perfect*)

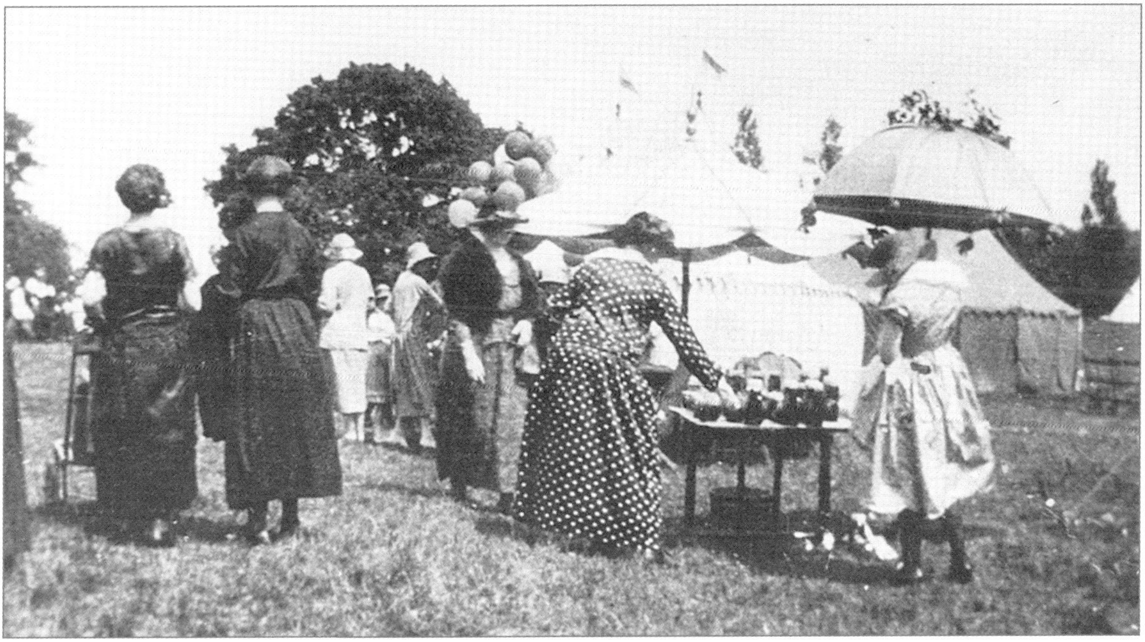

A fête, early 1900s. The fence to the right shows it was not on the common as was first thought. Before the Second World War most fêtes were held in Vicarage Meadow, or in fields off Hammersley Lane or Beacon Hill. Can anyone add any detail? (*CWPC*)

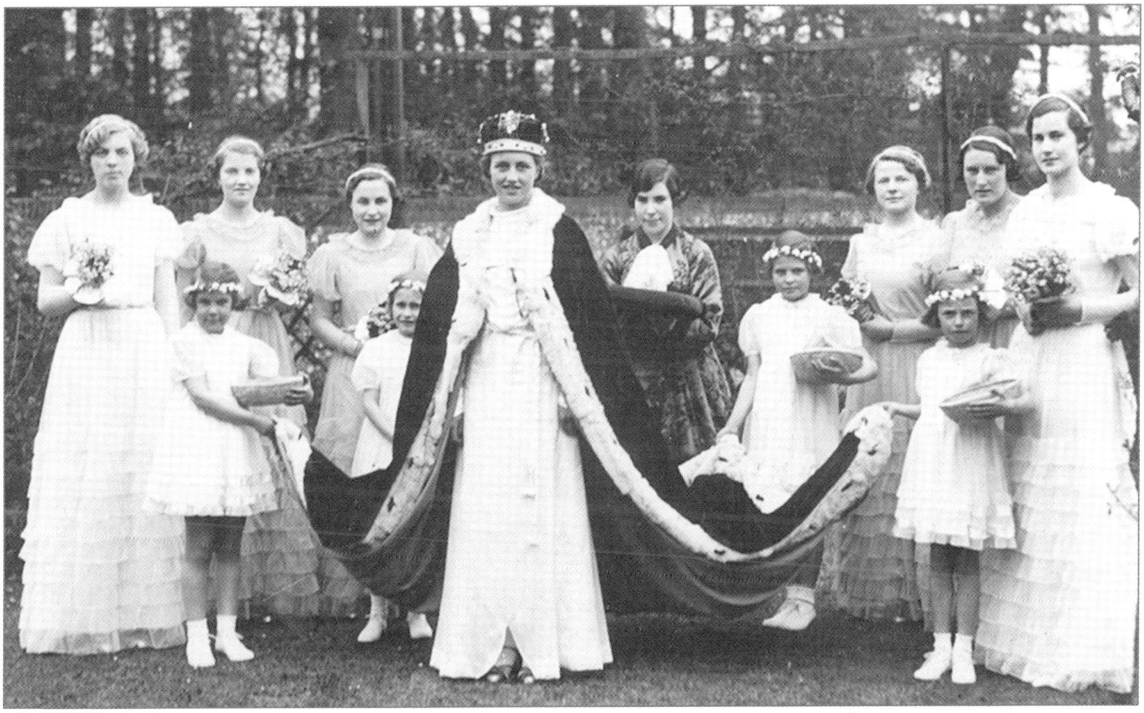

Coronation Queen, Molly Weedon, with her Court, 1937. Back row, left to right: Rene Randall, Evelyn Jones, Audrey Walcroft, Ann Simmonds, Laura Parrott, Nora Woodbridge, Sylvia Clark. Children: Joan Charlott, Doreen Meeks, June Hawes, Margery Burden. (*CWPC*)

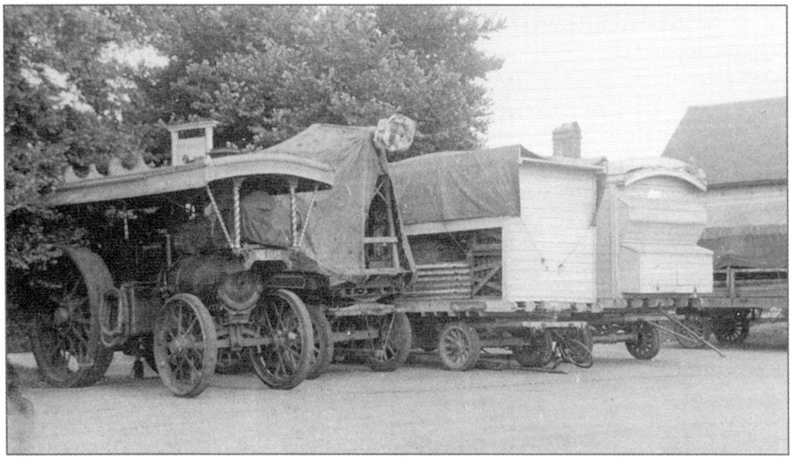

Fair vehicles parked outside the Red Lion waiting to move on to the common, 1941. They all belonged to Miss Sally Beach and were pulled by the Burrell showman's road locomotive, 'Lord Fisher', on the left. The next three trailers are all for the 'gallopers', with swing boats on the right. They featured in Alison Uttley's story, 'Merry-go-Round', in her book *Magic In My Pocket* (1957). (*P. Bradley*)

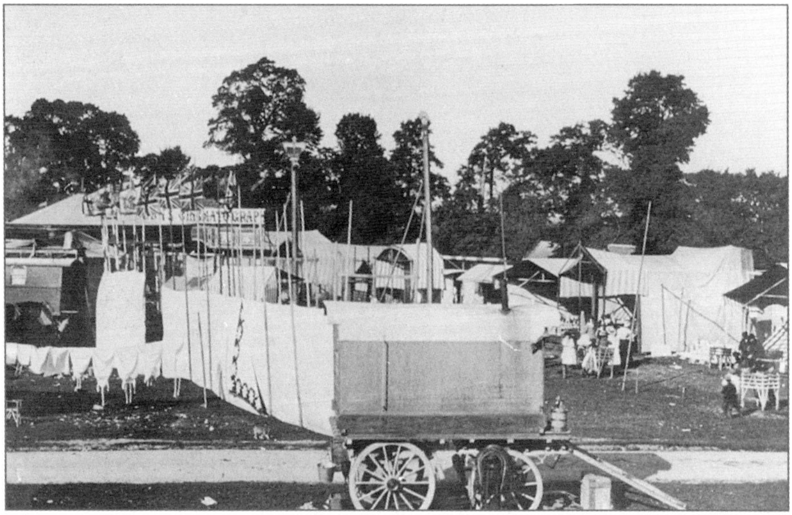

Penn Fair, with the elms of Elm Road in the background, *c.* 1908. This is the earliest photograph of the fair and may have been taken in September 1902, since one of the flags appears to be a still new coronation flag. The vehicles were all horse drawn. Billy Matthews's Steam Galloping Horses are on the far left, next to the cinematograph which brought the first flickering moving pictures. (*copy by Ron Goodearl from Stuart King's collection*)

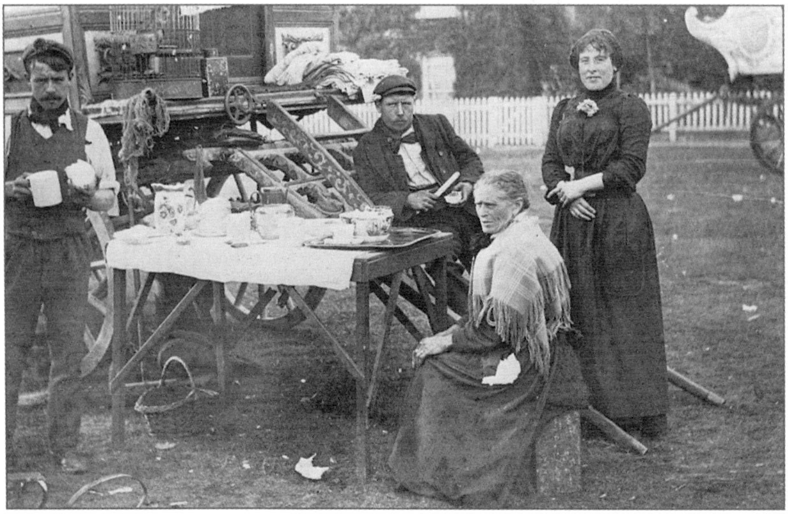

The family of Billy 'Redshirt' Matthews in front of Jasmine Cottage on the front common, *c.* 1908. Mrs Matthews is with her son and daughter. The man on the left is unknown. The fair is first recorded in the school log of 1874 but it is not known when it started. It has to be held on 17 September and on the day before or after, unless it is a Sunday. (*Peter Barnes*)

Mrs Edith White (née Saunders, b. 1894) in the uniform of the Navy & Army Canteen Board (now NAAFI) in the First World War, 1916. A video has been made of her memories, which include walking to Beaconsfield before the railway was built in 1906 and her time as housekeeper in the Penn Institute Reading Room from 1928 to 1960. She lived for a few years in Muddy Bottom until advised by her doctor 'to come out of that Bottom!' Five generations of her family have been to the village school. (*E. White*)

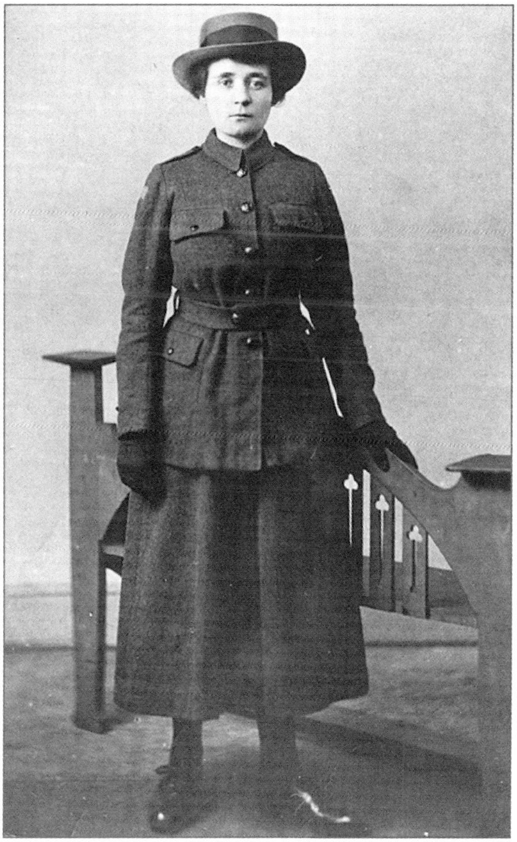

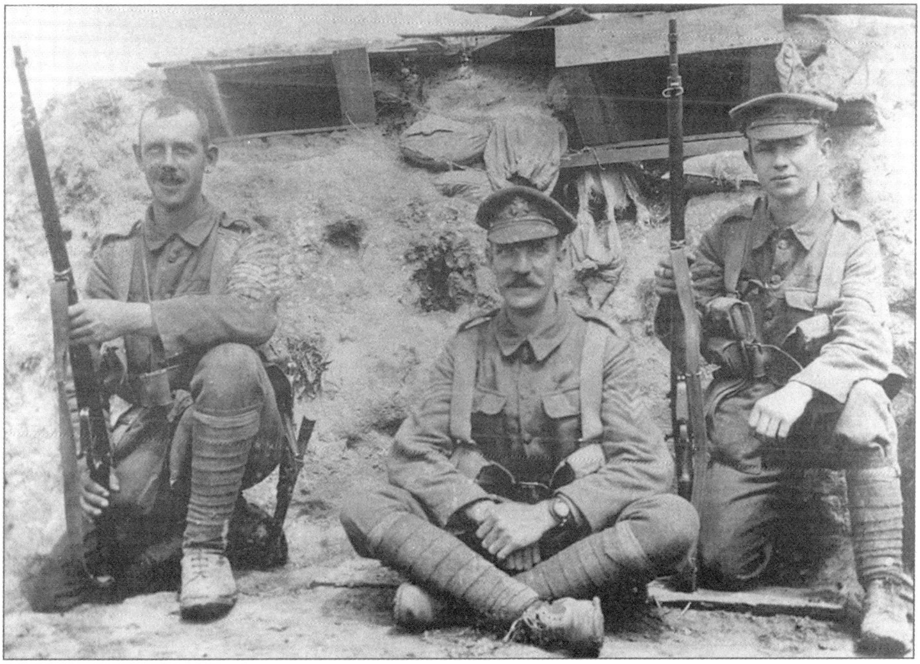

In the trenches in the First World War, 1915. Edith White's husband John is on the right wearing a hat. He was a Wycombe chairmaker and they married in 1915. (*E. White*)

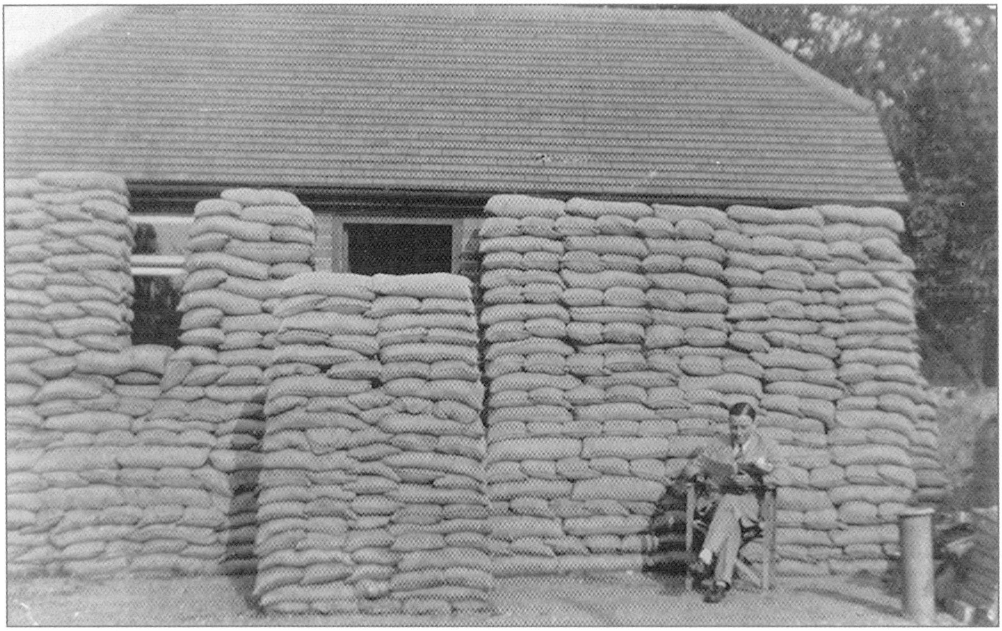

E.J. West's office in Hazlemere Road, opposite the present Coppice Farm Road, September 1938. Mr West was a local man, played in the brass band, became both a Penn and Chepping Wycombe Parish Councillor and was later Clerk of CWPC (1950–71). He was the head warden for Air Raid Precautions (ARP) and his office was the area command post with the siren. There was a searchlight at Rushmoor Corner. Several bombs fell on 1 October 1940, at Rushmoor Corner, in Manor Road, and off Hammersely Lane below the Danes. (*CWPC*)

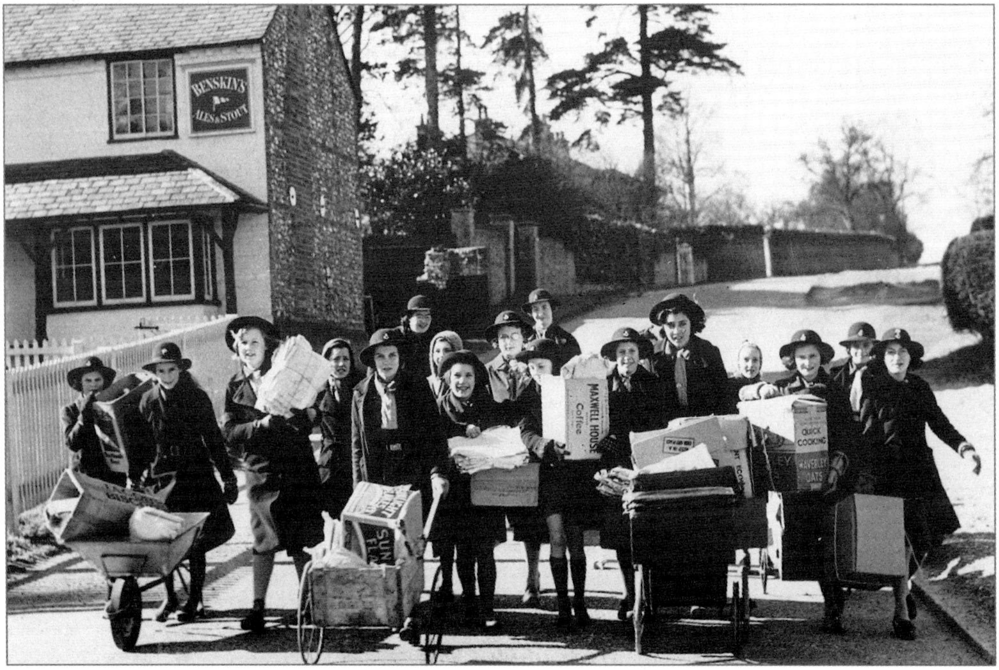

Girl guides collected cardboard boxes and waste paper from all the houses in the village every Saturday during the Second World War, seen here in the early 1940s. (*Norah Beattie*)

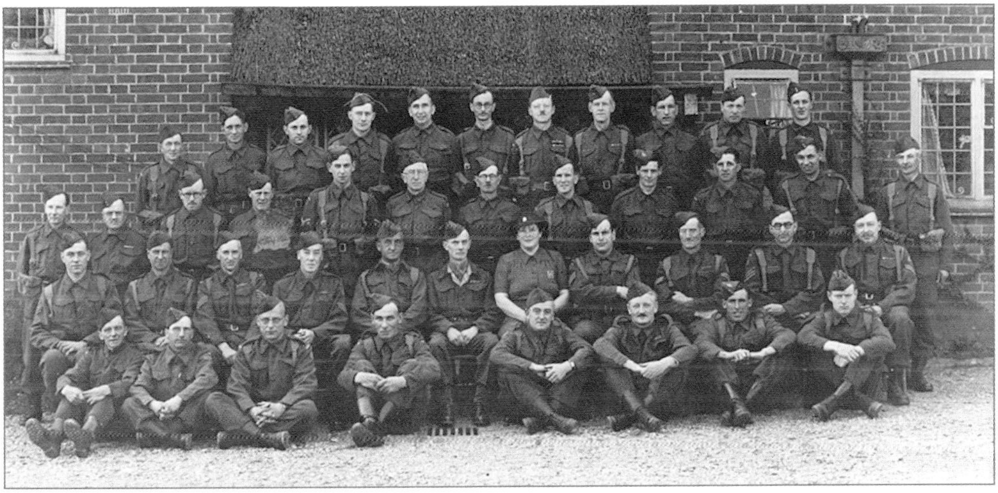

Home Guard outside Hatchits, Paul's Hill, the home of Lt S.A. Jollye, the Platoon Commander, *c.* 1944. When first raised as Local Defence Volunteers (LDV) at the time of Dunkirk, in 1940, they had only shotguns and armbands and some were well over seventy years old. They patrolled on bicycles every night and there were night observation posts on Penn Church tower and Beacon Hill. Rifles, sten guns and a Lewis machine gun were eventually issued and were kept in the hall of Hatchits with Mills bombs in the garage. The Home Guard, when disbanded in 1944, had become a well-organised and highly efficient unit. (*Betty Jollye*)

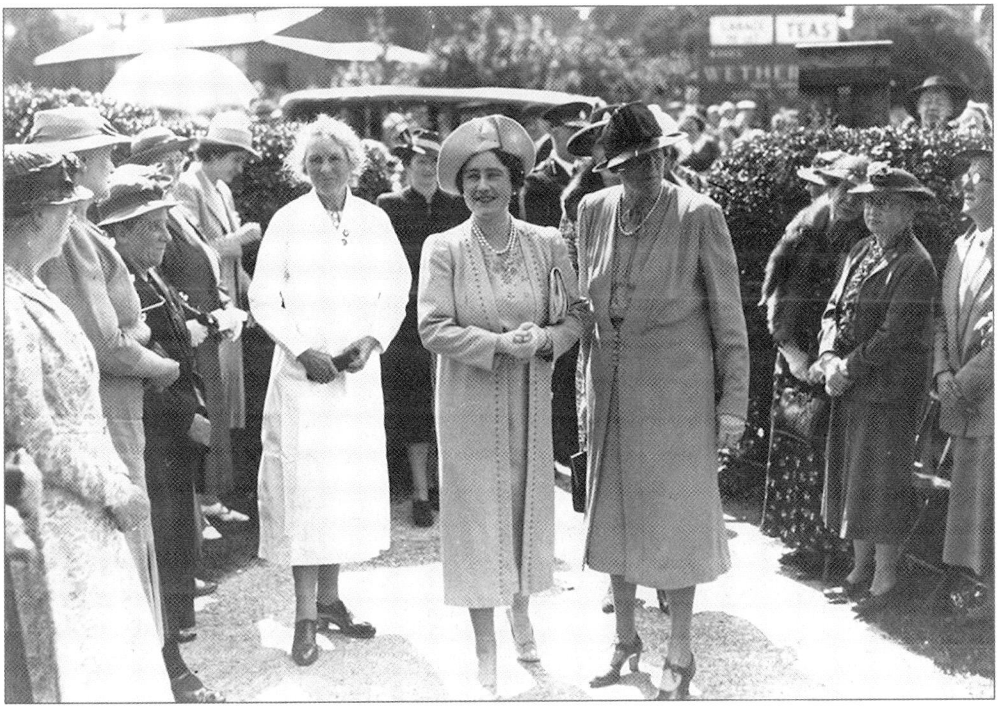

Visit of Queen Elizabeth to the Parish Room to see the WI jam-making centre, 29 July 1940. Mrs Nora Cuthbert, in the white coat, is to the left with her daughter Pat Cuthbert behind her, looking down. The WI had about 160 members at the time. 'I have been thrilled with what I have seen', said the Queen. Mrs Cuthbert was the first woman to stand (unsuccessfully) for election to Penn Parish Council in 1913. (*Pat Cuthbert*)

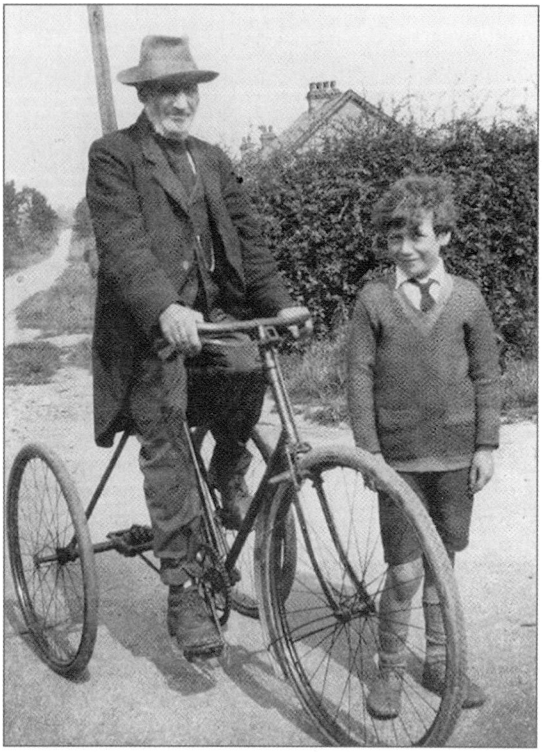

Mr Rodway on his tricycle at the junction of St John's Road and New Road with Georgie Knight beside him, *c.* 1920. Mr Rodway lodged in Victoria Cottages, Elm Road, and was a farm labourer at Inkerman Farm. George Knight (born *c.* 1912) lived in half of Pightle Cottage, Cock Lane. St John's Road, which was set out by the 1868 Inclosure Award as a 30 ft wide carriage road, had not yet been lined with houses. Len Barnes's shop on the corner, which gave 'Barnes Corner' its name, was not built until the early 1930s. The first bicycle in the village was a penny farthing, in 1880, owned by Mr Rees, headmaster of the village school. Riding downhill, he was pitched over a hedge, much to the delight of some of his pupils with whom he was not popular. They were punished for making fun of him. (*Ann Vieyra*)

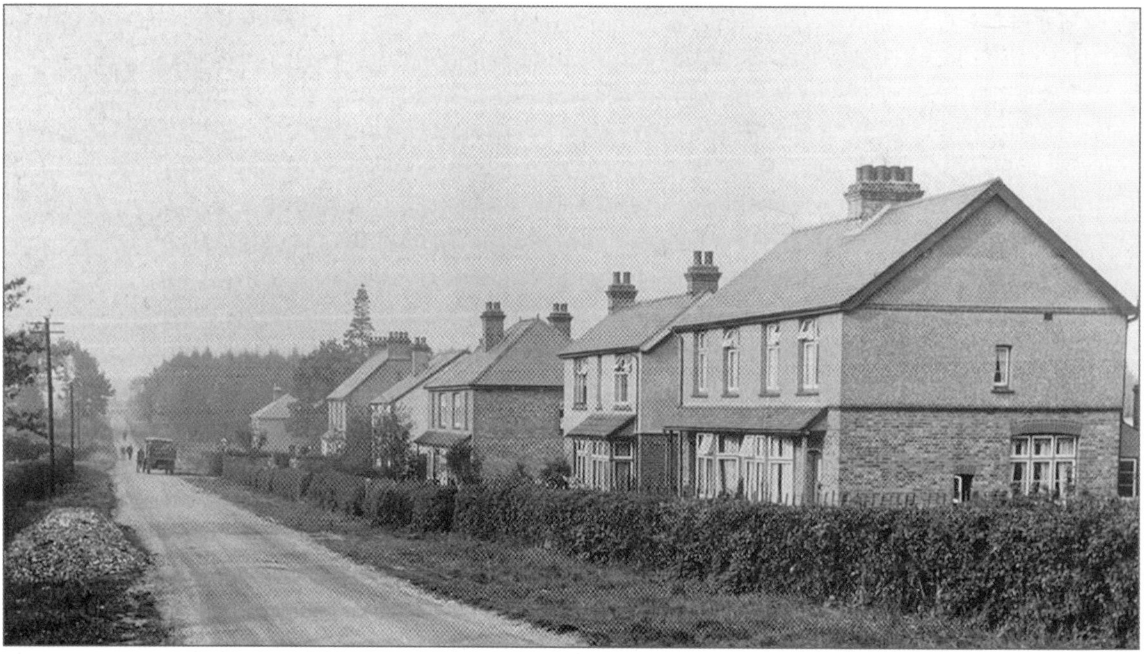

St John's Road, 1926, not long after these houses were built. The entrance to the Penn Bus Company depot (later the industrial estate) was between the last two houses. Mr Sugg, the owner of the bus company, lived in the house one from the end, and started his first service to Beaconsfield station in 1920. Plachet Pond was near the entrance and the depot area, once part of St John's Wood, was formerly Plachet Plain. (*Eric Britnell*)

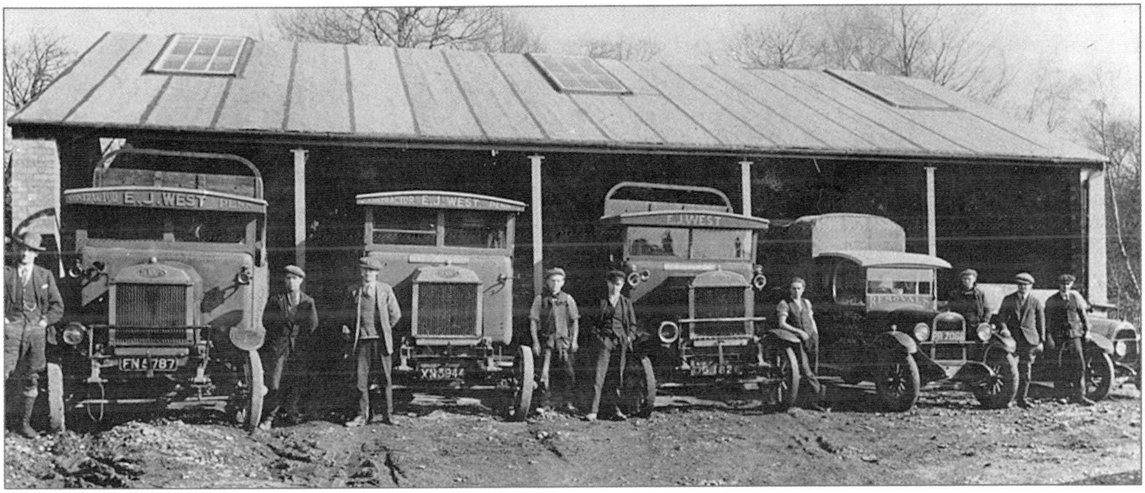

E.J. West's haulage and removal vehicles in his depot off Hazlemere Road, *c.* 1930. E.J. West is standing on the far left. The three lorries on the left are all Dennis, with a Ford to the right. They were mainly used to carry bricks and building materials for houses. (*CWPC*)

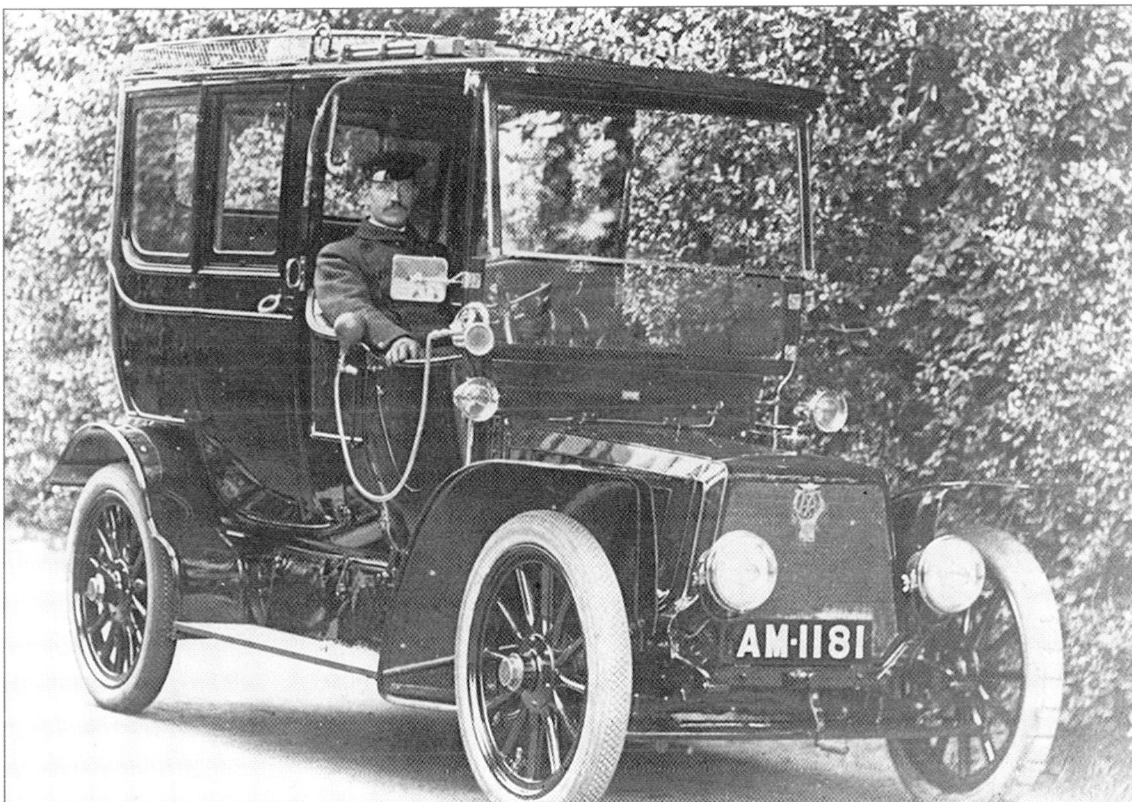

Edward Hunt, chauffeur to Mr Alston of Ashwells Manor, driving a Belgian car called a Metallurgique, *c.* 1914. Ashwells Manor had been built in 1905 by Professor William Rose, cousin of the second Sir Philip Rose. He died in 1910 and the estate of 58 acres and several cottages was sold to Mr Alston. The father of Christopher Soames, later Lord Soames, the last Governor of Rhodesia, owned the estate from 1919 to 1927. The Katherine Knapp Home now occupies the house. (*Ethel Wheeler, née Hunt*)

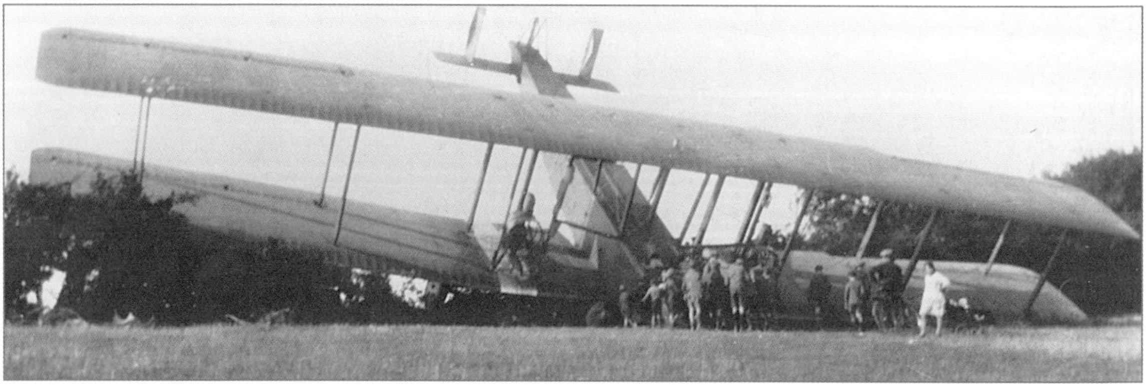

The first recorded presence of an aeroplane in Penn is this RAF Vickers Virginia night bomber from 58 Squadron, Worthy Down, which made a forced landing in fog near Puttenham Farm, August 1925. It was landing in an easterly direction, parallel to Common Wood Lane, saw Brook Wood ahead (to the right of the picture) and swung sharply to the right and into the hedge next to the footpath. The plane was dismantled and repaired, remaining in service until 1938. Alcock and Brown had flown much the same type of plane across the Atlantic in 1919. Arthur Whitten Brown's wife came from Sweethope Cottage in Manor Road, and he was buried in St Margaret's Churchyard in 1948. (*CWPC*)

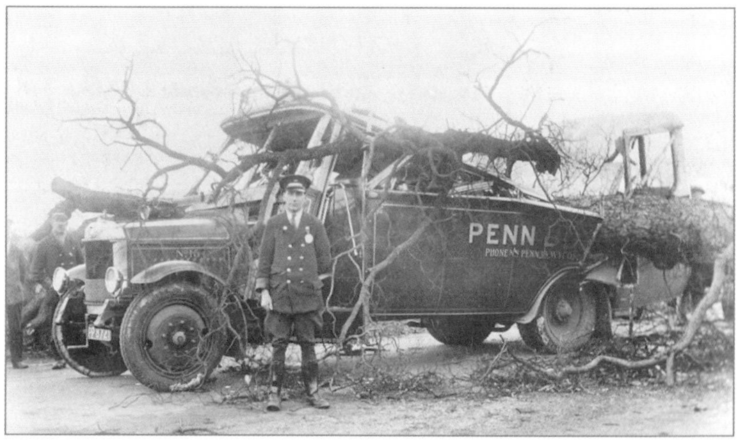

The twenty-six-seater Dennis bus of the Penn Bus Company, badly damaged by a falling tree at Pipers Corner, January 1928. It was the thirteenth bus to be delivered only six months earlier. Note the telephone number, Penn 18. The Tylers Green and Beaconsfield bus service was started by Frederick Sugg, in 1920, with one war surplus vehicle. He was already sixty years old but expanded the service rapidly. It became the Penn Bus Company in 1923, running twenty-one buses by 1930. In 1935 Thames Valley bought out the company. (*Eric Britnell*)

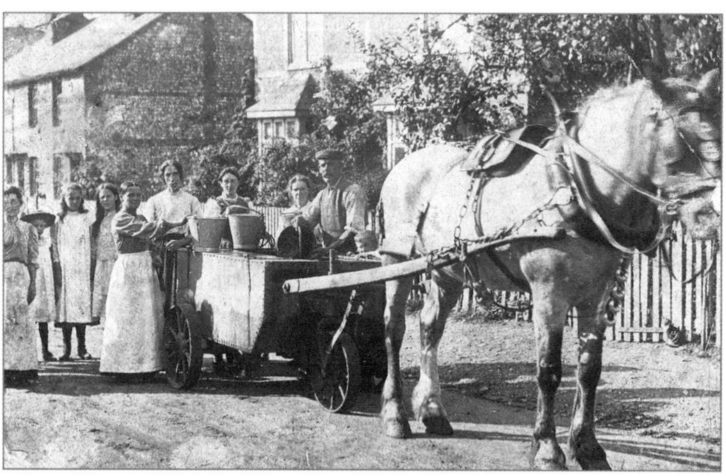

Rayners water cart, 22 September 1911. Water supply was often a very serious problem when tanks and ponds dried up. The first Sir Philip Rose sank a 350 ft well at Rayners and villagers were able to use it. This picture shows the water cart from Rayners in Hazlemere Road in front of the house later demolished for the entrance to Coppice Farm Road. Two buckets were allowed for each family. The cart had been sent round three times a day for the previous month as Widmer Pond was completely dry. Left to right: Mrs Chilton, -?-, Lucy Jarvis, -?-, Mrs Fryer, Mrs Plumridge, Mrs Bristow, Mrs Jarvis, Mr Timms (shepherd for Rayners). (*CWPC*)